JAPANESE PHILOSOPHY

JAPANESE PHILOSOPHY

H. GENE BLOCKER
CHRISTOPHER L. STARLING

State University of New York Press

Published by
State University of New York Press, Albany

For information, address State University of New York Press,
90 State Street, Suite 700, Albany, NY 12207

Production by Kelli M. Williams
Marketing by Fran Keneston

Library of Congress Cataloging-in-Publication Data

Blocker, H. Gene.
  Japanese philosophy/H. Gene Blocker and Christopher L. Starling.
    p. cm.
  Includes bibliographical references and index.
  ISBN 0-7914-5019-8 (alk. paper)—ISBN 0-7914-5020-1(pbk. : alk. paper)
    1. Philosophy, Japanese. I. Starling, Christopher L., 1948- II. Title.

  B5241.B56 2001

  181'.12—dc21   2001020222

CONTENTS

To
The Unknown Philosophers
who deserved a place in these pages

CHAPTER 1

INTRODUCTION

Japanese philosophy? Our very title poses a problem in that even influential figures among those we might assume to have a vested interest, those we might otherwise confidently call "Japanese philosophers," have long called into question the very existence of a body of work that would deserve the name.

Recall for example the lamentations of noted Meiji era thinker Nakae Tokusuke (pen name Nakae Chōmin), who declared in 1901 that "from antiquity to the present day, there has never been any philosophy in Japan" (8). Scholars of National Learning, he wrote, had done nothing but study ancient texts and imperial mausoleums, Confucianists had merely proposed new interpretations of the sages, and if some Buddhists had shown creativity, it had always been within the limitations of their religion. As for the Western-style thinkers among his contemporaries, all they were doing, he contended, was to parrot this or that European theory.

Some scholars would have it that a century after Nakae's lament, there is still no Japanese philosophy. Listen, for example, to this remark of Sakamoto Hyakudai:

> When asked at an international conference or some other occasion abroad to explain the essence of "Japanese Philosophy," one cannot but experience a twinge of regret to have to respond that "There is no such thing; everything is imported, imitated." (3)

Prominent thinkers Yoshimoto Takaaki, Umehara Takeshi, and Nakazawa Shinichi did little to allay doubts about the very existence of

Japanese philosophy when they named their joint 1995 work *Nihonjin wa shisō shita ka* (which we might translate as "Have the Japanese Done Philosophy?"). And another contemporary philosopher, Nakamura Yūjirō, goes as far as to ask rhetorically, "Is a Japanese philosophy possible?" before evincing some optimism that Japan can achieve the transition from what he terms its "culture of translation" to an authentic self-expression. Even if Nakamura comes to acknowledge the existence of Japanese philosophy today, like many Japanese intellectuals he would still hold that there was none before Nishida Kitarō's 1911 *An Inquiry into the Good* (*Zen no kenkyū*).

> One had to wait for Nishida for a work that could disprove [Nakae] Chōmin's judgment that there was no philosophy in Japan. . . . Nishida's work is *the first* to deserve the name of philosophy. (Nakamura Yūjirō, *Philosophie*, 20, our translation)

That there might yet be no established body of thought that we can characterize as Japanese philosophy is surprising in the light of the wealth of other non-Western philosophies that have emerged. The first of these to appear, as long ago as the end of the eighteenth century, were Chinese philosophy and Indian philosophy. (Of course, these thought systems are really much older, dating back to approximately the same time as the emergence of Greek philosophy in the sixth century BCE. But it was only toward the end of the eighteenth century that these ancient thought systems appeared as something called "philosophy," that is, labeled and packaged *as* Chinese or Indian "philosophy.") In the twentieth century the proliferation of non-Western thought systems laying claim to the term *philosophy* has intensified: Beginning around 1960, there appeared for the first time discussions of "African philosophy," "Native American philosophy," and, more interesting from the standpoint of the discussion of Japanese philosophy, something called "Korean philosophy," which has comfortably assumed that name despite its own indebtedness to the "imported" and the "imitated."

What is particularly surprising about the lack of anything packaged as "Japanese philosophy" is Japan's wealth of literature of the sort elsewhere classified without demur *as* "philosophy." This contrasts with such cases as African philosophy and Native American philosophy, which terms have found their place in academia despite a great deal of often heated debate as to whether there was anything in sub-Saharan Africa or pre-Columbian North America that could be reasonably classified as philosophy, especially as these peoples had no written literature until contact with European cultures in the modern period. In this respect the Japanese case would seem far less controversial. The same sorts of texts that are included within, and classified as, Indian, Chinese, and Korean philosophy are amply represented in Japanese literature. Nor has this literature been in any way hidden or "lost." It has simply been packaged and classified in other ways—as "literature," "culture," and so on, but not as "philosophy."

Yet why should this be so? Why is it that Japan fails to fit the mold of other cultures eager to claim for their rich intellectual questings the title of "philosophy"? As a first step toward determining the principal reasons for this, let us recall how the notion of "philosophy," as known in the West, first took shape in the Japanese intellectual world during the Meiji period (1868–1911). At that time the Japanese government was encouraging the wholesale importation of Western intellectual culture, including something called "philosophy," which was conceived as being exclusively Western (Plato, Aristotle, Descartes, Locke, Kant, Hegel, and so on).

To designate this newly-introduced Western study, Nishi Amane introduced in 1874 a new word, *tetsugaku* (a shortened form of *kitetsugaku*), which he formed using two Chinese characters, or *kanji*, meaning the "science of seeking wisdom." The first philosophy instructors were foreigners, who began to arrive three years later, and it was not until 1893 that they began to be replaced by Western-trained Japanese professors of philosophy. Naturally, this fostered the idea that that thing called philosophy was a strictly Western product standing alongside other Western disciplines such as chemistry, physics, and biology. Philosophy *(tetsugaku)*, in other words, was perceived as a part of the foreign knowledge that Japan felt it needed in order to compete with the West and avoid being colonized by the aggressive Western powers.

Here, however, we are merely recalling an initial stage in which the Japanese saw philosophy and their indigenous thought as separate fields. This does little to explain why intellectuals since the Meiji Restoration have not wanted to join the Indians, Chinese, Koreans, and others in claiming for certain parts of their ancient literature the honorific title of "philosophy." After all, the same two Chinese characters for the word *tetsugaku* (which the Chinese pronounce *zhu-shway*—pinyin, *zhe xue*) were also adopted by the Chinese around 1900 to mean philosophy, but whereas the Japanese used this term to refer only to Western thinkers, the Chinese ultimately came to accept that it should be used to refer not only to the likes of Aristotle and Kant, but also to the ancient Asian philosophers, including their own Kongzi (Confucius), Mengzi (Mencius), Zhuangzi, Laozi, Mozi, and so on.

The comparison of the Japanese and Chinese cases is both interesting and instructive. In China, too, many scholars initially thought that *zhe xue (tetsugaku)* was one of the Western *sciences*, and was therefore something previously nonexistent in either China or Japan except in very rudimentary form. However, as it gradually became clearer, partially through the efforts of John Dewey and Bertrand Russell, who visited China just after World War I, that Western philosophy was not a science but a metaphysical and speculative world view based largely on a sense of cultural values, Chinese scholars began to see greater similarities between Western philosophy and ancient Confucianism, Mohism, Taoism, and so on.

The final shift in definition was achieved following the great debates on this issue of 1922–1923, in which the dominant figures were Liang Shuming (*The Civilizations of Orient and Occident and Their Philosophies,* published in 1922 and using for the first time the term *zhe xue*) and Chang Chunmai (Carson Chang, *Science and the Philosophy of Life,* 1925). Chinese intellectuals now reached the consensus that much ancient Chinese writing (Confucian, Taoist, and some Buddhist texts) should indeed be considered *zhe xue* and that *zhe xue* must be divided into Western, Indian, and Chinese, each representing different value orientations or *Weltanschauungen* of these different cultures. Since philosophy was now deemed not a science but rather the expression of cultural values, Liang and his group successfully argued that the Chinese should embrace Western science but continue to espouse Chinese philosophy.

So, while Europeans began to refer to some Chinese writing as philosophy in the late 1700s and early 1800s, the Chinese themselves did not begin to refer to their own ancient writing by the term by which they translated "philosophy" until 1923.

Liang Shuming was probably the first to advance the idea, so popular today, that the philosophical systems of respective cultures represent different value systems, and are therefore a good way to understand the "spirit," character, or temperament of each given people. As Dewey and Russell had pointed out, philosophy is not science. Insofar as the sciences deal with hard facts and rigorous mathematical proof, they will be the same anywhere. Philosophy, on the other hand, insofar as it is concerned with values and metaphysical speculation, will vary from culture to culture. Liang took this to mean that one could use philosophy as a tool to learn about other cultures. What are the Indian people fundamentally like? What is their character, or temperament? One way to find out is to study their philosophy. Thus, the idea arose, from around 1923, that philosophy is culture-bound and a good culture indicator. A leading writer in this movement was the Japanese author Nakamura Hajime, who argued in his very influential *Ways of Thinking of Eastern Peoples* (written in the 1940s but not published until 1964) that each people has a distinctive conception or way of "seeing" the world that defines each as a distinct cultural entity.

The similarity of views of Liang and Nakamura was not, however, accompanied by a common use of the terms *tetsugaku* and *zhe xue.* Despite their common origin, these terms continued in their divergent destinies. If *tetsugaku* never came to have the broader definition *zhe xue* acquired through the influence of Dewey and Russell and the Chinese debates, a major factor in this was a difference in the respective degree of allegiance felt in Japan and China toward their own intellectual traditions. In Japan the zestful embracing of Western disciplines from around 1870, accompanied by a shift in state education policy away from Chinese learning (neo-Confucianism) toward Western learning, was conducive to the association of "philosophy" and the Occident.

The loss of favor suffered by neo-Confucianism at this time was facilitated by the fact that it was not truly indigenous. When, beginning in the Sui dynasty (seventh century), Chinese culture had appeared to the Japanese as superior in certain ways, they had imported it with enthusiasm, but with Western learning similarly appearing to have the edge a thousand years later, it now seemed advantageous to the Japanese to wholeheartedly adopt it in turn (and in so doing reject Chinese traditional thought). Later, in the Taishō period, a new nationalist trend began to take only the Western learning necessary for science, technology, and economics, reaffirming for morality, social relations, and lifestyle traditional culture of Nipponese (not Chinese) origin.

In China, by contrast, the resistance to Western learning and the loyalty to Chinese traditions were much stronger, leading to a long and lively debate between near equals from 1880 to the 1920s, which, as indicated above, finally ended in a compromise: to embrace Western science and technology and to retain (and reinterpret) traditional Chinese moral and social thought (i.e., "Chinese philosophy"), especially Confucianism. For the Chinese, whose cultural identity is enduringly linked with ancient Chinese thought systems, the shift from Chinese to Western has been far less easy than in Japan, and, even today, far less uniform.

It should be said that in neither China nor Japan was the policy on these issues the result of an immediate and unanimous decision. On the contrary, in both countries it was a fiercely contentious issue. On the one hand, some Chinese wanted to abandon *all* Chinese traditional learning (both scientific and moral, social, and political); while, at the same time, a powerful lobby of "liberals" in Japan almost succeeded in their advocacy of Western ideals of democracy, in addition to Western science, technology, and economics. On the other hand, there were in both China and Japan influential conservatives who advocated the complete rejection of all Western influence. As we now know, both countries ultimately embraced a compromise, accepting Western science, technology, and economics, while keeping their indigenous moral, social, and political culture. For the Chinese, this meant retaining their ancient philosophy; for the Japanese it entailed a reaffirmation of fidelity to their ancient pre-Chinese (and *non-philosophical*) traditions, manifested in a growing emphasis on Shintō.

What we have just said may satisfactorily explain the divergent emphases of *zhe xue* and *tetsugaku*, but does it really explain the continued eschewing of the term *philosophy* by Japanese to refer to Japanese traditional thought? After all, for all the enthusiasm displayed toward Western ideas this was not unanimous, and one could hardly say that the non-Western traditions in Japan have vanished or been forgotten. Moreover, even if the rejection of traditions had been total, Japanese philosophers from the Meiji era onward would still have had ample opportunity to review their country's thought and establish an account of it as a retrospective history of Japanese philosophy.

At this point, we might try pursuing a different line of inquiry. If we examine non-Western philosophies that have emerged, we find that a major motive in their elaboration has been the redressing of wounded cultural pride. In reaction to centuries of colonial and near-colonial rule by overbearing and ethnocentric European masters, intellectuals of suppressed nations justifiably strove to restore their peoples' cultural dignity. For many years, Chinese and Indian intellectuals had been told that their own culture was worthless or at least vastly inferior to that of Europeans. Finally, they reacted by sifting through their ancient literature, selecting the best examples, and packaging for the first time a new grouping that they could point to with pride as Chinese philosophy, or Indian philosophy. Other colonized peoples in the South Seas, Africa, and elsewhere followed suit: they had ancient oral wisdom literature; why should not this, too, be considered philosophy?

In this connection, what can we say of the Japanese case? Certainly we can point to individual works such as Okakura Tenshin's 1904 English work *The Awakening of Japan* and Watsuji Tetsurō's 1935 *Fūdo (Climate and Culture)*, which initiated a fresh emphasis on Japanese values in what can be seen as a reaction against the earlier passion for European learning. But, again, what we do not find is the comprehensive formulation *après coup* of a Japanese philosophical tradition. Could it be because they were never colonized or humiliated by Western imperialists that the Japanese never felt the need for such a comprehensive philosophic self-assertion? Could it be that they simply took it for granted that their culture was as good as or better than any other, except in the areas of science and technology that alone could yield the military strength necessary to resist European incursion? Each culture tends naturally to be ethnocentric, and at least as far as arts and letters are concerned, not to mention myths of superior national origins, the Japanese could be as spontaneously ethnocentric as anyone. Could it be, indeed, that they found the means of intellectual independence not by elaboration of philosophy but by assertion of myth? In later chapters we will return to this issue, but for now we can at least posit this as a plausible answer to our key question.

Yet another reason might be offered why Japanese scholars have not attempted to package parts of their traditional writing as philosophy *(tetsugaku)*. We have seen that following the work of Liang Shuming and Nakamura Hajime in the 1920s and 1930s, it was widely accepted that philosophy was the expression of the value orientation of each culture. However, this can be interpreted in one of two ways, according to the precise sense we accord the term *philosophy*. Sometimes the word refers to a general outlook or attitude toward life (as in "my mother's philosophy of life"), while at other times it denotes a scholarly discipline acquired by training and practiced by technical specialists (as in "studying philosophy at university," "reading a philosophy book").

According to the first interpretation, since each distinctive culture necessarily has its own value system, each distinctive culture necessarily has, in a broad sense, its own philosophy, regardless of whether this has been written down in some analytical, logical, systematic form or not. The second, equally plausible, interpretation is that while each distinctive culture has its own value orientation or way of seeing the world, this need not be expressed philosophically (that is, in the restricted sense), but can be equally well expressed mythologically, religiously, artistically, poetically, and so on, philosophy in the restricted sense being only one of the possibilities.

Any cultural group wishing to overturn Western Eurocentric cultural imperialism must decide which of these two ways to go. Formerly colonized African peoples, for example, can argue either that their oral wisdom literature (proverbs, myths, etc.) should be regarded as philosophy, or, following the Negritude movement, that in contrast to Europeans, who are cerebral, analytical, abstract, and in that narrow sense "philosophical," African people are more feeling, holistic, contextually oriented, and have therefore developed a more rhythmic, musical understanding of the world. Similarly, women's groups today can argue either that there is a feminist philosophy, which a male-dominated power structure has suppressed up to now, or that women see the world in a more emotional, holistic, contextual way that is fundamentally different from the masculine analytic, cerebral, abstract way that leads to what we know traditionally as philosophy. In every case what has previously not been called philosophy compares itself to what has traditionally been called philosophy. One then argues either that the term *philosophy* should be extended to include what had previously been unrecognized as such, or else that the term *philosophy* should be reserved for certain types of highly analytic, logically articulated thought systems and not extended to include alternative approaches to the world that are more holistic, contextual, integrative, and more in touch with emotion.

It is in this second way that most Japanese intellectuals have interpreted the theory of cultural *Weltanschauungen*. When Japanese intellectuals, such as Nakamura Hajime, approached the question of what was distinctive about their culture, how it differed from others, they concluded that it was not, on the whole, logical, analytical, abstract, intellectual, and philosophical, but was rather sensual, integrative, and aesthetic. Of course, they acknowledged that Japanese had over the centuries borrowed and made use of a great deal of Chinese philosophical thought, but that was not considered the strong point of Japanese culture; that was not what the Japanese did best. If the Indians and to a certain extent the Chinese approached the world rationally, intellectually, abstractly, analytically, the Japanese genius was to see the world in concrete, sensuous, holistic, and aesthetic terms. This vision and approach was thought to be in no way inferior to, and indeed was thought to be in a certain "romantic" way superior to, the more cerebral, analytical approach of the West and to a lesser extent those of India and China. The title of Nakamura's book is instructive in this regard. He does not title his work "*Philosophies of Eastern Peoples*" but "Ways of Thinking of Eastern Peoples." (Of course, all of this presupposes the stability of the long tradition restricting the technical use of the word *philosophy* to logical rigor and analysis, but in chapter 5 we will consider the postmodern challenge to this "logocentric" conception of philosophy and explore the implications for Japanese philosophy.)

Clearly, if, in accordance with Nakamura's outlook, the specifically Japanese elements in Japan's intellectual heritage are to be subsumed in the notion "ways of thinking," while the term *philosophy* is to be restricted to the narrower "logocentric" sense explained above, with all such thought in Japan supposedly "imported and imitated," be it from China, Korea, or Europe, then we may yield, momentarily, to the view that no, there has never been any such thing as "Japanese philosophy." Perhaps the term does not refer to anything distinctively Japanese, but simply to imported Chinese philosophy and, later, imported Western philosophy. Earlier we stated that *tetsugaku* was used exclusively to speak of imported Western thought. Having noted the influence of Liang Shuming in tracing the world's philosophical schools back to three original ones, the Greek, Indian, and Chinese, we might now surmise that Japanese intellectuals saw their non-Western thought as simply falling into the Chinese camp. Moreover, following Nakamura Hajime's line of thought, the Chinese thought imported to Japan remained, by its abstract character, fundamentally foreign to the Japanese way of thinking. The implication of all this is that there has been no Japanese philosophical originality.

This is, however, a contestable argument in that assenting to a common origin does not preclude the emergence or the recognition of originality. Acknowledging the debt to China would not logically prevent Japanese intellectuals from arguing for a Japanese philosophy as a distinct philosophy deriving from Chinese thought, in the same way that French, German, British, and even American intellectuals argue that they have distinct national philosophies, even though each of these can be ultimately traced back to the Greeks.

It is probably true that there are only three independent origins of philosophy, China, Greece, and India, all at roughly the same time (600 BCE). But whenever a subsequent group of people is able to transform any one of these original philosophies, adapting it to their own indigenous culture so that it becomes a stable, ongoing indigenous tradition in its own right, then we speak appropriately of Roman philosophy, British philosophy, and even of American philosophy. American philosophy appears at that extra remove when it is sufficiently different from British and German philosophy, addressing itself to peculiarly American concerns in a distinctly American style or voice, and when that way of doing philosophy and those sets of concerns become an ongoing stable tradition in their own right, something that did not occur in the United States until the end of the nineteenth and the beginning of the twentieth century. Before that there was British and German philosophy being done within the geographical area of North America but nothing that could properly be called American philosophy. The well-known twentieth-century Chinese philosopher, Fung Yulan, similarly distinguished Buddhism in China (Indian Buddhism that appears in China during the first and second centuries) and Chinese Buddhism (a distinctively Chinese style of Buddhism that does not appear until the fourth and fifth centuries).

Why should we not make a similar distinction between "continental Asian philosophy in Japan" and "Japanese philosophy of continental Asian derivation"? Might Japan be exceptional in some way so that its borrowed philosophy never matured into a local product? As we shall see, a case might be made that it is, based on allegations of a fundamental weakness in the very manner in which Japanese intellectuals assimilate foreign thought. This is the view we encountered at the outset, that there is no original Japanese philosophy because all philosophy in Japan is imported, translated, imitated, and so on.

Nonetheless, we reject this view, the fallacy of which can be ascribed to two things. The first of these is the exaggeration of an admittedly strong tendency to translate with little critical contribution. Ōe Kenzaburō, who sees this tendency as having subsisted from the Meiji era to the present day, writes:

> There was an inclination for people to think that an intellectual effort had been accomplished merely by transplanting or translating the new American and European cultural thoughts into Japanese; and both the translators and those who read the translations were inclined to think in the same manner. (204)

According to Ōe, this inclination resulted in the "diachronic, one-dimensional acceptance and discharge of new cultural theories . . . ; with only a few exceptions, the Japanese were not able to establish a cultural theory of their own" (209). In philosophy too, the exceptions may be few, but they count.

Secondly, we must point to a simplistic notion of translation itself. Examining the supposed lack of philosophy in Japan, Nakamura Yūjirō, in terms that recall those of Ōe, attributes it to an emphasis on the history of philosophy, philology, and the translation of foreign philosophers. Japan, he stresses, is a "culture of translation." Now, it may be that in restricted areas of philosophy, such as logic, a pure translation is possible. But much of what was translated to Japanese from Chinese and Korean, and from European tongues, dealt with epistemology, axiology, and other fields in which texts were redolent with implications of the cultures from which they had emerged. In the translation of this sort of writing, what is received is rarely the same as what is given. Even the furnishing of a fresh lexicon of Japanese words, for example, could not prevent Western philosophies from acquiring a fresh resonance within the cultural *Weltanschauung* of Japan.

In many cases, given the tendency mentioned above to translate without adequately considering local cultural applications, such ideas did indeed remain "remote" (Ōe's word) from Japanese realities. But where any attempt was made to creatively reformulate the foreign ideas, the new text could not but be distinctively Japanese. In other words, the notion that in truly entering Japanese cultural life, foreign philosophies could indefinitely retain the precise character proper to their foreign origins is difficult to accept and goes against all we know about acculturation. In general, we know that people are seldom aware of their own cultural biases as they translate from a foreign culture into their own. The tendency, for anyone, is to imagine we are "objectively" translating, merely transcribing, whereas it is clear to others (and perhaps to ourselves later) that we have unconsciously imposed on our transcription the indelible imprint of our own cultural *Weltanschauung*.

As we shall see, this notion of a purely "objective" translation also goes against the evidence: Chinese philosophy in Japan became something other than Chinese; Buddhism in Japan became something other than Chinese and Indian; European philosophy in Japan became something other than European. Just as the country's monks and scholars had done in centuries past when poring over freshly-acquired volumes from the Asian mainland, the earliest practitioners of Western-style philosophy in Japan were bound subtly to modify their subject despite themselves. As we shall see (in a similar way again to the case with Asian sources), this modification later became part of a conscious project as Japanese thinkers chose to use Western modes of expression to express local ideas and values.

Another way to put this is that what we have respectively called philosophy in the broad sense and philosophy in the narrow sense are rarely independent. It is true that philosophy in the technical sense sets out to critique the ambient world view, that is, what we may call philosophy in the broad sense, pressing for justification, pointing out contradictions, demanding clarity in vague areas, and so on. But in so doing it also reflects the cultural preconceptions of its exponents and in that sense tends to sustain an already existing set of beliefs, values, and attitudes. Thus, philosophy in the narrow sense both critiques and reflects philosophy in the broad sense. It is because the *Weltanschauung* thus pervades philosophy in the narrow sense that where the latter is brought in from an alien tradition, it loses its pristine character of the "imported." Chinese or Western philosophy imported into Japan is used by Japanese to reflect on, rationalize, clarify, justify their own indigenous Japanese *Weltanschauung* (that is, philosophy in the broad cultural sense). In that sense, imitation, too, is invention.

We can now perceive the validity of the term *Japanese philosophy* in the narrow, technical sense. Although it is debatable precisely how deeply Chinese and Western philosophy took root in Japanese soil, we think it will be clear in the chapters to come that there is a large body of Japanese writing that is both sufficiently philosophical and sufficiently Japanese to qualify as "Japanese philosophy." And despite the ongoing controversy whether, in the end, Japanese intellectuals accepted or rejected the rational and analytic "logocentric" style of much Indian, Western, and Chinese philosophy, there is no question that Japanese thinkers have been deeply engaged philosophically in these issues and, along with many Western, Indian, and Chinese philosophers, have contributed enormously to the ongoing critique of philosophy as the citadel of Reason. We can therefore state unequivocally that before the modern period (Meiji, 1868) we see a Japanese philosophy deriving from the Chinese (and Korean, which in turn ultimately derives from Chinese) and in the modern period a Japanese philosophy influenced by and contributing to the Western tradition.

What we propose to do in this book is, to our knowledge, unprecedented: to package, *as* philosophy, significant parts of Japan's intellectual tradition that we judge to merit the term, including much that has hitherto been subsumed under "literature" or "religion." In doing this we shall be referring to material that is familiar to anyone who has studied Japanese cultural history. We shall not be bringing to light any lost texts. We shall simply be putting this existing, well-known material together as philosophy. If we allow the existence of "Arabic philosophy," or "Korean philosophy," what is to prevent our proposing a Japanese philosophy?

Why, one might wonder, should we do this? What difference does it make whether these texts are called philosophy or not? Our response would be that to understand any culture, we need to be able to compare it to others, and in comparing cultures we must always attempt, as far as possible, to compare equals with equals. We need to be able to compare Japanese poetry with the poetry of other cultures, Japanese religion with the religion of other cultures, Japanese art with the art of other cultures, and in this sense it would be helpful to compare Japanese philosophy with the philosophy of other cultures.

Of course, this still leaves us to decide our criteria for what is to count as "philosophy." How will we know what to include and what to exclude? We have already seen that the word *philosophy* is commonly used in two senses: a very broad sense and a narrow, specialized one. In the broad sense, we may say that every person and every culture necessarily has a particular philosophy, where this means a general sense of things and how they ought to be, an inarticulate and undeveloped sense of values, a general and intuitive *Weltanschauung*, which might appear in a culture's myths, legends, popular sayings, songs, poetry, art, and so on. To study the philosophy of an ethnic group in this broad sense would be the work of a social anthropologist trying to derive from these elements some sense of the general outlook and basic attitudes of the group as a whole. Such research might conclude, for example: "They tend to see the world as threatening," or, "They see themselves as divinely appointed to lead their neighbors." This is not, however, what we would expect to learn, except incidentally, in a study of French or German philosophy. Here we would be looking for a particular kind of written text, by an identifiable author (Descartes, Kant, Hegel, for example), logically and systematically developing a more or less original view with which other individual philosophers could then disagree in whole or in part, and thus contributing to a tradition, or history of philosophical theories sharing a common methodology of rational scrutiny and the imperative of logical justification.

If we are thinking of philosophy in this latter narrow, specialized sense, as something comparable to British, or French, or American philosophy, then this must be our criterion in selecting material for inclusion in Japanese philosophy. As Kwasi Wiredu has said in talking about African philosophy, we must compare equals with equals. Hence, it would be misleading to compare German philosophy in the narrow sense with Japanese philosophy in the broad sense. If we want to talk about the social psychology of the Japanese (how they think, how they tend to act, what their basic values, attitudes, etc. are), then we will want to compare this with the Germans' social psychology (the fact that they tend to be well-organized, disciplined, or whatever), rather than with the writings of Immanuel Kant, for example. In this book we are interested in comparing Japanese philosophy in the narrow, technical sense with Indian, Western, and Chinese philosophy in the narrow, technical sense. As we will see, *all* philosophy in the narrow, technical sense is related to philosophy in the broad, sociological sense in that the former is a reflection on and refinement of the latter. But this is no more true of Japanese philosophy than it is of Chinese or Indian or Western philosophy.

In this second sense of "philosophy," European philosophy arose at a particular point in Greek history. Greeks before Thales did not have philosophy in this second sense. And if the Greeks before Thales had no philosophy or philosophers, it is possible that this was true of other societies and cultures as well. By the same token, however, just as philosophy did arise in European culture at a particular time and place, so it is possible that philosophy arose at various moments in other, non-European cultures. In this second sense of "philosophy," it may turn out that some cultures have philosophy and some do not, and we cannot dogmatically assert before examining the facts either that all cultures must have philosophy or that none do except European cultures. We must patiently and empirically look at each culture to see whether it does or does not have philosophy, and, of course, if it does, then we will naturally want to study it, either alongside European philosophy or perhaps by incorporating all the different regional philosophies into a more comprehensive world philosophy.

Of course, this way of defining philosophy might be challenged as being ethnocentric and Eurocentric. The question of whether there is any non-European philosophy was originally one raised by European philosophers about some other, non-European group, and this certainly raises the possibility of cultural bias. Whose conception or definition of philosophy are we using when we ask of the thought systems of other cultures whether they count as philosophy? Well, naturally, with our own, Western, European philosophy. And, of course, a lot is at stake in this question. Philosophy is an enormously value-laden term. To say that a culture did not develop a philosophy sounds demeaning and to say that they had a philosophy sounds like a compliment. As each region of our planet tries to define itself in the postcolonial period in as positive a manner as possible, it becomes highly sensitive to pejorative or belittling assessments of its own culture, especially those assessments made by outsiders (and even more so those made by former colonial masters).

But the reason we use our own value-laden conception of philosophy is that this is all we have, at least at the beginning! From the beginning of the discussion of the possibility of non-Western philosophy, *philosophy* is a Western term. One might note minor variations of meaning among its cognates: the French *philosophie*, for example, has its own specific associations of the encylopedists arising from the Enlightenment, but whether practicing "philosophy," *philosophie*, or *filosofia*, the Western scholar treads essentially the same path, inspired by the same "love of wisdom" (in Greek: *philosophia*) and using a term whose meaning has been determined by Western thought.

For better or worse, any description of another culture's thought systems must be comparative, entailing the comparison of their thought with our own, whoever "we" and "they" may be. Since Europeans or European-trained scholars are the speakers, they must use their language (with the standard meanings of their words, terms, and concepts) to talk about (and judge) non-European thought systems. If Indian or Chinese intellectuals began the discussion, exactly the same principle would apply; they would use their respective language, each with its distinctive web of meanings, taking account of European concepts by comparing these with concepts of their own, ever referring to homegrown notions as models and standards.

Perhaps Hindu scholars asked Alexander's generals whether there were any *rishis* among the Greeks. We can imagine Marco Polo trying to satisfy the curiosity of Yuan dynasty Confucian administrators concerning the presence or absence in Europe of *zi*. "We have a long tradition," they might say, "of important thinkers we call *zi*—Kongzi, Mengzi, Laozi, Zhuangzi, Mozi, Xunzi, Han Feizi, and many others, who have made our culture great. What about you? Do you have any *zi* among your people?" We can imagine Marco Polo's dilemma; it is hard to say "yes" and hard to say "no." It is hard to say yes since there really is no tradition in Europe identical or even very similar to the Chinese *zi*. There were European saints, and academics, for example, but these are not the same as *zi*. On the other hand, if he admits there are no European *zi*, he seems to belittle his own culture, admitting, in effect, that his people had produced none of those intellectual giants prerequisite to a great culture.

Initially, then, there is no alternative but for the culture initiating the investigation to use its own concepts to approach the culture under scrutiny. Because of European military, economic, scientific, and technological hegemony during the eighteenth and nineteenth centuries, it was

Europeans who judged Chinese and Indian cultures by comparing them to their own European standards. From now on, as Europeans learn enough to recognize significant similarities between their thought systems and those of China and India, and begin to consider them together, it is likely that European concepts will be influenced by Asian ones and vice versa, and that all these will undergo a gradual modification and mutual accommodation toward the others. Comparing Asian thought with Western philosophy might, for example, shift the European sense of the center of philosophy farther from the more rigorous, scientific, analytic regions of philosophy (Aristotle, Descartes, etc.) and toward the more mystical and wisdom-oriented European philosophers (Epicurus, Epictetus, Spinoza, Kierkegaard, etc.). In chapter 5 we will explore the possibility that this is already occurring, in the alliance of postmodernism's attack on "logocentrism" with a heightened regard for Japan's holistic and aesthetic traditional culture. But initially, if Europeans begin the investigation, then they must begin with their own language and their own cultural baggage, with all the admitted dangers of bias and misunderstanding that this approach inevitably involves. To understand another culture is necessarily to misunderstand it, at least at the beginning and to a certain extent.

This is true more generally. All cultural descriptions are comparative; unavoidably culture A must use A's words and concepts to describe culture B. Even when we ask about Japanese *religion*, "religion" is, after all, an English word that we are trying to impose on an alien culture. Perhaps people of that culture have no word that translates exactly as our word *religion*. A similar case is that of "African *art*" or "American Indian *art*." The very question, "What kind of art did the American Indians have?" presupposes something that may well be false. It assumes that the American Indians not only made things that we see as fitting our concept (in English) of "art," but also had themselves a similar concept, that is, a word reasonably accurately translated as "art," a word that they understood to mean something very much like what we understand the word *art* to mean.

One reason it may well be a mistake to think that other cultures have concepts such as art and religion is that these concepts in English and other European languages presuppose a division of society and culture into distinct functional regions, such as exists in our culture. Art is thus seen as more or less separated from religion, which is in turn more or less separated from agricultural, military, political, and scientific concerns. In many cultures, no such separation ever took place, and in cultures where what we call artistic activities are inseparable from religious, agricultural, military, and political activities, concepts like our concept of art and religion simply do not arise. In such cultures it makes no sense (even if you speak their language and they yours) to ask, "What is your religion, what is your art?" They may make wooden statues for ancestor spirits to temporarily "occupy," and to which they make offerings of food and drink, and of which they ask (that is, "pray") for help for a successful harvest, battle, or marriage; but they have no sense of which part of this complex is their "art," which part is "religion," which part is "agriculture," and so on. These questions will make no sense to them, though they will, of course, make sense to us. We are the ones interested in their "art" and "religion." Even in the cases of art and religion, then, where it might seem obvious that all cultures and societies have something separably identifiable under both concepts, the possibility of bias and misunderstanding arising from cross-cultural comparison presents a serious problem.

Suppose we now return to the word *philosophy*, as defined in our second sense (that is, as a critical, reflective, rational, and systematic approach to questions of very general interest), and apply that definition to different thought systems around the world. As mentioned earlier, by applying this definition of philosophy as a criterion, at least three independent original thought systems would seem to qualify—Greek, Indian, and Chinese, all arising around 500 BCE.

Cultures that are not philosophical in this sense are those that tend to accept their own mythological world view simply on the authority of tradition. "We believe this because it is our ancient belief; our people have always believed this." Philosophy, by contrast, arises precisely at that point when, for various reasons, that traditional outlook is called into question. "We have always been taught to see the world in this way, but how can we be sure that this is really correct?" At this point individual philosophers come forward with the boldness and the audacity, and we might even say the arrogance, to start utterly afresh, questioning everything, assuming nothing, and confident that they can figure it all out by themselves! No longer do we say, "This is how our people see the world," but rather, "Anaximander advanced this theory; Thales held another view; Aristotle disagreed with both and developed a radically different position." Or, to give a second example: "Gaozi denied there was any human nature; Mengzi held that there was a human nature that was fundamentally good; Xunzi agreed with Mengzi (against Gaozi) that there was a human nature, but disagreed with Mengzi that it was fundamentally good." Far from a traditional uniformity of opinion, the onset of philosophy, whether in China, India, or Greece, is generally marked by a proliferation of many different, competing views, whose proponents engage in endless debates, arguing for their favorite doctrines and against all the others.

But why should we believe any of these philosophers with their new and radically different ideas? Certainly not from any traditional authority, but only from the weight of rational evidence that they adduce. In this sense early Greek, Indian, and Chinese thinkers tried to prove their individual theories by carefully defining their terms, by drawing distinctions, and by constructing arguments for their positions and counterarguments against the positions of their opponents. Notice how Sarvepalli Radhakrishnan characterizes the beginnings of Indian philosophy.

> The age of Buddha (596–483 BCE) represents the great springtide of philosophic spirit in India. The progress of philosophy is generally due to a powerful attack on a historical tradition when men feel themselves compelled to go back on their steps and raise once more the fundamental questions which their fathers had disposed of by the older schemes. The revolt of Buddhism and Jainism . . . forms an era in the history of Indian thought, since it finally exploded the method of dogmatism and helped to bring about a critical point of view. For the great Buddhist thinkers, logic was the main arsenal where were forged the weapons of universal destructive criticism. . . . The conservative schools were compelled to codify their views and set forth logical defenses of them. The critical side of philosophy became as important as the speculative. (17)

Of course, this characterization represents only the beginning stages of philosophy, when it first arises in Greece, China, and India. Later, its criticism of tradition itself becomes traditional, so that later Greek and Roman philosophy, as well as later Chinese and Indian philosophy, become orthodox and conservative. When alien cultures borrow these original philosophies, they generally receive them in their well-established, conservative late phase. To the Romans, Greek philosophy was a highly revered, virtually complete system of thought. As we will see, Chinese philosophy was introduced into Japan with much the same aura of an established tradition. It is also true that there occur from time to time within well-defined philosophical traditions, whether Indian, Chinese, or Western, philosophical movements (romantic, existentialist, etc.) that philosophically challenge philosophy itself, calling into question the privileged role of reason as the final arbitrator of Truth and Goodness. But where this is carried out philosophically, using logic to combat logic, analysis to overcome analysis, reason to recognize the limits of reason, it, too, has an important place within philosophy, however short-lived these revolts against the "logocentric" mainstream of philosophy may have been.

This, then, is our working definition of "philosophy," as critical, logical, and systematic, and it is this more narrow and technical sense of philosophy that we will use in our reconstruction of Japanese philosophy. It is in this sense that scholars now typically refer to the six orthodox and three unorthodox schools of Indian philosophy and to Confucianism, Taoism, Mohism, and Legalism as different schools of Chinese philosophy.

A first question now for Japanese philosophy is at what point Chinese philosophy became Japanese, and one of the most important themes to examine is precisely how Japanese philosophers interpreted, criticized, modified, developed, and used imported Chinese philosophical ideas and methods in accordance with Japanese predilections and needs, and how their writings contributed to an ongoing tradition of thought that is distinctively Japanese. Exactly the same criteria should be used to distinguish twentieth-century Japanese philosophy of a Western or international style (that is, a Japanization of Western philosophy) from the earlier study of European philosophy in Japanese universities (in the late nineteenth and early twentieth centuries).

Naturally, the development of a distinctive philosophical subregion (such as Japan within the larger Chinese tradition) is influenced by the selections the subculture makes from the grand tradition, whether these occur by chance or design, with distinctive local cultural predispositions a factor both in the selection and in the modification of what is selected. Indeed, one big difference between Japanese and Chinese philosophy arises from the fact that Japanese philosophy is highly selective of the much larger range of philosophical schools that arose in China. Partly this is due to the historical accident whereby by the time Chinese philosophy was imported to Japan in the eighth century many earlier Chinese schools had already become obsolete or absorbed into other philosophical schools. Thus, when Chinese philosophy was first introduced to Japan during the Sui and Tang dynasties, China had already gone through a thousand years of extremely diversified philosophical development—the original teachings of Kongzi (Confucius), then centuries later his most important followers (though very different from one another), Mengzi (Mencius) and Xunzi, in addition to many other quite different and competing schools of philosophy, such as the philosophical (as opposed to the religious) Taoism of Laozi and Zhuangzi, Mohism (Mozi), The School of Names (Hui Shih, Gong-Sun Lung), legalism (Han Feizi), and so on. By the Tang dynasty, Confucianism had been accepted as the official Chinese school of philosophy and many elements of earlier schools had been absorbed into later Confucianism, including *Yin Yang*, Five Agents, as well as elements from the *I Jing* (the *Book of Changes*). In addition, by the time of the Song dynasty, Mengzi (Mencius), and not Xunzi, had been selected as the orthodox follower of Kongzi (Confucius), with the result that *Mengzi* became one of the four classical Confucian texts, while Xunzi's writings were more or less ignored. Therefore, when the Japanese first began to learn Chinese philosophy, they were introduced only to this late Confucianism, ignoring all the other previous schools of philosophy, as well as neglected Confucianists such as Xunzi.

However, part of the selection process reflected Japanese political priorities and cultural preferences. In China philosophy had developed independently of government. At first (sixth through third centuries BCE), various schools of philosophy vied with one another trying to persuade the state authorities that their particular philosophy could best guide the nation. When government leaders politely refused the political advice of these sages, philosophers turned to teaching promising individuals in small schools as a means of self-cultivation, an important conception of the role of philosophy for more than two thousand years. Even later, when Confucianism became the dominant official state philosophy, the other schools were not outlawed, and the teaching, writing, and development of Confucianism was never directed by the government but remained in the hands of a class of scholars, known as the *ru*. An important indication of the traditional independence of Chinese philosophers is the ancient tradition of Chinese philosophers protesting government policy, or even refusing, or resigning government service under corrupt regimes. Confucian philosophers cultivated moral standards to which they held governments accountable.

In Japan, by contrast, philosophy was admitted by the government for the aid it could provide the government in the service of the state. Hence, there never developed until quite late an independent class of literary specialists among whom scholars could be selected for government service, as was the case in China with its famous meritocratic examination system. In Japan, government positions tended to be hereditary.

For all these reasons Japanese tended to select only those aspects of Chinese philosophy best suited to the perceived needs of Japanese government leaders and advisors. So, for example, because it was not considered important for the running of the country, Japanese never developed (until the late Tokugawa era—eighteenth and nineteenth centuries) the idea, so prominent in China, of the role of philosophy as a tool for self-cultivation. Also, the Japanese were never very interested (again until late Tokugawa) in China's second most important and popular philosophy, philosophical Taoism *(Tao Jia)*, which the Japanese government leaders thought encouraged anarchy, rebellion, and lack of loyalty to the government and devotion to the state. As a result, Japan never developed the kind of alternative, "personal" philosophy of Taoism that flourished in

China as a kind of counterculture to the dominant official public Confucianism, an alternative to which Confucian scholars could turn at the end of the day or toward the end of life or as a solace when they lost or resigned their government jobs or the government they worked for was overthrown.

For similar reasons, Japanese tended to exclude Kongzi's theory of the "mandate of heaven," the view that to be successful, governments must be acceptable to a moral order of Heaven, without which they could be legitimately overthrown (not a popular idea among government leaders anywhere). Mengzi (Mencius), who was the most philosophical of the earlier "orthodox" Confucianists, was almost completely ignored for nearly a thousand years because Mengzi held the firm and outspoken belief that, in addition to serving Heaven, governments must also serve the people, for it was from this service that governments derived their legitimacy. If such service was lacking, rebellions would be morally justified. Where Mengzi and the Confucian tradition generally tended to offer advice to governments on how they ought to rule in order to fulfill their moral obligations to their people and to Heaven, this tended to be excluded from Japanese Confucianism, at least until very late in the Tokugawa period (eighteenth and nineteenth centuries). Also, Japanese Confucianists tended to emphasize loyalty to the state government over filial piety (family loyalty), whereas for the Chinese it was just the reverse.

Japanese Buddhism in its early centuries was similarly politically enmeshed, being introduced into Japan by government leaders as a way to protect and bring good fortune to the state, and not as a popular movement of personal faith among ordinary Japanese people. Contrast this with China where the monasteries maintained their independence throughout, refusing even to pay allegiance to the emperor as their sovereign, and relying not on government sponsorship but on a broad popular base of support and private contributions by individual families.

The particular selection of texts the Japanese made from the Chinese and Korean traditions and the interpretations these texts received were also much affected by Japanese cultural predispositions. In the later neo-Confucianism of the Tokugawa period, for example, Japanese philosophers tended to reject the more abstract, transcendental, and rationalist elements of the philosophy of Zhu Xi (Shushi) in favor of material, phenomenal, sensual, immediate, intuitive principles. Japanese philosophers often explicitly criticized Chinese philosophers for being too intellectual, abstract, logical, and otherworldly, odd as this may sound to Indian or Western philosophers, who tend to think of Chinese philosophy as being less abstract and analytical, and more intuitive and holistic.

Clearly, as far as the non-Western components of Japanese philosophy are concerned, the comparison of Chinese and Japanese Confucian and Buddhist texts and their emphases and implications will be highly instructive. Before we select texts to consider, however, we must specify our criteria: which of the texts imported from the Asian mainland are themselves truly philosophy? This is a major issue, in that much of what we would probably want to include as Japanese philosophy (and the same is true of Chinese philosophy) is often classified as religion, that is, as religious writing, especially Buddhism. This is a problem that can arise in the study of all the major traditions. Most Western philosophy during the medieval period in Europe is Christian philosophy. Much, though by no means all, Indian philosophy is Hindu and Buddhist. And here we must acknowledge that there is no firm consensus among scholars. Some Chinese experts exclude Buddhist writings from the catalogue of Chinese philosophy, while others, such as Fung Yulan and Hu Shih, include certain Buddhist texts as Chinese philosophy. Similarly, Indian scholars cannot agree on whether some parts of Hinduism, Buddhism, and Jainism qualify as philosophy or whether all such writing should be considered religion.

We will argue on the side of those who support a distinction between religious and philosophical writings within Hinduism, Jainism, Buddhism, and Christianity. But, within Christianity, Hinduism, and Buddhism, how do we separate the religion from the philosophy? This is a very large and difficult question, but we would argue that religion is primarily a combination of personal faith (felt inner experience) and communal ritual activity (so that there can be and are religions, as in Africa and among American Indians, without any written texts), while the associated philosophy is the attempt to intellectually explain and systematize problems that arise in interpreting and defending religious texts.

Religious texts speak, for example, of the difference between body and soul, but do not bother to explain exactly what that distinction is or how the two are related; or we find scattered throughout religious texts statements that, taken together, appear contradictory (the problem of evil, for example, is the problem of how to reconcile the religious beliefs that God is all-powerful, and all-good, and that evil, nonetheless, exists). Similarly, there is the problem of intellectually reconciling in Buddhism how the soul can be born into a different body after death when, according to Buddhism, the soul does not exist. How can God be said to be eternal, supreme, perfect, and still be worried about human beings (though this may be a problem that philosophers themselves have created)? Indian Hindu, Jain, and Buddhist schools all accepted the doctrine of karmic causality, but this opened up the philosophical debate concerning precisely what is meant by causality, and in particular, whether causality produces something new, or whether the effect already exists in some sense in the cause. Finally, there is the intellectual problem of the meaning of religious language. If God is so completely different from us, how can we apply words such as "love," "caring," "knowing," "making," etc. to God? And if we do not use words of ordinary language (normally used to describe ordinary human beings and their relationships to one another), then how can we talk about God at all?

These are not *religious* problems, not problems for religious belief. But they can become problems for intellectuals, creating a stumbling block to religious belief. They are intellectual problems that must be resolved before these intellectuals can continue their religious progress. And of course it is precisely these intellectual (philosophical) problems associated with religious texts and religious beliefs that the critics of any religion will focus on in attacking that religion. So defenders of a particular religion will have to be prepared to answer such attacks, not those from the inside, so to speak, but attacks from the outside seeking to undermine the religion and supplant it with another.

For many religious thinkers, these intellectual problems and philosophical solutions are a decidedly nonreligious distraction to be tolerated, at best, if at all, only temporarily, as one might need to clear a roadblock before getting on with the really important task of continuing the journey. The early Christian church father, Tertullian, and the original Śākyamuni Buddha were very concerned that philosophical questions not replace or become a substitute for religious concerns. After approximately a century and a half of Islamic philosophy, Islamic religious leaders decided that it was not a good idea to try to mix religion with philosophy, but that it was better to keep the religion pure and free of philosophical theorizing. But Islam is exceptional among the world religions in that regard. Christianity, Buddhism, and Hinduism made an early decision that however different philosophy and religion were, and however much more important, from their point of view, religion was than philosophy, nonetheless philosophy was necessary to remove intellectual obstacles to religious progress, to justify faith to skeptics and to defend the religion against attack. In that sense, Nāgārjuna, Seng Zhau, Hui Neng, Kūkai are Buddhist philosophers, Shankara is a Hindu philosopher, and Aquinas a Christian philosopher.

We have felt it important here to clarify the distinction between philosophy and religion, but in fact, the selection of Chinese texts considered to be philosophical has already been made with considerable consensus. That is, among the majority of philosophers considering "Chinese philosophy," there is wide agreement on the body of Confucian, Taoist, Mohist, Legalist, and Buddhist texts, which ought to be included. It follows that if

we know which Chinese texts conventionally count as being philosophical, we can be reasonably sure that where these same texts have Japanese
derivatives or offspring the latter are prime candidates for inclusion in
Japanese philosophy. Similarly, where the debate between followers of the
Chinese philosophers Zhu Xi and Wang Yangming is continued by
Korean writers in a peculiarly Korean way, this is widely accepted as an
example of Korean philosophy.

Having established our criteria, what then shall we include in our
survey of Japanese philosophy? There are three main groups, corresponding to three main historical periods. Early Confucian and Buddhist philosophy (from the eighth century on); neo-Confucianism of the Tokugawa
period (1603–1868); and philosophy inspired in style and content by the
Western thought introduced in the Meiji period (beginning in 1868),
which has in the decades since come to engender its own fresh and distinctly "Japanese" scion. In the following chapters we will follow this historical progression. In chapter 2 we shall discuss pre-Tokugawa Japanese
Buddhist philosophy; in chapter 3, Tokugawa Japanese Confucianist philosophy; in chapter 4, Western-style Japanese philosophy following the
Meiji Restoration; and in chapter 5, Japanese postwar philosophy, as well
as Japanese responses and contributions to the displacement of modernity by postmodernity.

CHAPTER 2

THε BⵣDDHIꟅT PHAꟅε

We said in chapter 1 that philosophy arises out of a reflection on an ancient, highly developed traditional civilization, precisely at the point where traditions underlying that civilization are called into question as being no longer able to support it. In China, well over a millennium of feudal civilization spanning the Xia, Shang, and Zhou dynasties achieved remarkable sophistication in many fields, including painting, architecture, writing, written history, bronze work, and military science. When this civilization began to decay, that heritage provided the rich ground from which philosophical reflection could sprout and flourish in the sixth century BCE.

The contrast between China and the Japanese archipelago at this time is stark. In China, the literate, bronze and iron, feudal civilization is already old and degenerating, and Kongzi (Confucius), China's first philosopher, has risen to condemn the existing political morass and seek healthy new directions for the tradition. Japan, meanwhile, is still evolving slowly from its Stone Age magico-fertility culture, known as Jōmon (5000 BCE–200 BCE), toward the early metal-using shamanistic and hierarchical Yayoi culture (200 BCE–200 CE). Even a whole new millennium later, when Japan finally came into contact with Chinese civilization (directly, or indirectly via Korea), Japanese culture was still at a comparatively early stage of development.

All this is significant for us in that what had taken China thousands of years to evolve arrived in Japan all at once. Thus, in the fifth century CE, bronze was being introduced to the Japanese through Korea while

China's techniques of using iron (discovered in the Han dynasty, 200 BCE–200 CE) were transmitted to western Japan directly at almost the same time. The same telescoping occurs in the field of culture: whereas writing (2000 BCE), literature (1000 BCE), philosophy (500 BCE) and Buddhism (100 CE) appeared in China hundreds of years apart, they all arrived in Japan simultaneously.

The most significant consequence of this for us is that philosophy appears in Japan fully formed, and more importantly, is perceived as being an essential, perhaps indispensable part of a more advanced and more successful alien civilization. In this lies its appeal to Japanese rulers of the period, and a first contrast between Chinese and Japanese philosophy. In China, philosophy arises from individual thinkers systematically criticizing ancient traditions (and then one another), and pleading with their political rulers, usually unsuccessfully, to give them the chance to apply their new theories to the reordering of society. In Japan, philosophy is brought largely by the rulers themselves as a way to learn and benefit from the advanced, rich, and powerful Chinese (and this is something we shall consider at greater length in chapter 3).

A second contrast between Chinese and Japanese philosophy occurs through what we have already referred to as "acculturation." The Japanese project was at first, to be sure, one of imitation in the interests of development, with the distant goal of emulating, or even surpassing, China. However, needless to say, the Japanese could only approach this project with the preconceptions and predilections of their own culture, where these had been reinforced over centuries of isolation to the point where they appeared to have an absolute justification. Where the local culture encountered elements alien to its own understanding or taste, it was bound either to reject them or to interpret them in some more satisfying way. The same occurred when the imported ideas did not correspond precisely with the Japanese political scheme.

Given this, we ourselves are not likely to be able to understand Japanese philosophy and its divergence from Chinese models unless we examine the beliefs, tastes, and customs that prevailed in Japan before the arrival of philosophy from the Asian continent, and the mutual influence of the preexistent culture and the new. Also, we should investigate the social and political scene at the time, and the manner in which the Japanese rulers selected and modified the imported thought according to their purpose.

The absolute nature accorded by the Japanese to their beliefs of that time is evidenced by the fact that these had, and indeed needed, no collective name. What later became known as Shintōism was at this point an amorphous set of shamanistic folk practices of a basically animistic nature. We should hesitate to call this a religion. As we pointed out in chapter 1, it is always potentially misleading to refer to any non-Western culture by Western labels, and this includes the label *religion*. We can refer to Judaism or Buddhism as distinct religions, but not to shamanistic and animistic practices, which are so immanent in the total fabric of life that no entity identifiable as "religion" can be abstracted.

By animism we mean the belief in the power or force of many varied things of everyday life—clouds, trees, rocks, animals, and so on. This special power, force, or potentiality is greater in some things than in others, and more important in some than others from the standpoint of human well-being. What we might be tempted to call "religious" practices in such societies focus on various magical techniques for harnessing and controlling these powerful natural forces. Early Japanese called these forces *kami*. *Kami* is often translated as "gods," but since the word *gods* usually connotes conscious, anthropomorphic beings with distinct personalities and gender (e.g., Zeus, or Venus), which most *kami* (with some notable exceptions) did not have, it is probably a mistake to think of the *kami* in this early period as gods. Pre-Buddhist Japanese religious practices were probably very much like those of other early agriculturalists, a celebration of life in the here and now, supported by shamanistic techniques in which the forces of good were appealed to and those of evil appeased in order to maintain the bountiful rhythm of earthly life.

As with Taoism in China, it was the introduction of Buddhism that gave contours to this animism for the first time and gave it a name, Shintōism ("the way of the gods," in contrast with "the way of the Buddha"), and made it appear for the first time as a distinct "religion" (although the Japanese word *shūkyō*, meaning religion, was until the Meiji era a Buddhist term meaning Buddhism). When Buddhism first appeared in Japan, it was as a distinct, self-contained entity, complete with elaborate forms of ritual, written texts, initiation procedures, a priesthood, a set of moral codes, etc. set off from other aspects of Japanese culture and something that one could either join or not. If one decided not to become a Buddhist one could still function as a member of one's Japanese village. In this it contrasted with Shintō: it would be literally unthinkable for a member of such a community not to participate in a hundred and one daily acts of respect and devotion to various local *kami*, in crossing a stream, walking by a large tree, climbing a hill, and so on. Such practices were as natural as breathing.

It was only by way of comparison with the novel Chinese Buddhism that Japanese began to think of their own ritual conduct as a similar and perhaps competing "religion." This was similar to what had happened in China with the recognition of various traditional ritual practices as an indigenous "religion," later called Taoism, to counter (or complement) the alien Indian "religion" known as Buddhism. To complete the parallel, Shintō then simply added whatever Buddhism had that it lacked: if Buddhism had texts, then so must Shintō; if Buddhism had uniform practices, then so should Shintō; if Buddhism had an organized hierarchy of priests and temple complexes, then these too must be added to Shintō. So it was that a Shintō religion parallel to Buddhism was gradually constructed. Buddhism also transformed Shintō. Buddhism gave the *kami* personalities and human-like representations in painting and sculpture (treating the *kami* like the Indian pre-Buddhist *devas*); also, through writing and by providing a model to emulate, it gave indigenous Japanese magico-mythological shamanism a more systematic and coherent theoretical foundation, in short, what could be called "a religion." Later an accommodation was worked out between Buddhism and Shintō, whereby the Shintō *kami* protected the sites of Buddhist temple complexes in mountainous areas and often themselves became followers of Buddhism, or, as with Indian *devas*, minor Buddhist deities.

Despite Japan's adoption of Buddhism, and its Buddhist transformation of Shintō, many elements of primitive Shintō have continued undiminished well into the twentieth century. The *kami* not having been anthropomorphized or systematized into abstract principles, the distinctively Japanese emphasis of ancient Shintō on the here-and-now, sensual aestheticism, and ritualized ceremonialism has endured. Indeed, as we will see, this seems to be a permanent pattern of Japanese absorption of alien cultures: whatever Japanese borrow from other cultures is reinterpreted to coincide with traditional Japanese beliefs and practices. In the end it is debatable to what degree alien cultures have really changed Japanese culture. Because the Japanese never had foreign cultures forced on them by invading armies, they felt free to selectively choose what they needed to improve their military, technology, economy, and science, but not in a way that would seriously undermine their own non-Chinese (and later non-Western) culture. In most cases the alien, borrowed culture was simply used to justify and defend existing Japanese beliefs and practices, rather than to introduce entirely new ones. Where a new practice was brought in (e.g., the Confucian pattern of governmental organization introduced into Japan in the seventh century), it was almost always a failure that had to be later abandoned or else brought into line with Japanese traditions.

In short, then, whereas Buddhism developed gradually in China as a religion, independent of government support or inhibition, it was brought to Japan by the government for the protection of the government. And whereas Chinese saw Buddhism as very different from traditional Chinese culture, and not at all as a way to bring sophisticated intellectualism to China (after 600–700 years of highly developed Chinese philosophy, letters, etc.), Japanese saw Buddhism as part of a package of Chinese cultural superiority and intellectual sophistication, in writing, history, government, literature, and so on. For these reasons, in China Buddhism spread among all classes of people, in all parts of the country, whereas in Japan it was limited for several centuries to aristocratic families living in the capital. Moreover, whereas Chinese Buddhists tried and largely succeeded in staying out of government service, Japanese Buddhists were from the beginning heavily involved in the affairs of state.

Although Confucianism and Buddhism arrived more or less simultaneously in Japan as part of a "package deal" of Chinese culture, for various reasons Buddhism played by far the greater role before Tokugawa (seventeenth century). One reason for this was the rising power of Buddhism over Confucianism in China at the time significant contact with Japan occurred. In the Sui dynasty Buddhism was at its peak in China and was strongly supported by the Sui rulers. A more practical reason inhibiting the spread of Confucianism was the enormous difficulty for Japanese people to read Chinese. Although the characters were the same, the grammar of the two languages is completely different. Not until the Tokugawa period a thousand years later were these problems sorted out, affording Japanese greater access to Chinese sources. Yet another reason for the greater impact of Buddhism in the early centuries was the Japanese government's interest in the magical power of the new religion to protect the nation, and especially to safeguard the capital and the ruling families. Indeed, if the Japanese did give attention to Confucianism at this time, one of the main reasons, besides the general conservative tendency of Chinese Confucianism to encourage discipline, duty and loyalty to rulers and the state, was the *Yin Yang* and *I Jing* magical and ceremonial aspects that had become attached to Chinese Confucianism. Government leaders saw these as useful means to ward off evil and predict the success or failure of risky projects, including military campaigns. In the end, however, it was not Confucianism but Buddhism that was to dominate, its monastic organization helping it to spread out in a series of temple complexes, and to propagate itself through a program of indoctrination and education.

Indeed, for nearly a thousand years (that is, from the introduction of Chinese culture in the seventh century until the Tokugawa period in the seventeenth century) Buddhism played much the same educational role in Japan as Confucianism had in China. Apart from a few aristocratic family members who were educated in elite Confucian schools, the most educated people in Japan were the Buddhist monks. Throughout most of this long period, the Buddhists ran the schools and educated most of the ruling and military elites. Ironically, it was the Zen Buddhists who introduced neo-Confucianism (Zhu Xi and Wang Yangming) to Japanese in the seventeenth century.

In China, on the other hand, education had been in the hands of the Confucianists since the Han dynasty. To become a civil servant an aspiring young Chinese had to pass a statewide examination based almost exclusively on the Confucian classics. It was the most gifted of those who had studied for these exams in small Confucian schools that constituted China's literate, educated class, regardless of whether they came from the smallest village or the largest city.

Because Buddhism in Japan predominated over Confucianism before the Tokugawa Shōgunate, Buddhist *philosophy* flourished in Japan a thousand years before Confucian philosophy took root. As we will see in chapter 4, even today the most successful and distinctively Japanese philosophy is that of the Kyōto school, combining Zen Buddhism with the European philosophies of Hegel and Heidegger. This is why we want to devote this chapter to the development of Buddhist philosophy, before turning in chapter 3 to Tokugawa Confucian philosophy. It is important to emphasize our focus. In chapter 1 we saw how difficult it is to disentangle Buddhist religion from Buddhist philosophy, and we also suggested there how we proposed to make that separation. This is not, then, an account of the history of Japanese Buddhism, but only an outline of some of the main points in the development of Japanese Buddhist *philosophy*.

In light of what we have already said concerning the Japanese traditional preference for the aesthetic surface of the world as it directly appears to us, it should come as no surprise that in their reception of Buddhism (and, as we shall see in the next chapter, Confucianism too), the Japanese in general rejected any transcendent, other-worldly, metaphysical reality "behind" appearances, and embraced instead the "here-now" phenomenal world sanctified and glorified as aesthetic ritual. To fully appreciate the novelty of the manner in which Japanese interpreted Buddhism, we need first to be familiar with earlier, Chinese interpretations.

The philosophically most sophisticated Buddhism to emerge in China (Tien Tai, Hua Yen, and Chan) endorsed the profound and paradoxical idea that the changing, dependent phenomenal world is simply a false way of seeing the eternal, ultimate reality. This striking theory results from carrying to its logical conclusion the idea that there is nothing in the world but this one Buddha reality. There is nothing else. There is therefore no dualism by which we might contrast the Buddha reality with the ordinary space-time physical world. What we experience as ordinary mundane existence is simply the one Buddha reality misunderstood. Chinese Buddhists said, for example, that the real nature of dried grass is the Buddha, meaning that there is no ghostly Buddha-thing behind the grass, or in addition to the grass. If you really understood the grass in its essential nature you would see that it is the Buddha Nature. The Buddha Nature is the real nature of everything, including dried grass.

Looking now at the Japanese Buddhists' interpretation, we find them taking all this a step further: they infer that "the Buddha is *nothing but* this dried grass" in a kind of reduction of unseen metaphysical entities to the sensual, aesthetic delight in ordinary sense perception. Should the Japanese feel guilty cherishing and ritualizing the aesthetic beauty of everyday objects as they had been doing for thousands of years? Not at all! The most profound Buddhist metaphysics says this everyday world of sense objects is identical to the most profound metaphysical and spiritual entities. This is similar to the difference between Hegel's identity of artistic form and content in Classical art and the neo-Hegelian aestheticians' identity of artistic form and content. Like Chinese Buddhists, Hegel understood this to mean that material form points to spiritual content, while neo-Hegelian aestheticians, like Japanese Buddhists, took it to mean that there is no spiritual content apart from its material embodiment in artistic form. Hegel, like Chinese Buddhists, utilized the sensual and phenomenal to get to the transcendent; the neo-Hegelian aestheticians, like Japanese Buddhists, used this identity to bring us back to the here and now, to the sensuously aesthetic, immanent, empirical world.

Of course, if two things are really identical, the relation between them should be symmetrical: if A is B, then B is equally A; if understanding A leads to understanding B, then understanding B should also lead to understanding A; if the real nature of A is B, then equally the real nature of B should be A. But epistemologically and psychologically, our human way of understanding one thing is not necessarily identical with our way of understanding the other, though the first may lead to the second. It is not therefore symmetrical, but a one-way street.

In Christian symbolism, for instance, the Holy Ghost is not identical with the icon of the dove in religious paintings; it is just that it is easier for ordinary people to understand the visual imagery of the dove descending from God to man (specifically to Mary in the traditional imagery of the Annunciation) than it is for them to grasp something so profound, mysterious and, above all, so imperceivable as the Holy Ghost, the Third Person in the Trinity. Similarly, God is often represented as a father and as a shepherd without being identical to (without literally being) a father or a shepherd.

On the other hand, nineteenth-century "natural theologians" held that God was nothing but human relations, like the love of a father for his children. They believed, that is, that God did not exist over and above human relations. In a similar way, Naturalists or Pantheists held that God was simply another name for Nature, or for all there is. Likewise,

Japanese Buddhists, in keeping with the cultural predispositions we noted in their ancient, pre-Buddhist traditions, tended to reduce any transcendental, metaphysical aspects of Buddhism to ordinary phenomenal reality. The difference between the Chinese and the Japanese understanding of the intimate relation of the Buddha reality to ordinary sense appearances may seem slight, but its implications for Japanese Buddhist philosophy are enormous. So, we need to look at this cultural difference more closely.

In China there was a long Taoist tradition before the introduction of Buddhism in which the principle of spontaneity, known as the *Tao*, governed the growth and form of everything in the world, from ducks to bamboo leaves, and could therefore be represented (at least in the minds of educated Chinese) as any ordinary thing whatever, from ducks flying to bamboo leaves. But, of course, when these Taoists talked about flying ducks or bamboo leaves they were not just talking about ducks and leaves but about the principle of spontaneity which differentiates ducks from bamboo leaves and which internally governs the life of each. And this Taoist perspective carried over into many forms of Chinese Buddhism.

This is not to suggest that Chinese Taoists or Buddhists, especially late Mādhyamika/Yogācāra Mahāyāna Buddhists, embraced dualism. Far from it. Chinese Buddhists explicitly *denied* any absolute transcendence of Buddha from the immanent empirical, sensual world. They rejected the idea that there were two separate things, or two separate realms—one sensuous appearance, the other spiritual reality. Nonetheless, they did not simply identify the two, much less reduce the transcendent to the phenomenal. The reality of, the real nature of each and every thing, they said, is the Buddha (not that each and every thing simply *is* the Buddha), just as the Taoists had earlier held that the underlying, governing principle of each and every thing is the *Tao* (without saying that everything simply *is* the *Tao*). The first is a metaphysical claim concerning the essential reality of a thing; the second is a rejection of metaphysics in favor of an aesthetic acceptance of phenomenal surface.

Just as in Western philosophy, the notion of "identity" is notoriously tricky. In the strictest sense, if two things are identical, then whatever is true of the one must be true of the other. That is, the two are different in name only. "Śākyamuni" is identical with "Siddhartha" in the strong sense that these are simply two different names for the same individual. Therefore whatever we truthfully say of "Siddhartha" holds equally for "Śākyamuni." If Siddhartha's mother was named Maya, then so was Śākyamuni's mother named Maya.

But we often use the term *identity* in a weaker, less strict sense, meaning only that B is the essential or most important element of A, not that A and B are simply different names for the exact same thing. If we say that Śākyamuni was the Buddha, we don't mean that "Śākyamuni" and "Buddha" are simply two different names for the same thing, since, if we are Buddhists, we also hold that there are many Buddhas, indeed, that everyone (and indeed every sentient being) is potentially a Buddha. We mean that in addition to being a man and a prince and a son and a husband and a father, Śākyamuni was also a Buddha and that that was the most important, essential, significant thing about him. When the mystic says, "I am God," it does not follow that if he was born in Aberdeen, Scotland, in 1930 that God was born in Aberdeen, Scotland, in 1930. It only means that the essence or core of his being is divine. According to our commonsense, ordinary understanding, there are many things we can truthfully say of him that we cannot truthfully say of God. The mystic means that God is the essential part of every person, and that it is this part of him or herself with which the mystic wants to identify as his or her most important, essential nature.

From the ordinary, commonsense perspective, of course, the two are not strictly identical; only from an enlightened perspective can the two be claimed to be in a sense the same. Even when we reject dualism, there is still a difference, in other words, between the ordinary way of seeing the bamboo leaves and an enlightened way of seeing those same bamboo leaves. A famous Chan saying is, "Before I began studying Chan I saw mountains as mountains and rivers as rivers, but when I had studied Chan for thirty years I no longer saw mountains as mountains and rivers as rivers; but now that I have finally mastered Chan I once again see mountains as mountains and rivers as rivers." What is the difference between the first and the third stage? In both cases he sees mountains as mountains and rivers as rivers; why spend a lifetime learning something so obvious as this, something he presumably knew as a child? In the first stage of ordinary experience he saw mountains simply as mountains, while in the third stage he saw the real Buddha Nature of the mountains, that is, he saw the mountains as mountains exemplifying the Buddha.

Thus, throughout the vast Mahāyāna literature, especially that of Mādhyamika and Yogācāra, the rejection of dualism and the assertion of the identity of all things with the Buddha Nature can be interpreted in slightly different ways, and between Chinese and Japanese interpretations a slight but significant difference of emphasis may be observed. On the one hand, this identity can be understood to diminish or reduce the ordinary phenomenal world in favor of its metaphysically "real Buddha Nature." On the other hand, this identity can be understood to reduce the traditionally transcendent, metaphysical Buddhist reality to the here-now empirical reality of everyday life. Chinese Buddhists tended toward the

first, moving gradually away from a strong dualism of empirical appearance versus Buddhist reality, common sense ignorance versus Buddhist
enlightenment, toward a weak identity of the ultimate Buddha reality
with the essential, underlying, inherent nature of each thing. Japanese
Buddhists, on the other hand, tended to concentrate on the second, focusing on the immanent, empirical, sensual reality at the expense of the inner
metaphysical nature, or underlying principle of these empirical, sensual
entities.

It would be false, of course, to portray all this as the Japanese incom-
prehension of Chinese Buddhism; they simply understood it in their own
way. Remember, the pre-Buddhist Shintō *kami* were not perceived as independently existing anthropomorphic gods understood as transcendent
beings, much less as abstract metaphysical principles, but simply as the
power or strength that certain natural objects, such as a tree, a stream, a
large rock, a mountain, or even a person, exemplified. Even to speak of a
kami as the "power *of*" some natural object suggests too great a separation
of the power from the object. If a large tree had been split by lightning, it
could become a *kami*, that is, recognized as a powerful object, as a source
or center of extraordinary natural strength and power. If we ask, "What
did the Japanese people worship, respect and revere, the tree or the *power
in* the tree?" our question would probably make no sense to these early
worshipers of *kami*; the question presupposes a distinction they themselves did not draw.

In many similar so-called "animistic" religions, everything is perceived to be animated by a force, power, or character: from a drop of
water to a butterfly to a cloud. Some objects have greater force or power
than others, and these must be respected and revered. Such a conception
of the world is prior to any mind-body, matter-soul distinction, so that it
would be a mistake to read into the reverence for *kami* the idea of an
immaterial indwelling spiritual soul that inhabits rocks or trees, just as it
would be a mistake to interpret the *kami* as gods, in the sense in which we
think of gods as anthropomorphic beings such as Zeus or Odin. The result
of such an "animistic" world view is an aesthetic sense of the dynamic
energy immanent in all of nature.

We see, then, no radical transformation of Japanese thinking on
the Chinese Buddhist model. Rather, Japanese interpreted Chinese
Buddhism, as everything else, in accord with their own tradition. Indeed,
what is most interesting about Japanese culture is the paradox that while
they borrowed almost everything from other cultures, they never really
renounced or gave up anything in their own. In every case they accepted
the new, alien culture and then interpreted it in a uniquely Japanese way.
The Japanese have always lived according to the rhythm of the seasons,

feeling a part of nature, and engaging in sensual and ritual celebration of this participation. Nature, it is true, is not always benign, and faced with typhoons, earthquakes, and similar catastrophes, few know better than the Japanese its destructive force. As Ivan Morris has written, "Human life . . . is full of sad vicissitudes, fleeting, impermanent like the seasons. Helplessness and failure are built into human enterprises . . ." (39). In a different culture, all this might drive the populace to seek solace in the otherworldly, but the Japanese, lucidly facing misfortune and fate itself, find an aesthetic consolation: "In the very impermanence and poignancy of the human condition, the Japanese have discovered a positive quality . . ." (40). Morris is referring of course to the "special beauty inherent in evanescence, worldly misfortune, and the 'pathos of things' *(mono no aware)*" (40). It is this aesthetic sense (also to be expressed in concepts such as *wabi* and *sabi*) that comes to inhabit Chan Buddhism in Japan and ensure the distinctiveness of Zen.

With these preliminary remarks now before us, let us return to the early beginnings of Japanese Buddhism in order to trace the development of Japanese Buddhist philosophy. It is through decisive efforts of the Japanese government, and for government purposes, that Buddhism entered Japan along with Chinese learning. This occurred around the middle of the sixth century CE. Before this there were a number of foreign, mostly Korean, Buddhists living and worshiping in Japan, but this had limited impact on society at large. The exact chronology of Buddhism's advance to official recognition is unclear. It may have been in 522 when a Chinese monk, Shiba Tachito, built a small Buddhist temple, or, according to the *Nihon shoki,* in 552 when the ruler of the Korean Kingdom, Paekche (Japanese, Kudara), presented a Buddhist image and various sūtras to the Yamato court as part of a political treaty. Whichever the case, Buddhism came to Japan as part of a government plan for advancement and protection. Arriving with it were various other forms of Chinese culture, including writing, elementary forms of Confucianism, Taoism, and the idea of official government historical documents.

Before the *Kojiki* (*Record of Ancient Matters,* 712 CE) and *Nihon shoki* (*Chronological History of Japan,* 720 CE), along with its sequel *Nihongi* (797), all modeled after Chinese historical records, there were many aristocratic families *(uji)* claiming descent from various tutelary deities *(ujigami)*. In the latter half of the sixth century the two most powerful of the aristocratic *uji* were the Soga and Mononobe clans. The Soga served as managers of the imperial estates, thus coming into contact with foreign immigrants. In this way, they encountered more advanced foreign technology and learning (directly or indirectly from China), which they felt Japan should adopt. This progressive outlook contrasted with that of the Mononobe, who wanted to maintain the status quo.

Emperor Kimmei (531–571) worked out a compromise that allowed the Soga to embrace Buddhism as a kind of test to see whether the local Japanese *kami* would accept the new religion or would be angered (and take out their anger on the people). When natural disasters then occurred, they were indeed attributed to the gods' anger over the new religion and Buddhist images were thrown into the canal. However, Emperor Yōmei (585–587) embraced Buddhism in the hope he would be cured of a grave illness. When he nonetheless died the Soga and Mononobe (joined by the Nakatomi) went to war over the accession to the throne. With the victory of the Soga, Yōmei's son, Prince Shōtoku became regent to his mother, Yōmei's wife, Empress Suiko, and Buddhism's future in Japan was assured.

By the eighth century the Yamato clan had gained the upper hand and could cement their position by commissioning the two historical records (the *Kojiki* and *Nihongi*) that made it appear that they had been the imperial family from time immemorial, going all the way back to direct descent from the Sun Goddess, Amaterasu Ō Mikami, and fitting into this construction important but secondary roles for other prominent family clans previously in competition with the Yamato. According to these official historical accounts, the first Japanese Emperor was Jimmu, whose reign began in 660 BCE. In fact, however, the Yamato clan, which later became the imperial family, had only begun to gain hegemony over other competing clans in the fourth century CE.

Historically, Prince Shōtoku is credited with great learning as a Confucian scholar and a Buddhist adept. Doubtless, some of this praise is exaggerated, but Shōtoku was surely well educated in the new Chinese learning and largely responsible for its Japanese reception. A well-known example of this early Chinese influence, whether written by Shōtoku himself or for which he was ultimately responsible, is the so-called "Seventeen-Article Constitution," which was not so much a constitution as a set of precepts of social behavior. For our purposes it is interesting for the clear indications of Chinese influence, certainly Buddhist and Confucianist, and perhaps even Taoist and Legalist.

As we will see in the next chapter, Confucianism at the level of official state policy had (by the seventh century) come to mean a moral and cosmological justification for a hierarchical feudal relationship of duties and obligations between higher and lower social orders, of "lord" to "vassal" and "vassal" to "lord," as well as the Confucian notion that good government is the rule by morally good rulers who set the ethical example for their subjects, practicing the Confucian virtues of human-heartedness *(ren)*, propriety *(li)*, righteousness *(yi)*, and so on. Just as Heaven *(tian)* is above Earth *(di)*, so the ruler should be above the subjects, and just as the universe can only function if Earth does not usurp the proper function of Heaven, so human affairs are best managed if the subjects do not attempt to wrest control from the rulers. Ethically, if the ruler is a morally good person, then, just as a child will tend to follow the example of his father, so the subjects will tend to follow the example of their ruler and all affairs will be handled according to principles of righteousness, fairness, and humanity. From the Han dynasty (approximately 200 BCE to 200 CE) there was also the notion, reflected in Shōtoku's "constitution," of a reciprocal causal relation between Man and Heaven: if human affairs are not properly ordered, this will cause a breakdown in the cosmos, causing eclipses and the like; also, vice versa, if the relation between Heaven and Earth is in some way damaged, this will be reflected in human disasters—both natural and civil, causing flooding, earthquakes, war, and famine. Thus, in this post-Han Confucianism, the affairs of Earth, Man, and Heaven are all interconnected.

Here are some obviously Confucian excerpts from Prince Shōtoku's "Constitution":

> Harmony should be valued and quarrels should be avoided. Everyone has his biases, and few men are far-sighted. Therefore some disobey their lords and fathers and keep up feuds with their neighbors. But when the superiors are in harmony with each other and the inferiors are friendly, then affairs are discussed quietly and the right view of matters prevails. Then there is nothing that cannot be accomplished! . . . Do not fail to obey the commands of your Sovereign. He is like Heaven, which is above the Earth, and the vassal is like the Earth, which bears up Heaven. When Heaven and Earth are properly in place, the four seasons follow their course and all is well in Nature. But if the Earth attempts to take the place of Heaven, Heaven would simply fall in ruin. That is why the vassal listens when the lord speaks, and the inferior obeys when the superior acts. Consequently when you receive the commands of your Sovereign, do not fail to carry them out or ruin will be the natural result. . . . The Ministers and officials of the state should make proper behavior their first principle, for if the superiors do not behave properly, the inferiors are disorderly; if inferiors behave improperly, offenses will naturally result. Therefore when lord and vassal behave with propriety [Chinese *li*,] the distinctions of rank are not confused: when the people behave properly the Government will be in good order. . . . Every man has his own work. Do not let the spheres of duty be confused. When wise men are entrusted with office, the sound of praise arises. If corrupt men hold office, disasters and tumult multiply.

. . . Good faith is the foundation of right. In everything let there be good faith, for if the lord and the vassal keep faith with one another, what cannot be accomplished? If the lord and the vassal do not keep faith with each other, everything will end in failure. . . . To subordinate private interests to the public good— that is the path of a vassal.

The second article is obviously Buddhist. "The three treasures, which are Buddha, the Buddhist Law, and the Buddhist Priesthood, should be given sincere reverence, for they are the final refuge of all living things. Few men are so bad that they cannot be taught their truth."

There are also passages that sound more like the skeptical, relativist, and subjectivist Taoist philosopher Zhuangzi.

Let us control ourselves and not be resentful when others disagree with us, for all men have hearts and each heart has its own leanings. The right of others is our wrong, and our right is their wrong. We are not unquestionably sages, nor are they unquestionably fools. Both of us are simply ordinary men. How can anyone lay down a rule by which to distinguish right from wrong? For we are all wise sometimes and foolish at others.

There are even a few passages indicating the influence of the Legalist philosopher of the Qin dynasty (255–207 BCE), Han Feizi, who argued that a system of strict rewards and punishments was far more effective in good government than trying to encourage rulers and subjects to behave morally.

Punish the evil and reward the good. This was the excellent rule of antiquity. . . . Know the difference between merit and demerit, and deal out to each its reward and punishment. . . . You high officials who have charge of public affairs, make it your business to give clear rewards and punishments. (In Tsunoda et al., vol. 1, 47–51)

With Buddhism in official favor and more and more of its texts arriving, Japanese Buddhist scholars began to be overtaken by enigmas that had earlier perplexed the Chinese. Both were unaware that Buddhist doctrines had emerged from a long and tortuous past. With the notable exceptions of Chan and Pure Land Buddhism, nearly all Buddhist schools had developed not in China but in India. There, for more than a thousand years, Buddhism had gone through vast transformations. Hundreds of schools had emerged to dispute each other, each claiming to be the true interpreter of the original Śākyamuni, with some surviving (usually in a new mutation) and others fading into oblivion. However, when Buddhism began arriving in China, the scholars there had no knowledge of these antagonisms. They assumed all Buddhist schools and sects must have a common core. Yet, as wave upon wave of new Indian schools of Buddhism reached China, Chinese Buddhists could not help recognizing (and being deeply troubled by) differences and even contradictions they perceived among the many different Buddhist doctrines being introduced. Unlike Indian Buddhists, who were engaged in vigorous debates among competing doctrines, Chinese Buddhists strove to find (or construct) some form of unity underlying the apparent diversity.

The preferred principle of unity most often employed (first developed in India) was a developmental schema in which earlier schools were interpreted as steps toward a final doctrine (the "final" doctrine being the particular one that the drafters of the schema themselves embraced). Naturally, each new sect claimed for its doctrine that it sprang directly from the mouth of Śākyamuni. Indeed, every Buddhist sūtra begins with the words, "Thus have I heard . . . ," followed by an account of a conversation between Śākyamuni and his disciples on some particular historical occasion. Discrepancies among different doctrines attributed to Śākyamuni were generally explained by Śākyamuni's *upāya,* or "skillful means." This was the technique of saying to the listener or listeners only what they were capable of understanding at their particular level of spiritual and intellectual development, just as one explains electricity differently to a five year old and to a high school student. In spite of this reasoning, Indians remained aware of the history of competition and antagonism among different Buddhist sects, some of which they might dismiss as having been discredited. Chinese Buddhists, in contrast, tended to accept all incoming doctrines as equally authentic forms of Buddhism "direct from the source in the West." Their successors in Japan did likewise.

This being so, we see, for example, that both Hīnayāna and Mahāyāna were accepted, the former as a beginning stage completed by the latter at a more developed stage. Similarly, different schools of Mahāyāna were all accepted as different stages in the gradual development of the final and complete doctrine. To this policy of tolerant accommodation must be added the fact that the different "schools" of Chinese and Japanese Buddhism, at least in the early stages (the Nara period in Japan), were not housed in separate temple monasteries. Different texts and doctrines might be treated in the same monastery, and a student might even study and later practice and teach two or three different doctrines, without renouncing any of them. Indeed, some of the early Nara schools (e.g., the Sanron) were only academic subjects to be studied in preparation for becoming a monk and had no practitioners at all (in much the same way Western philosophy students today study Stoicism without becoming card-carrying Stoics). Apart from Hui Neng's *Platform Sūtra* (the only non-Indian sūtra and the only Buddhist sūtra not presented as a historical conversation with the original Śākyamuni), the primary texts for Chan (Zen) Buddhism were at first the Lotus and Diamond sūtras, and later the Mādhyamika and Yogācāra sūtras. The net result of all this mutual absorption is that there is a large measure of theoretical commonality among all the different Buddhist schools, differences lying, for the most part, in the final twist each school adds to the top of its opponents' hierarchy in order to appear as the "final doctrine." As an example of this ploy, some of the early schools transitional between Hīnayāna and Mahāyāna, in a manner recalling the early Greek atomists, held that ordinary physical objects were constantly changing and so unreal, although their constituent parts were eternal and unchanging. The San Lun (Japanese, Sanron) school of Nāgārjuna, Kumārajīva, and Seng Zhao argued that this was true so far as it went but that it did not go far enough. Not only are the complex objects of everyday life changing and so unreal, but so are their constituent parts. Nothing is eternal; all is empty *(Śūnyatā)*. This was followed by the Yogācāra school, which agreed with all this but felt the Sanron had nonetheless failed to explain how so many unreal things can *appear* to be real to everyone in everyday commonsense experience. Their explanation was that they are all appearances produced by the mind *(xin)*. Chan (Zen) Buddhism is primarily a Chinese (and later Japanese) version of a combination of Mādhyamika and Yogācāra, with a twist of Taoism. Similarly, while some of the early schools distinguished the many changing and hence ultimately unreal physical objects as opposed to the one absolute Reality (whether empty or mental), later schools argued that since the Buddha reality includes everything, and excludes nothing, it must also be acknowledged that, properly understood, each of these everyday things is really the absolute, ultimate Buddha Nature, that properly understood each of these things is the Buddha reality. And then, pushing this last point one step farther, Hua Yen (Japanese, Kegon) argued that if a brick is in its real nature the Buddha reality and if a frog in its real nature is also the Buddha reality, then the brick and the frog are in a sense the same. Finally, Tien Tai (Japanese, Tendai), pushing this last point still further (without renouncing any of the previous steps, but simply according them a preliminary, partial status), argued that since the Buddha reality includes, in a sense, everything in the world and this brick contains the Buddha reality, it follows that this brick contains everything in the world. The whole world is contained in a grain of sand.

Within this sequence of steps, ascending higher and higher toward the final Buddhist goal of complete truth and enlightenment, each stage was often presented as corresponding to the length of time after his enlightenment that the relevant doctrine was first preached by Śākyamuni. So, for example, Hīnayāna is presented (by Mahāyānists) as Śākyamuni's very first sermon delivered to his pre-enlightenment fellow ascetics, while more advanced doctrines (Hua Yen (Kegon), Tientai (Tendai), Shingon) were presented as Śākyamuni's sermons delivered much later (and therefore presumably to a much more sophisticated and advanced and better pre-pared audience). Even Chan (shortened from Chan-na from the Sanskrit *dhyāna*, meaning "meditation" and pronounced Zen in Japanese) Buddhism, which pretty clearly developed over a thousand years after the death of the historical Śākyamuni, explained the fact that none of the old Indian sūtras ever talk about Chan (Zen) ideas by saying that Śākyamuni realized that this was too difficult even for his most advanced disciples. In fact, the only person, according to Chan (Zen) traditions, who understood the Chan (Zen) ideas from Śākyamuni was Kāśyapa. Once when Śākya-muni held up a flower, only Kāśyapa got the point, which he indicated simply by smiling. In short, it was by using the Indian notion of *upāya* or skillful means that Chinese and Japanese Buddhists were able to overcome initially baffling inconsistencies. Where contradictions appeared in differ-ent texts attributed to the very same Śākyamuni, they argued these away as the difference between a partial truth delivered to someone incapable of understanding the more complete truth and a fuller account given to those more advanced and better prepared.

In one way Japanese Buddhism carried still farther a movement already begun in China away from certain tendencies in Indian Buddhism. Indian Buddhism is based on a very firm pre-Buddhist foun-dation of the doctrine of reincarnation. Since we are born and reborn many times, we have the opportunity to gradually perfect our practice and understanding of Buddhism until "we finally get it right" and at last achieve Nirvāna (salvation), however thousands upon thousands of lives this may take. Eventually, all sentient beings, even monkeys, frogs, and grasshoppers, can and will achieve final enlightenment. But although Chinese and Japanese Buddhists accepted the notion of reincarnation, it did not have for them the same deep cultural and historical roots as it did in India. Consequently, Chinese Buddhists, especially Chan Buddhists, sought ways to short-circuit this long process and achieve sudden enlight-enment attainable in this life. Chanists sought sudden enlightenment through intuitive leaps of insight; with late Tantric Buddhism the same immediate illumination was sought through secret, magical means. Japanese Buddhists carried the movement toward sudden enlightenment in this lifetime even farther. Zen taught that enlightenment was simply a way of looking at ordinary things that could be achieved by a sudden shift in perspective. Japanese Tantric Buddhism (Shingon) became very popular in Japan precisely because it preached instant enlightenment through magical incantations and secret formulas.

Another point worth attention is that many schools of Buddhism, while originating in China, lasted far longer and developed much farther in Japan. This has to do with the rising and falling fortunes of Buddhism in China, which were not mirrored in Japan. When Buddhism was introduced into Japan in the sixth and seventh centuries as a novelty forming part of a package of cultural and social innovation, it already had a five-hundred-year history of development in China. More important, when Buddhism was first introduced into China in the first century CE, that country had already experienced its "golden age" (more than 500 years) of philosophy and several thousand years of a highly developed feudal culture (writing, music, literature, history, art, and so on). In contrast with the case of Japan, therefore, Buddhism was introduced into China as an alien religion in competition with an ancient, well-established, and equally sophisticated and advanced culture. Thereafter, the history of Chinese culture can be roughly divided into alternating periods of Buddhist ascendancy over traditional Chinese (mainly Confucian) culture followed by the ascendancy of traditional Chinese/Confucian culture over Buddhism.

For nearly two thousand years these two have alternated, back and forth, like a see-saw, with Buddhism gaining the upper hand when the central government was weak and the country divided, say, from the fall of the Han dynasty until the Tang dynasty (more precisely from the fifth through the ninth centuries), and Confucianism gaining preeminence over Buddhism with the reestablishment of a strong central government, starting with the Tang, but more so in the Song and Ming dynasties. With the rise of neo-Confucianism in the Song and Ming dynasties Buddhism never regained its cultural and philosophical prominence (though it long continued to exist as a popular religion). As Buddhism declined in China most of the schools of Buddhism simply died out, never to be revived. Indeed, only Chan (Zen) and Pure Land Buddhism survived the emergence of neo-Confucianism.

In Japan, on the other hand, Buddhism continued to flourish right up to the Tokugawa period (seventeenth century), when Song and Ming neo-Confucianism was finally introduced. Until Tokugawa there was no sense in Japan of the tension the Chinese felt between Buddhism and Confucianism. Thus, many Japanese schools that originated from China continued in Japan long after they had ceased to exist in China. The best example of this is tantric Buddhism. This was one of the last schools of Indian Buddhism to be introduced into China—indeed just before the rise of Confucianism and the decline of Buddhism. But to the Japanese, the tantric Buddhism of Kūkai and the new Shingon sect was the most important sect of all, not only because it was the newest, and presumably most advanced, but especially because it promised this worldly, in fact instant, enlightenment through secret, magical formulas. Long after its Chinese demise, tantric Buddhism continues even today as a major Japanese school.

Now that we have taken a quick look at the historical context in which Buddhism took root in Japan, let us examine in more detail the philosophical developments within Japanese Buddhism, beginning with Saichō's articulation of the Tendai sect, moving on to Kūkai's introduction and systematization of Shingon (tantric) Buddhism, and ending with Dōgen's unique interpretation of Zen. We will begin then with Tendai, the Japanese interpretation of the Chinese Tien Tai school of Buddhism.

Since Tendai (Tien Tai) has theoretical connections to Kegon (Hua Yen), for a better understanding we should examine the Kegon doctrine first. Kegon was one of the Six Nara schools, the earliest branches of Buddhism introduced into Japan and associated with Japan's first permanent capital at Nara. During this early period of Japanese Buddhism all Buddhist temple schools were clustered in and around the capital. They were primarily centers of academic study by Buddhist monks, and only members of the ruling elite participated in worship. This was the original Buddhism, which had been brought to Japan by its rulers for the benefit and protection of the nation. Kegon (Hua Yen) is based on the third century Indian sūtra, *Buddhavatamsaka Mahāvaipulya,* commonly referred to as the *Avatamsaka,* which means "flower-wreath," of which Hua Yen and Kegon are the respective Chinese and Japanese translations.

This is one of the most highly evolved and complex of all the Mahāyāna sūtras. Earlier we indicated how Buddhists attempted to mark the precise stage of evolution of different schools and sects by the timing of Śākyamuni's sermons after his enlightenment. The *Avatamsaka* is said to have been first preached fourteen days after his enlightenment, indicating a very advanced form of Buddhism that would have been incomprehensible to ordinary people.

The nominal founder of Hua Yen in China was Fa-shun (557–640), but the doctrine was systematically worked out by the third Chinese patriarch, Fa-tsang (643–712), who saw the Avatamsaka Sūtra as the "middle way," or reconciliation of the two leading Mahāyāna schools to reach China, the Emptiness *(Śūnyatā)* doctrine of Mādhyamika (Nāgārjuna) and the Mind-Only idealism of Yogācāra (Vasubandhu). Putting the point another way, it was the reconciliation between the transcendence of non-being *(Śūnyatā)* and the immanence of phenomenal empirical reality. According to Nāgārjuna's Mādhyamika (Chinese San Lun, Japanese Sanron—the fourth of the six Nara schools), reality is empty (neither existent nor nonexistent, and therefore completely beyond verbal description or conceptual thought). According to Vasubandhu's Yogācāra (Chinese

Fa-xiang, Japanese Hossō—the fifth of the six Nara schools), reality is mental (and therefore, while not existing independent of mind, contains all the phenomenal richness of ordinary experience, which can therefore be verbally described and conceptually thought).

Hua Yen (Kegon) was brought to Japan around 740 where it was well received by Emperor Shōmu, primarily because its main theme of the interrelatedness of all things seemed a good political principle and symbol of national unity. Shōmu showed his strong support for Kegon Buddhism by ordering the construction of the Great Buddha Mahāvairocana which may still be seen in the Tōdaiji in Nara and by naming the *Kegongyō* (Avatamsaka) as one of the principal sūtras of the nation.

According to Kegon, the entire universe is reflected in a grain of sand. An individual grain of sand is therefore an organic part of the whole universe (but without giving up any of its individuality). This is very similar to the Hegelian concept of the "internal relations" among the parts of an organic whole. As in a well-ordered work of art, or a living organism, each part contributes to the whole and is in turn defined and determined by that whole. For example, in isolation from the whole organism of which it is a part the eye would not function as an eye, and, by the same token, without the eye the organism could not function as a seeing, mobile entity. The part is necessary to the whole and the whole is necessary to the part. Without the part the whole would not be what it is and without the whole the part would not be what it is. As we will see in chapter 5, twentieth-century Japanese philosophers have been quick to recognize and to revive this connection between Hegel's notion of the whole/part relation and early Japanese Buddhist philosophy.

Realization of this complex view is said to evolve from the commonsense point of view in four stages. The first stage (the *ji*, or thing, perspective) is the commonsense point of view in which each individual thing is assumed to exist independently of all others, and to exist just as we normally perceive it. This is like seeing the waves in the ocean without noticing the underlying ocean itself. The second stage (the *ri*, or principle, perspective) grasps the underlying reality or principle behind the changing multiplicity of everyday experience. Here we are aware of the ocean as the real basis for the waves, which we now realize do not exist as independent entities, this nonexistence being expressed as *Śūnyatā*. The third stage (the *ri-ji*, the relation of principle to thing, or reality to appearance perspective) is awareness of the underlying principle in each individual thing; that is, we are aware of individual things, but only as manifestations or revelations of the underlying reality or principle. This is like the third stage in the famous Chan (Zen) saying, "Before I studied Chan I saw mountains as mountains and rivers as rivers; but after I had studied Chan for thirty years I no longer saw mountains as mountains and rivers as rivers; but now that I have grasped the essence of Chan I once again see mountains as mountains and rivers as rivers." In the third stage the monk sees mountains as expressions of the underlying Buddha nature of everything. The fourth stage, which is unique to Kegon (the *ji-ji*, thing to thing perspective), sees the whole universe as the interrelatedness of individuals, and not as some underlying substratum, or unperceived reality (or principle).

To use again our Hegelian analogy of the living organism or the art work, the whole is nothing over and above the sum of interrelations among all the parts; the parts define the whole and the whole defines the parts. Whereas in the third stage there is still a reality *(ri)* lurking beneath the appearance *(ji)*, which we nonetheless see by way of the things *(ji)* in the ordinary empirical world, the fourth stage is pure immanence, pure here-now phenomenal appearance. Somewhat like Leibniz's windowless monads, every individual object reflects within itself every other without losing its own individuality, and every single moment of time contains within it every other without losing its unique characteristics. The middle of a story, for example, implies both the beginning and the end of the story; an action cannot be understood apart from the earlier intention and the later consequences of the action.

Tendai appeared in Japan at about the same time (750) as Hua Yen, but it was not recognized as one of the Six Schools of Nara. China's Tien Tai was very close in theory to Hua Yen, but in Japan Tendai was much affected when its leader, Saichō, broke away from Nara and moved to a retreat high on Mount Hiei, near Kyōto. The result was that Tendai became more concerned with practice, both Zen and tantric. Tendai is rather odd in that its leading sūtra, the famous Lotus Sūtra, does not explain Tendai metaphysics, as Avatamsaka Sūtra explains the Hua Yen (Kegon) Sūtra. The Lotus Sūtra is a much simpler, more direct, and far more popular sūtra with lay Buddhists, the oral repetition of which later became a Japanese Buddhist practice: simply repeatedly saying aloud the name of the Lotus Sūtra was said to bring salvation.

One of the most distinctive features of Tendai theory is its doctrine of the threefold nature of truth. In Sanron (from Nāgārjuna and the Chinese Chi Tsang) truth is said to be twofold: the relative truth of everyday life (e.g., that many things exist) and the absolute truth known only to the enlightened (e.g., that all is empty, and nothing exists, that there are no individual things). Tendai went on to urge a third truth that would reconcile the first two.

In the first stage, "Follow the temporary and enter into the realization of emptiness *(kū),*" that is, emptiness is to be found within the relative world of multiple things (there are things and they are ultimately empty). In the second stage, "Follow emptiness and enter the temporary *(ke),*" that is, do not get so absorbed in Emptiness that you cannot function in the ordinary space-time world (but neither should you thereby become so enamored with the empirical world that you forget all about Buddhism). The best is the third stage, the middle way *(chū),* or the balance between knowledge of reality and its application in the ordinary empirical world.

The Tendai third stage is like the relation of *ri* and *ji* in Kegon. We need to get beyond seeing individual things as real in themselves and existing just as they normally reveal themselves to us in everyday life. So we begin to see the *Śūnyatā* reality, or principle *(ri)* behind these individual things *(ji).* But we do not want to embrace the *Śūnyatā ri* to the exclusion of the manifold *ji,* nor do we want to interpret the relation of *ri* to *ji* to imply a dualism of *ji* and *ri.* So we begin to see the *ri* in the *ji.* That is, the *ji* lead us to *ri,* and because we know that all is one, we can equally be led back again from the *ri* to the *ji* (the fourth stage of *ji-ji* in Kegon). But we must not take either of these too literally and become attached to either formulation. The two are really like two sides of the same coin. So it is that we come at last to the middle way between *ri* and *ji.*

Actually, there is very little theoretical difference between any of the late Mahāyāna doctrines, even between Nāgārjuna's Mādhyamika and Vasubandhu's Yogācāra, much less between Hua Yen (Kegon) and Tien Tai (Tendai). As we pointed out in chapter 1, Buddhism is not primarily philosophy, although there is philosophy in it. Buddhism is a religion, and as such, has a practical, not theoretical goal. Its objective is some sort of salvation from life's most basic problem, and however variously envisaged, that most basic problem is never perceived as a conceptual, theoretical one. Nonetheless, as discussed in chapter 1, as soon as we begin to talk about that problem and its solution, intellectual, theoretical, and conceptual problems, that is, philosophical problems, inevitably arise.

If we say that the commonsense view of the world is false, we are unavoidably drawn into a discussion of the distinction between "true" and "false," "knowledge" and "ignorance," "appearance" and "reality." If we say that individual things in everyday life are not self-sufficiently real, we find ourselves talking about "reality" and "appearance," "being" and "non-being," what is "independent" and what is "dependent." And then if we are going to talk this way, to make these sorts of statements, then we need to explain them, and of course, this will not be easy. What are we talking about, what do we mean when we say, for example, that the chair I am sitting on is not "real," that it is "empty," or has no "being." Is that not just plain nonsense in terms of ordinary language, whether the language be Indian, Chinese, Japanese, English, or any other? And so we must attempt to explicate these strange sayings philosophically, entering now into the arcane realms of logic, epistemology, and, above all, metaphysics.

But our theoretical problems are far from over. Indeed, they have just begun, since every metaphysical explanation is liable to misunderstanding, requiring further metaphysical clarification, in need of still further clarification, and so on, ad infinitum. If we say that ordinary physical objects are "unreal" or that they are "empty," that seems to suggest a kind of duality between "appearance" on the one side and "reality" on the other. But that is not what we want to say at all. We mean to say that all is one, that there is no duality anywhere. But in order to explain what we mean by nonduality, we have to point out, at least initially, that if all is one, then there really is no difference between the chair I am sitting on and the desk I am writing on. But to say that is to contradict our entire commonsense outlook.

A careful reading of each of the major Mahāyāna texts reveals that what they mean, or intend to say, is essentially the same. Differences arise because each worries that the claims made by the others will be misinterpreted, blocking the way to enlightenment, hindering rather than aiding the practical task of what is, after all, a religious quest. Simultaneous with all the theoretical (metaphysical, epistemological, logical) debate, therefore, there has always been the search within Buddhism for practical methods. The Chinese, and even more so the Japanese, gave special attention to this concern.

Having discussed some of the philosophical background to Tendai, let us turn now to Saichō (767–822), the founder of Japanese Tendai. Saichō was born of a very religious (Buddhist) family, the Mitsuobi, in the town of Ōmi. At twelve he entered the Kokubunji monastery there, studying under Gyōhyō, and at nineteen was ordained as a monk at the Tōdaiji in Nara. Almost immediately upon ordination Saichō left Nara, the established center of Buddhist life, to live in a small hermitage on Mount Hiei. When we think of Chinese or Japanese Buddhism today we often think of remote mountain monasteries, but Saichō was the first in Japan to move away from the centers of political intrigue to a place of beauty and solitude where he could concentrate on effective Buddhist practice purified of political involvement.

In Nara the study of Buddhism was primarily theoretical and scholarly. Any practice was mainly ceremonial ritual in the service of the state. Not satisfied with this, Saichō sought out a method of Buddhist practice designed to lead the serious devotee to enlightenment. This he found in Tendai (Tien Tai) scriptures, especially the writings of Chih-I, the Chinese founder of Tien Tai. Saichō's reputation as a Buddhist scholar grew, and in 802 he was asked to lead a discussion of the Lotus Sūtra at what is now

known as Jingoji temple. This made a significant impression on Emperor
Kammu who promised Saichō the opportunity to travel to China on an
official visit to learn more about Tien Tai.

In 804 Saichō and the Shingon founder Kūkai (774–835) left in two of
four Japanese ships that were sailing for China. Saichō's ship arrived in
Ningbo, just south of present Shanghai, and he proceeded south the short
distance to Tien Tai mountain. There he studied under Tao-sui and Xing-
man and also received meditation instruction from Xiu-jan. While await-
ing his return ship to Japan, Saichō met a master of the new Tantric techniques (involving magical mantras and mandalas of the sort now more
associated with Tibetan Buddhism) and was initiated into this magical
esoteric Buddhism.

After nearly a year in China Saichō returned to Japan officially sanctioned to transmit the Tien Tai doctrine in Japan. But Saichō's Tien Tai
(Tendai) was not identical with Chinese Tien Tai. Saichō had already studied a Japanese version of Tien Tai before leaving for China, and was also
interested in Chan (Zen) practice, which he continued in China and upon
his return to Japan. More important, Saichō's Tendai was heavily laced
with Tantrism (Mikkyō). Monks studying with Saichō on Mt. Hiei studied
both the Lotus Sūtra and Tantric techniques and, to show their serious-
ness, had to promise not to leave the mountain for twelve years.

Also while Chinese Tien Tai was universalist in scope, Saichō's Tendai
had a nationalist aim of rendering service to the state and the country,
using a purified and reformed Buddhism to protect and strengthen the
country. Saichō, who was the first to use the nationalistic phrase, dainip-
ponkoku (the great country of Japan), often said, "For the sake of the nation
chant the (Lotus) sūtra, for the sake of the nation, lecture and expound the
sūtra." Finally, while Chinese Tien Tai and its close affiliate, Hua Yen
(Kegon), were highly aloof, contemplative, and idealistic, envisioning the
complex one-in-many Hegel-like metaphysics outlined earlier, Saichō's
Tendai was practical and reformist. Saichō opened one branch of Tendai
for lay practitioners and fought tirelessly for political reform of the corrupt
Nara sects. Combining this with his nationalist fervor, Saichō sought a revolutionary transformation of Japan into a thoroughly Buddhist country.

The relation between Saichō and Shingon's Kūkai is fascinating.
Saichō was temperamentally modest, idealistic, and fiercely opposed to
any compromise with the corrupt Nara sects. The brilliant Kūkai, on the
other hand, was supremely confident, and politically adept at compromise. In addition Saichō had become associated with an older Chinese
school of Buddhism (Tien Tai) and one that was already fading in China,
while Kūkai had mastered the newest and what promised to be the most
practically powerful (magical esoteric Tantric). At first, when Saichō was

the better known and established, he helped Kūkai and the two men had several exchanges of views. But as Kūkai gained influence he distanced himself from the older man.

In 813 Kūkai refused to let Saichō borrow a Tantric text, the *Rishushakukyō,* on the grounds that such an esoteric text could only be studied with an established master (i.e., Kūkai) and not merely read on one's own (even by someone as well-versed as Saichō). The final break in the relation came when the man Saichō had named as his successor, Taihan, went to study with Kūkai in Nara and never returned, even after Saichō's repeated entreaties.

Previously Saichō had hoped to find a middle ground between Kūkai's Tantric Buddhism and his own Tendai, creating a grand synthesis of the two systems as a nationalist Buddhism for the whole of Japan, but the break with Kūkai led Saichō more and more to work for Tendai's independence. He wrote the *Ehyō Tendaishū (Fundamentals of Tendai),* which the famous Hossō scholar, Tokuichi, criticized in a well-known essay. Saichō responded in 817 with *Shogon jitsukyō (Reflections on the Provisional and the True).* The main point of contention between the two scholars was the Hossō (Yogācāra) three-point path to salvation, the triyana (Sravaka, Pratyeka Buddha, and Bodhisattva careers) versus Saichō's Tendai concept of one path, the *ekayāna.* Tokuichi envisioned a very long road to enlightenment, traversing many lifetimes, while Saichō sought a more direct route.

Toward the end of his life Saichō sought permission for Tendai to conduct its own ordination, independent of Nara. While this was bitterly opposed during his lifetime, permission was granted shortly after his death.

Ironically, despite the race to find and adopt the latest Buddhist practices, a race that Kūkai clearly won, in the long run Saichō's Tendai had a greater influence precisely because it proved a better blend of theory and practice. What Saichō sought to do was to wed the sophisticated Nara theoretical Buddhism, especially Sanron, Hossō, and Kegon, with Chan and Tantric practice under the banner of the Lotus Sūtra and Tendai *ekayāna.* Tendai interprets the Lotus Sūtra to mean that each stage on the road to enlightenment contains all the others, so that while in one sense there are many stages, in another, there is only one. Though Saichō never worked out this complex program in detail, it provided a greater stimulus to subsequent Buddhist development in Japan than Kūkai's Shingon, which we shall now proceed to examine in turn.

Kūkai (774–835) was born of an aristocratic family. In 791 he entered the Confucian college in the capital. Some scholars even think it was as a student that he wrote *Sangōshiki (Indications to the Teaching of the Three Religions),* in which he dealt with Confucianism, Taoism, and Buddhism in a quasi-fictional manner. A later version of this work was Kūkai's first major publication. In this 797 version he indicates the superiority of Buddhism over the other two religions, containing everything they contain but going beyond either of the other two. All his life Kūkai sought a synthesis or integration of all the partially truthful doctrines, especially all the many schools of Buddhism that existed in Japan at the time. As he wrote,

> Three vehicles, five vehicles, a dozen sūtras—there were so many ways for me to seek the essence of Buddhism, but still my mind had doubts which could not be resolved. I beseeched all the buddhas of the three worlds and the ten directions to show me not the disparity but the unity of the teachings. (*Testament*, 134)

As we have seen, in 804 Kūkai sailed to China, where, in the capital, Chang-an, he studied with the great esoteric tantric master, Hui-kuo (746–805). Returning to Japan less than a year later he received permission to build a monastery on Mount Kōya which later became the center of Shingon Buddhism. In 822, shortly after Saichō's death, he was appointed Abbot of Tōji, the famous temple in Kyōto.

Shingon means "true words," or "speech," one of the Three Mysteries, body, speech, and mind. Every person has these faculties, each of which contains within itself secrets not known to everyone, secrets that hold the key to enlightenment "in this life." The mystery of the body involves different ways of holding the hands (*mudras*), postures of meditation, and ways of handling ritual artifacts such as the *vajra*. The mystery of speech involves the secret formulas and incantations (the "true words," or *mantras*). The mystery of the mind involves the "five wisdoms." None of these mysteries can be learned from books, which could be read by anyone (and so are "exoteric"), but must be transmitted orally from teacher to student, in a highly individualistic manner suited to the peculiar qualifications of both teacher and student (and so are "esoteric").

In 830 Emperor Junna ordered the Six Nara Buddhist sects to present in writing an outline of their beliefs. It was in response to this that Kūkai wrote his famous *Ten Stages of the Religious Consciousness*, in which, as pointed out earlier, he related Shingon to all the other schools of Buddhism, and even Taoism and Confucianism, as the final stage of a gradually expanding, evolving consciousness. But in Kūkai's version, written in impeccable classical Chinese, Shingon is not only the highest (the tenth stage), but it alone is the true "esoteric" doctrine, the others falling far below it. Perhaps Kūkai's greatest philosophical genius lies in his ability to systematically synthesize all the various major schools of Buddhism, as well as Taoism and Confucianism, into one grand hierarchical ten-stage schema.

1.

The mind animal-like and goatish in its desires.

The mass-man in his madness realizes not his faults.

He thinks but of his lusts and hungers, like a butting goat. (the ordinary person)

2.

The mind ignorant and infantile yet abstemious.

Influenced by external causes, the mind awakens to temperance in eating.

The will to do kindnesses sprouts, like a seed in good soil. (Confucianism)

3.

The mind infantile and without fears.

The pagan hopes for birth in heaven, there for a while to know peace.

He is like an infant, like a calf that follows its mother. (Brāhmanism and popular Taoism)

4.

The mind recognizing only the objects perceived, not the ego.

The mind understands only that there are Elements, the ego it completely denies.

The Tripitaka of the Goat-Cart is summed up by this verse. (Shravaka Hīnayāna Buddhism)

5.

The mind freed from the causes and seeds of karma.

Having mastered the 12-divisioned cycle of causation and beginning, the mind extirpates the seeds of blindness.

When karma birth has been ended, the ineffable fruits of Nirvāna are won. (Pratyeka Hīnayāna Buddhism)

6.

The Mahāyāna mind bringing about the salvation of others.

When compassion is aroused without condition, the Great Compassion first appears.

It views distinctions between "you" and "me" as imaginary; recognizing only consciousness it denies the external world. (Hossō or Yogācāra Buddhism)

7.

The mind aware of the negation of birth.

Through eightfold negations, foolishness is ended; with one thought the truth of absolute Voidness becomes apparent.

The mind becomes empty and still; it knows peace and happiness that cannot be defined. (Sanron)

8.

The mind which follows the one way of Truth.

The universe is by nature pure; in it knowledge and its objects fuse together.

He who knows this state of reality has a cosmic mind. (Tendai)

9.

The mind completely lacking characteristics of its own.

Water lacks a nature of its own; when met by winds it becomes waves.

The universe has no determined form, but at the slightest stimulus immediately moves forward. (Kegon)

10.

The mind filled with the mystic splendor of the cosmic Buddha.

When the medicine of exoteric teachings has cleared away the dust, the True Words open the Treasury.

When the secret treasures are suddenly displayed, all virtues are apparent. (Shingon) (*Recapitulation*, 150–51)

Although close in many ways to Tendai and Kegon, Kūkai's concept of Vairochana Buddha is more absolute, all-encompassing, and cosmic. Also, Kūkai rejected the Yogācāra (Hossō Idealist) doctrine that all is mind. For Kūkai, mind is only one of six basic substances, the other five being the Chinese *wu xing*, the "five elements" of earth, water, fire, air, and space (substituting "space" for the Chinese "metal").

Although esoteric doctrines could not be articulated in written form, they could be effectively suggested in painting and sculpture. As Kūkai wrote,

> In truth, the esoteric doctrines are so profound as to defy their enunciation in writing. With the help of painting, however, their obscurities may be understood. . . . Art is what reveals to us the state of perfection. (*Memorial*, 138)

Part of the magic of "true words" (Shingon) is the look and sound of words in their original language. Since Buddhism originated in India, Kūkai introduced elements of Sanskrit signs into Japan as powerful visual and auditory, nonintellectual symbols of mysterious, inarticulate forces.

Notice how strongly Kūkai privileges the esoteric over the exoteric, and how forcefully he expresses this.

> The ocean of the Law is one, but sometimes it is shallow and sometimes deep, according to the capacity of the believer. Five vehicles have been distinguished, sudden or gradual, according

to the vessel. Even among the teachings of sudden enlightenment, some are exoteric and some esoteric. In Esotericism itself,
some doctrines represent the source while others are tributary.
The masters of the Law of former times swam in the tributary
waters and plucked at leaves, but the teachings I now bring
back reach down to the sources and pull at the roots. . . .

According to exoteric doctrines, enlightenment occurs only
after three existences; the esoteric doctrines declare that there
are sixteen chances of enlightenment within this life. In speed
and in excellence the two doctrines differ as much as Buddha
with his supernatural powers and a lame donkey. (*Transmission*,
142–143)

As Kūkai defines esotericism, it is, first of all, a truth that is too difficult to be understood by ordinary people and even fairly advanced students, and therefore useless to try and explain in writing designed for a
wide audience. It is not, as Kūkai says, the truth adapted for a particular
audience (using *upāya*, or skillful means); it is the truth expressed for its
own sake, just as it is in itself.

The Buddha has three bodies [*Nirmana*, i.e., Śākyamuni;
Sambhoga, i.e., Amitābha; and *Dharma*, i.e., Vairochana]; his doctrines are in two forms. The doctrine expounded by Nirmana
Buddha is called exoteric, since the words are open and brief,
and adapted to those taught. The doctrine taught by Dharma
Buddha is called the esoteric treasury; the words are secret and
of absolute truth. The sūtras used in exotericism number in the
millions. . . . The reason why these complicated doctrines arose
was clearly explained by the Great Sage. According to the esoteric *Diamond Crown Sūtra*, Buddha manifested himself in
human form and taught the doctrine of the Three Vehicles of
gradual enlightenment for the sake of . . . the believers of
Hīnayāna and Quasi-Mahāyāna. Buddha also manifested himself in his Sambhoga-body and taught the exoteric doctrine of
the One Vehicle of universal enlightenment [Saichō's brand
of Buddhism] for the benefit of boddhisattvas on earth. Both of
these teachings were exoteric. The Dharma Buddha who manifested himself for his own sake, for his own enjoyment,
expounded the doctrine of the Three Mysteries, with only his
own retinue present. These were the esoteric teachings.
(*Difference*, 144–145)

More important, however, the esoteric doctrine is not a *theoretical* truth at
all; the truth of Shingon is not something that can be mastered by even the
keenest intellect, but, as Kūkai says, something which must be "attained"

in actual practice, in one's life, and not just in one's understanding. In this sense it is truly beyond words. As we have seen, and will see later, this notion of a nontheoretical intuition never fails to strike a deep and responsive chord in Japanese sensibilities.

> The doctrine of the Three Mysteries lies in the realm of the inner wisdom of the Buddha, and even bodhisattvas who have attained ten steps of enlightenment cannot penetrate it, much less the ordinary believers of the Hīnayāna and Quasi-Mahāyāna. Therefore, though the *Jiron* [commentary by Vasubandhu] and *Shakuron* [commentary by Nāgārjuna] declare that the Truth does not depend on the faculties, and the *Yuishiki* [commentary by Dharmapala] and *Chūkan* [commentary by Kumārajīva] praise the Truth as a thing beyond words or thought, the absolute truth of which they speak was known to the compilers of these commentaries only in theory; they were not the work of men who had attained Buddhahood. (*Difference*, 145)

Completing our trio of outstanding Japanese Buddhist philosophers is Dōgen (1200–1253), author of *Shōbō Genzō (Treasury of the True Dharma Eye)*, and the man who put Zen on a firm, independent footing in Japan following its introduction to the country by his predecessor, Eisai. Born of an aristocratic family and benefiting from an excellent education, Dōgen rejected the political opportunities afforded by his family connections in favor of a religious life. He was disappointed, however, to find so few serious students of Buddhism at that time on Mount Hiei. Leaving Hiei he went to study with Eisai who unfortunately died shortly afterward. Dōgen then went to China, entering the Tien-tung monastery where Eisai had studied. But still he was unsatisfied. After moving from monastery to monastery he finally achieved enlightenment on hearing his teacher, Ju-ching's explanation that the practice of Zen meant "dropping off both body and mind."

Interestingly, some scholars think that Dōgen may have misunderstood the Chinese expression used by Ju-ching. More likely, however, is that Dōgen interpreted the statement in his own creative way. Since the introduction of Mādhyamika Buddhism to China and later Japan (the Nara school of Sanron), reality was said to be empty *(Śūnyatā)*. This means that everything is empty, or void of permanent substantial being, though it is far easier to recognize the impermanent, transient (empty) nature of physical objects than it is to see the impermanent, transient nature of ourselves. As we study Buddhism and practice meditation, we naturally have a sense of ourselves looking out on a world of impermanent, transient entities, as though we ourselves were permanent unchanging observers.

Indeed, it may seem obvious that in order for us to observe change, the same observer must witness the object changing from "before" to "after," thus ensuring that the observer remains constant and unchanged. But this is an illusion, nonetheless, according to Dōgen, however obvious it may seem to us. In his analogy with looking at the shore from a boat, Dōgen urges us not to center our understanding of the world from the vantage point of ourselves (e.g., my mind in my particular body located in this specific time and place). If you only look at the shore from within the boat, then it appears that the shore is moving; but if you look at yourself sitting in the boat, then you realize that it is you who are moving and not the shore. Of course, *you* are examining objects in the world; *you* are thinking about the philosophical and religious issues; *you* are gradually attaining enlightenment; but this does not mean that you are a substantive, permanent entity, much less the center of the universe. Rejecting the abstract metaphysical Idealism of Yogācāra, Dōgen, like Kūkai and indeed like most Japanese philosophers, argues that the universe does not exist "in your mind." You (mind and body) are like everything in the world, a changing particle in an ever-changing world. In Dōgen's analysis the boundaries between self and world fall away; you are in the world and the world is in you.

> To study the way of the Buddha is to study your own self. To study your own self is to forget yourself. To forget yourself is to have the objective world prevail in you. To have the objective world prevail in you is to let go of your "own" body and mind as well as the body and mind of "others". . . .
> When you go out on a boat and look around, you feel as if the shore were moving. But if you fix your eyes on the rim of the boat, you become aware that the boat is moving. It is exactly the same when you try to know the objective world while still in a state of confusion in regard to your own body and mind; you are under the misapprehension that your own mind, your own nature, is something real and enduring (while the external world is transitory). Only when you sit straight and look into yourself, does it become clear that (you yourself are changing and) the objective world has a reality apart from you. (*Solution*, 245–246)

Dōgen frequently uses analogies having to do with water and boats. In another famous analogy, borrowed from ancient Chinese tradition, Dōgen compares our enlightenment with the reflection of the moon in one of millions of drops or pools of water. Earlier we discussed the tendency of language to generate misleading and false metaphysical pictures of the world. When we say a person gained enlightenment it sounds as though there are two things involved, the person's mind and the Buddha reality or Truth, and that with enlightenment the Buddha Truth has entered the person's mind. Taking this metaphysical picture literally might lead us to ask, for example, whether entering someone's mind alters either the Truth or the person's mind (as eating a sandwich alters both the sandwich and the person eating it). Suppose two people become enlightened, does that mean that the Truth is somehow divided, half entering one person's mind and the other half entering the mind of the second person? But then how can either be enlightened if each has grasped only half the truth? But, on the other hand, how can the whole truth enter each of the two minds? However we look at it, there is a problem. But the problem, Dōgen tells us, is a bogus problem, one created by the metaphysicalizing tendencies of our own intellect. "Truth entering the mind," "the mind becoming enlightened," these are merely figures of speech. Just as the moon and all the pools of water are unaffected by the moon's reflection in the pools, so nothing in the Buddha Truth or in oneself is fundamentally altered in one's becoming enlightened. Similarly, despite our way of talking about two or more things ("myself," "my mind," "the Buddha Truth"), there is only one Reality.

> Our attainment of enlightenment is something like the reflection of the moon in water. The moon does not get wet, nor is the water cleft apart. Though the light of the moon is vast and immense, it finds a home in water only a foot long and an inch wide. The whole moon, the whole sky find room enough in a single dewdrop, a single drop of water. And just as the moon does not cleave the water apart, so enlightenment does not tear man apart. Just as a dewdrop or a drop of water offers no resistance to the moon in heaven, so man offers no obstacle to the full penetration of enlightenment. (*Solution*, 246)

Looking at another aspect of Dōgen's analogy of the moon's reflection in many pools of water, we can see that although enlightenment may be occurring simultaneously in millions of people around the world, each person nonetheless tends to think *his* understanding is pivotal, that the enlightenment is being generated *in him*, and this tends to perpetuate the illusion of ourselves (or at least our minds) as permanent real entities (perhaps the only real entities), rather than *Śūnyatā*. Again, the idea is to discourage us from centering the enlightenment experience on ourselves, as natural as that may seem. Because I have been practicing meditation for years; because I have been steadily gaining enlightenment; because I have been mastering the sūtras, it may seem to me that enlightenment is now centered in my own mind. But that is an illusion, though a very persuasive and persistent one, like the illusion, in another of Dōgen's analogies, of seeing the horizon from a boat in the midst of a huge lake or ocean as a complete circle with oneself at the center.

However profound our understanding may be, it is only a single facet or aspect of the ultimate reality, which can never be exhausted by our understanding, or contained within our grasp, but must always transcend any human understanding of it. As Dōgen points out, a truly enlightened person realizes that he does not know the whole of reality. We might wonder, at this point, if Dōgen is, in effect, admitting the truth of Kūkai's claim that all previous Buddhist doctrines are only partial truths while Kūkai's Shingon is the only complete and absolute truth. Dōgen's point seems to be that a complete and absolute understanding is impossible for human beings; as human beings the most we are ever capable of is a realization that reality exceeds our grasp, but not, contra Kūkai, what that ultimate reality is. Finally, despite the enormous influence of Idealistic Yogācāra on Chinese Chan Buddhism, Dōgen's firm rejection of subjective idealism follows the pattern of Japanese intellectuals who tend to reject any abstract, metaphysical entities in favor of an exalted vision of the infinite richness of the phenomenal world of everyday life.

> When your body and mind are not yet filled with enlightenment, you may feel that you are enlightened enough. But when enlightenment fills your whole body and mind, then you may be aware that something is still lacking. It is like taking a boat out into a vast expanse of water. When you look in all directions, that expanse looks round all around and nothing more. But the ocean is not merely round or square; its virtues are truly inexhaustible, like the Dragon's palace with its innumerable reflecting jewels. Only as far as our eyesight can reach does the ocean appear to be round. It is the same with the real world; inside and out it has numerous features, but we can see only as far as our spiritual eyesight reaches. Once we learn the true features of the real world, it is more than round, more than square. Its virtues are illimitable, as is the vastness of the ocean and the immensity of the mountain. There are worlds on all four sides of us, and not on all sides only, but underneath as well and even in the little dewdrop. (*Solution*, 246–247)

In his creative understanding of "dropping off both mind and body," Dōgen constantly battles against the dualistic tendency of monks and scholars to see their minds as separate from their bodies (a tendency no doubt supported by Yogācāra Idealism). It was natural for students engaged in the academic study of the Buddhist sūtras, especially in the highly scholastic atmosphere of Nara, to think of enlightenment as a process occurring exclusively in their minds. But for Dōgen the mind is simply part of the body and the complex mind/body is but part of the entire universe. Often Dōgen exhorts his students to "just sit (in meditation)," that is, not to worry so much about intellectually understanding the complex, paradoxical aspects of Zen doctrine. Enlightenment, he tells us, is a transformation of the whole person, mind and body, becoming one with the whole of nature.

> Is the Way achieved through the mind or through the body? The doctrinal schools speak of the identity of mind and body, and so when they speak of attaining the Way through the body, they explain it in terms of this identity. Nevertheless this leaves one uncertain as to what "attainment by the body" truly means. From the point of view of our school, attainment of the Way is indeed achieved through the body as well as the mind. So long as one hopes to grasp the Truth only through the mind, one will not attain it even in a thousand existences or in eons of time. Only when one lets go of the mind and ceases to seek an intellectual apprehension of the Truth is liberation attainable. Enlightenment of the mind through the sense of sight and comprehension of the Truth through the sense of hearing are truly bodily attainments. To do away with mental deliberation and cognition, and simply to go on sitting, is the method by which the Way is made an intimate part of our lives. Thus attainment of the Way becomes truly attainment through the body. That is why I put exclusive emphasis upon sitting. (*Body and Mind,* 248–249)

Theoretically, there is little to distinguish Zen from other late Mahāyāna doctrines (Mādhyamika and Yogācāra). It is rather in their unique cultivation of Buddhist practice that Zen sects differ from other schools of Buddhism. The Rinzai Zen sect, in particular, developed and perfected the practice of posing and trying to answer intellectually baffling and indeed theoretically insoluble puzzles, known as *kōan*. Like Kūkai's "esoteric" Buddhism, the Rinzai method insists upon the direct "mind to mind" transmission from a particular teacher to a particular student, in a way that cannot be generalized and cannot therefore be expressed in words or put in writing, which anyone could learn by reading such writings. Only the teacher can know if the student has solved the *kōan*; the same verbal solution the teacher sees as a sign of insight in one student might be judged inadequate when expressed by another student.

Of course, as Dōgen says, *all* understanding is a personal, individual achievement. Nonetheless, written documentation of such personal, individual achievements of the past (including that of Śākyamuni, himself) are not only possible but, as Dōgen insists, are highly useful for those seeking instruction in the Way. Although Dōgen stressed the need to go beyond intellectual theory in achieving enlightenment, he nonetheless differed from the Rinzai sect's concentration on the *kōan* to the exclusion of studying the sūtras. Both are needed, Dōgen felt, and he argued consistently for the integration of theory (study of the sūtras) and practice (mainly sitting in meditation). It is this more balanced integration of theory and practice, gradual and sudden enlightenment, realism and idealism, that differentiates Dōgen's Sōtō (Chinese Cao-tung) from Rinzai.

> There are Zen masters of a certain type who join in a chorus to deny that the sūtras contain the true teaching of the Buddha. "Only in the personal transmission from one patriarch to another is the essential truth conveyed; only in the transmission of the patriarchs can the exquisite and profound secrets of Buddha be found." Such statements represent the height of folly, they are the words of a madman. In the genuine tradition of the patriarchs there is nothing secret or special, not even a single word or phrase, at variance with the Buddhist sūtras. Both the sūtras and the transmission of the patriarchs alike represent the genuine tradition deriving from Śākyamuni Buddha. The only difference between them is that the patriarchs' transmission is a direct one from person to person. (*Contempt,* 249)

One of the most striking peculiarities of Japanese, as opposed to Chinese, Zen is its influence on the Japanese warrior class of *samurai,* which we should examine if only briefly. Although we tend to think of Zen as highly intellectual and sophisticated, it was and is in many ways much more down-to-earth, direct, and practical than most other forms of Buddhism or other forms of Chinese culture. It is above all a form of practice, not theory. There is no preliminary literature to be grasped, no foreign script to study, no arcane metaphysical doctrine to fathom, no scholastic dialectical intricacies to master. Only a way of looking at quite ordinary things, a way that, however, puts everything in a quite different perspective. This perspective diminishes the importance of individual things, including the individual ego of the individual samurai soldier, thereby diminishing his fear of death. From a Zen perspective, the individual does not really exist at all and so one's sense of the importance of one's self (and hence the importance of preserving one's self, mind-and-body) is simply a deep-seated illusion.

One of the reasons the samurai were attracted to Zen is that most of
the education of young men, samurai or otherwise, was by Zen masters in
Zen monastery schools. An important function of Zen Buddhism in pre-
Tokugawa Japan was to educate Japanese young people. Even today, traditional Japanese cultural education (Nō drama, tea ceremony, sword
play, calligraphy) is carried out in a Zen tradition. This is why, strangely
enough, the Song and Ming neo-Confucianism of Zhu Xi and Wang
Yangming was introduced to a new generation of Tokugawa bureaucrats
by Zen masters in their Zen monastery schools. Indeed, all known forms
of Chinese learning were housed and available in Zen monasteries. Since,
as we will see in the next chapter, neo-Confucianism is heavily influenced
by Chan Buddhism, Japanese Zen educators had already been studying
neo-Confucianism as a minor aid to Zen mastery.

While it is true that Zen Buddhism arises out of a long literary tradition of Mādhyamika and Yogācāra sūtras (enough written material to fill
a vast library), it is also true that the Zen rhetoric has always been that all
this is ultimately unnecessary, that enlightenment is either sudden or not
at all and that sudden enlightenment requires an instant shift in perspective and not the mastery of dozens of difficult books or meditation techniques. To some extent the debate between gradual enlightenment
(through scholarly study and lengthy meditation) and sudden enlightenment (dispensing with study and meditation) is semantic. The early Chan
masters all acknowledge the normally lengthy period required to "pre-
pare" oneself for the sudden insight into Chan. They simply refused to
call that lengthy period (of twenty to thirty years!) stages of a gradual
enlightenment. It was, they said, a prerequisite to a sudden enlightenment, which lasts less than a second. The peculiarity of Japanese Chan
(Zen) is to take the rhetoric of sudden enlightenment quite literally: in
Japan Zen becomes the religious celebration of the ceremonial beauty in
the here and now aesthetically perceived from the detached "standpoint
of eternity."

In the twentieth century debates between D. T. Suzuki and Hu Shih,
Suzuki lays the Japanese stress on sudden enlightenment, taking the Chan
rhetoric seriously, while Hu Shih emphasizes the place of the earlier
Chinese Chan within the larger context of late Mādhyamika and Yogācāra
Buddhism, with its stress on mastering the sūtras and years of meditation
practice. The theoretical base of Chan (Zen) is, as we pointed out above,
the complex Mādhyamika and Yogācāra metaphysical sūtras. It is true that
Chan develops in China as a move toward a simpler, more practical, more
straightforward, less cerebral approach to enlightenment. Nonetheless,
Chinese Chan Buddhists studied the Mādhyamika and Yogācāra texts as
well as the Chan meditation and *kōan* techniques. In general Japanese Zen

monks paid less attention to the Indian Mahāyāna metaphysics and more to the Chinese meditation and *kōan* practice, and this may underlie the debate between Hu Shih (speaking more of Chinese Chan Buddhists) and Suzuki (speaking more of Japanese Zen Buddhists, especially the Rinzai sect). The difference, finally, is one of degree. Just as Chan Buddhism is a mixture of Indian Mādhyamika/Yogācāra Buddhism and indigenous Chinese Taoist traditions, so Zen is a fusion of Chinese Chan and indigenous Japanese aesthetic and ceremonial traditions.

Unlike Chinese Chan, Zen Buddhism came to lend its essence to a great many activities in Japanese society at large. In the pre-Tokugawa period, many of the most typically Japanese cultural institutions and traditions were developed within Zen Buddhism: cherry blossom viewing, for example, is a custom almost every Japanese participates in, although only a very small minority would have any affiliation with a Zen temple. Of more consequence historically is the relation of Zen to the Japanese warrior class, the samurai, and the role Zen has had in the nation's education.

In Zen we find all that is most distinctive about Japanese Buddhism: its antimetaphysical, antitranscendental stance, its stress upon an immediate, aesthetic point of view celebrating the wonder and richness of ordinary commonsense reality. There is no Reality behind this world that it could take thousands of lives to figure out; there is just this world, which one must see directly, immediately, from a heightened aesthetic perspective as the entirety of Buddha. The peculiar strength of Japanese Buddhism is to call attention to the everyday world of nature as the focus of extraordinary aesthetic delight and exalted ceremonial importance, as we find in the tea ceremony, Zen archery, rock gardens, special occasions for viewing the moon or cherry blossoms, and so on. In contrast to Indian transcendentalism, the Japanese have made of Buddhism a religion of the here and now.

CHAPTER 3

THE RISE OF TOKUGAWA CONFUCIANISM

Although Confucianism was introduced into Japan at approximately the same time as Buddhism, it did not develop there philosophically until the Tokugawa period beginning in the seventeenth century. In general Japanese Confucianism follows closely movements in Chinese Confucianism. So, we need to understand the various stages within Chinese Confucianism in order, first, to understand the parallel developments in Japan, and second, to understand differences between Chinese and Japanese Confucianism.

Naturally, we would expect a philosophical movement lasting more than two thousand years (from the time of Kongzi [Confucius], in the sixth century BCE to Wang Yangming in the sixteenth century) to go through many important changes. But the situation is complicated still further by the tendency of Chinese intellectuals to incorporate the theories of different and even opposed schools within their own once they have gained supremacy over their rivals. Confucianism in particular gained ascendancy, first in the Han and later in the Song dynasty, by absorbing practically all other schools of philosophy. Many people today associate Confucianism with anything Chinese; if it is Chinese then it must be Confucian. And indeed Confucianism has been the dominant philosophical and cultural influence on China for more than two thousand years. Yet Confucianism has not always enjoyed such dominance and it has never enjoyed an exclusive position relative to other schools of thought. In Kongzi's own day, and for several hundred years following his death, China was blessed with the "flowering of a hundred schools of

philosophy." Or if not literally a hundred, certainly at least a dozen equally prominent, equally important, and equally popular, very different
schools of philosophy. During this period (roughly 500–200 BCE)
Confucianism was but one of many schools of philosophy vying for public attention. In 213 BCE, during the short-lived Qin dynasty (the first post-
feudal dynasty in China to unite the whole of what was then China into a
single military empire), the government banned all schools of philosophy
except the Legalists *(Fa Jia)*, actually killing many Confucian scholars and
burning all the Confucian and other philosophy books they could find,
excepting only the Legalist books.

As Confucianism reemerged in the Han dynasty (roughly 200 BCE–200
CE) as the officially sanctioned philosophy of China, this newly triumphant Confucianism (of Dong Zhongshu) had already incorporated
the most important elements of its now defeated rivals, *Yin Yang*, the Five
Elements, the *I Jing* (*Book of Changes*, actually written hundreds of years
before Kongzi), Mohism, Taoism, and others. As such, Han dynasty
Confucianism incorporated many religious, ceremonial, and superstitious
elements not in keeping with the early pre-Han, Warring States
Confucianism of Kongzi, Mengzi, and Xunzi, whereby Confucius was
officially revered (perhaps for a time even worshipped as a deity) in elaborate ceremonies by government officials in Confucian temples (where
Confucian students often came to pray for good grades).

When Chinese Confucianism emerged triumphant once again, after
years of Buddhist ascendancy during the sixth through ninth centuries,
the Song and Ming "neo-Confucianism" of Zhu Xi (and more so, Wang
Yangming) incorporated many elements of late Taoism and Buddhism
(especially Chan). Despite these borrowings, Zhu Xi and other neo-
Confucianists explicitly criticize and reject Taoism and Buddhism and
claim to be returning to the pre-Han teachings of Masters Kong and Meng
(Confucius and Mencius). At the same time neo-Confucianism rejected
the religious and superstitious elements of Han Confucianism, returning
to the rationalistic and humanistic side of the pre-Han Confucianism of
Mengzi and Xunzi. Part of the success of Confucianism was thus its ability to flexibly adapt to the changing times and to coopt and absorb, however secretly and perhaps unconsciously, competing schools of thought.

In short, then, there are many quite different philosophical movements in China stretching over some twenty-five centuries calling themselves "Confucianist." The first, ironically, is the "Confucianism" that
existed before Confucius himself was born! Part of Kongzi's agenda
was to support and defend ancient and dying Chinese feudal traditions
(of the Zhou dynasty, the last truly feudal dynasty and the one Kongzi
greatly admired). Because Confucius defended this ancient tradition and

conservatively urged a return to it, his name has always been associated with these ancient traditions. But these traditions are not philosophical theories; they are ancient ethnic cultural customs of the Chinese, such as filial piety, respect for elders, a hierarchical chain of command and respect (from the emperor to the male head of the family to the oldest son, and so on), social unity and conformity to authoritarian central government, and so on.

Part of the tendency to identify Chinese cultural traditions with Confucian philosophy is due to the "culturalist" theories of Liang Shuming and Nakamura Hajime in the 1920s and '30s which we discussed in chapter 1, namely, that the *Weltanschauung* of each ethnically distinct group of people is expressed in their distinctive philosophy, that of the Indian people in Indian philosophy, that of the Chinese people in Chinese philosophy, and so on. So, today when Japanese, Korean, Vietnamese claim to be "Confucianist" they often mean no more than the fact that they share with the Chinese some of these ancient ethnic customs and traditions, not that the Confucian classics are still a prominent part of their educational curriculum or that people today bother to read Kongzi, Mengzi, Xunzi, Dong Zhongshu, Zhu Xi, or Wang Yangming.

The second "Confucian" movement entails the writings attributed to Kongzi himself, though most probably written by his disciples' disciples (i.e., the *Analects*, the *Great Learning*, and the *Doctrine of the Mean*).

The third Confucian movement is the first group of interpreters of Confucius, Mengzi (Mencius) and Xunzi. Mengzi's is the more "idealist," "humanistic" reading of Kongzi; Xunzi's, the more "rationalist," "scientific" reading. For many centuries Xunzi and Mengzi were held in equal esteem by Confucianists, but eventually (around 1200) Mengzi emerged as the "legitimate" interpreter of Kongzi and his book, *Mengzi* (and not Xunzi's book), became one of the Confucian classics (one of the "Four Books," alongside the *Analects*, the *Great Learning*, and the *Doctrine of the Mean*), and Xunzi largely was ignored for more than a thousand years.

The fourth Confucian movement is that inaugurated by Dong Zhongshu in the Han dynasty, bringing into Confucianism, as we said earlier, the *Yin Yang* and Five Elements metaphysics.

And the fifth, and last, Confucianist movement (before significant contact with the West) is the neo-Confucianism of Zhu Xi and Wang Yangming (incorporating further elements, as we indicated above, of Taoism and Buddhism, especially Chan or Zen Buddhism).

As we indicated in the previous chapter, Confucianism came to Japan from China, via Korea, as early as the sixth or seventh century as part of a package of Chinese culture, including Buddhism, writing, poetry, history, philosophy, and a system of governmental bureaucracy. As such it did not make much immediate impact, and was for a time not studied in any detail; it was mainly that part of Confucianism we are calling "Confucianism before Confucius" (i.e., ancient Chinese customs that Kongzi defended and systematized and that therefore became attached to his name, many of which were similar to ancient Japanese customs). Mainly it was understood as a general justification and theoretical support for hierarchy in society and cohesion within the family and more generally within society, that is, loyalty to the superior and loyalty to the group, as we saw in Shōtoku's "Constitution" in chapter 2.

In its Japanese reception, many of the details of Han dynasty Confucianism were ignored and many others were specifically rejected, especially Mengzi's (Mencius's) interpretation of the "mandate of heaven" as requiring the government to support the interests of the ordinary people and the right of the ordinary people to rebel against tyrannical government. According to ancient Confucianism, governments only have the right to rule when they enjoy the "mandate of heaven." But what is the criterion for enjoying or failing to enjoy the mandate of heaven? That is, how do we know when a particular ruler has gained or has lost that mandate? Mengzi's answer is, the expressed will of the people. That is, people will generally make it clear whether they approve of a particular government or not. So, when the people rebel that indicates not only that the people are unhappy but also, according to Mengzi, that the ruler has lost the mandate of heaven.

It should come as no surprise that this would not please de facto governments, who would obviously prefer to interpret the "mandate of heaven" as their own de facto power. This is especially true in Japan where, unlike China since the fall of the Zhou dynasty, there has been only one ruling family since the sixth century, and the primary justification for kingship was hereditary. After the assertion of Confucianism during the Han dynasty as the officially sanctioned school of philosophy, Chinese emperors played down Mengzi's interpretation of the mandate of heaven and tended to substitute for it the later, more superstitious Chinese criteria popularized by Dong Zhongshu in the second century BCE, namely, the appearance of good and bad omens (two-headed cows, birds flying backward, etc.), the reporting of which the rulers could more easily control. Nonetheless, Mengzi continued to be studied in China in the Han dynasty, along with other Confucianists and other schools of philosophy, whereas in Japan only those aspects of Confucianism suitable to Japanese government leaders were allowed into the country.

Hence, while Mengzi is the most important Confucian before the Song dynasty, second only to Kongzi himself, Mengzi was not studied in Japan until late in the Tokugawa period (1603–1868). Japanese in the early pre-Tokugawa period also tended to accept more of the ceremonial, religious, and superstitious trappings of Han dynasty Confucianism, rather than the more humanistic and rationalistic side of Confucianism.

Why was the detailed study of Confucianism ignored during the first centuries after the introduction of Chinese culture into Japan? As pointed out in chapter 2, it was mainly because this was the period of Chinese intellectual history (sixth through eighth centuries) when Buddhism was in the ascendancy and Confucianism temporarily in decline (from the end of the Han until well into the Tang dynasty). This also helps explain why Confucianism was introduced at the beginning of the Tokugawa era (in the first decade of the seventeenth century) through Zen Buddhists in whose monastery schools Song dynasty neo-Confucianism was studied as a "sideline."

What Western scholars call neo-Confucianism Chinese call *Tao Xue Jia*, the School of the Study of Tao. And this name indicates the new metaphysical and spiritual direction of late Taoism, beginning in the Tang dynasty but coming to maturity in the Song dynasty. Although neo-Confucianists rejected Buddhism because it was not Chinese either in origin or in tradition, they absorbed into Confucianism many elements of both Buddhism and Taoism. Neo-Confucianists also selected those Confucian texts more in line with Tang dynasty Buddhist-Taoist spiritualism, and then interpreted those texts in the new way. It was during this period (Song dynasty, around 1200) that the *Great Learning*, the *Doctrine of the Mean*, and the *Mencius* were lifted from relative obscurity among many other Confucian texts and added to the *Analects* to become the central Confucian classics. Mencius is selected over Xunzi and interpreted spiritually and idealistically, emphasizing the idea in Mengzi that everything lies within us, that we share the goodness of human nature with Heaven, that the direct, spontaneous feeling or intuitive thought is the best insight into reality. Key virtues during this period are not so much the social virtues of propriety and benevolence, but rather the self-cultivation of an inner quality of Buddhist-like mental tranquility and sincerity.

Nonetheless, Buddhism and Taoism are firmly and explicitly renounced. Neo-Confucians rejected Buddhism because they claimed it seeks to selfishly escape the suffering that is a natural part of life; their rejection was all the more forceful insofar as such a move might imply abandoning one's family (a Confucian sin against filial piety). Taoism they rejected in turn because it seemed to them to reject the natural order of life and death by seeking to avoid death altogether.

Cosmologically, the *ba gua*, or trigrams (and the sixty-four hexagrams of paired trigrams), were added to the older Taoist cosmology of *qi* in an effort to explain the evolution of the natural world from a single element into the multifaceted world we are familiar with (what is called "the ten thousand things"). The original *qi* ether is said to divide into the *yin* and *yang* ethers (representing the passive and active forces in nature), which in turn evolve into the five elements (*wu xing:* earth, wood, metal, fire, and water), which finally produce the "ten thousand things." Philosophically the most important element added during this period is the notion of *li* in opposition to *qi. Qi* is the material stuff of the world and *li* is the formative principle that shapes it into relatively stable and predictable forms. Despite constant fluctuations of *yin* and *yang,* tomato seeds tend fairly regularly to produce tomato plants which regularly produce tomatoes which look and taste pretty much the same from year to year. What is responsible for this order in the midst of change? *Li.* This is similar to the Taoist *de* (in the *Tao De Jing*).

This idea probably comes from Buddhist Tien Tai and Hua Yen metaphysics (which may, in turn, have been influenced by Taoism, suggestions of which are found still earlier in the *I Jing*), where the root idea is that the inner nature of everything is the same, namely the Buddha Nature. In neo-Confucianism the emphasis is more specific and somewhat more secular, each *kind* of thing being governed by its own principle, or *li.* The *li* of chickens makes their eggs hatch into chicks which then grow into chickens, and so on. But as in Yogācāra Buddhism, an understanding of all the *li* lies innate within each person's mind. By quietly reflecting within our own minds we can come to realize the inner *li* of all things.

Zhou Tunyi, Shao Yung, and Chang Cai are all "fathers" of neo-Confucianism, but it really begins with the Cheng brothers, Cheng Hao and Cheng Yi (eleventh century). Cheng Yi and Zhu Xi (late eleventh century) form the Cheng-Zhu *Li Xue* school (also called the Rationalist school), while Cheng Hao, along with Lu ChiuYuan, better known under his literary name Lu Xiangshan (twelfth century), and Wang Yangming (fifteenth-sixteenth century) form the Lu-Wang *Xin Xue* school (also called the Idealist school).

Li Xue held that *li* exist independently of particular things and also independently of human consciousness (or minds), and, as Fung Yulan points out, it is therefore somewhat like Plato's theory of Forms. Xin Xue held that *li* do not exist independently of human consciousness (or particular things). So, for the Li Xue we discover *li* by examining things in the world, whereas for the Xin Xue we discover *li* by examining our own minds. Also, for the Li Xue human nature is *li,* whereas for the Xin Xue human nature is mind (human consciousness). That is, for Li Xue human consciousness is part of the *qi,* the material stuff, or body, whereas for Xin Xue it is the essential characteristic of human beings. As we will see, another difference between Wang Yangming and Zhu Xi is that for Wang (as for Plato) knowing the good is enough to do it, whereas for Zhu (as for Aristotle) there is a gap between knowing and doing.

The first phase of Tokugawa Confucianism in Japan is basically a variation of the neo-Confucianism of Zhu Xi. Zhu Xi is clearly the most important neo-Confucianist and the one who had the greatest influence outside of China (he is the central figure in Korean and Vietnamese Confucianism, as well). Zhu Xi incorporates the Taoist, *Yin Yang*, Five Elements metaphysics, as well as the most sophisticated late Chinese Buddhist attitudes and assumptions. His metaphysics is basically a dualism between *qi* and *li*.

Qi is the active ether that provides the material stuff of all existence. Everything in the world (heaven and earth) is made of *qi* in some form or other. *Li* is the eternal, immaterial and abstract principle that determines the form, shape, and character *qi* will take to form all the different sorts of things we find in the world of everyday experience. Bamboo is different from carp because bamboo has a different *li* from carp. Much of Zhu Xi's metaphysics reads like Plato's theory of the abstract, immaterial, eternal, unchanging Forms responsible for the characteristics that actual entities acquire in their material embodiment and that differentiate one kind of thing from another, the Form of Tree being responsible for the form, shape, characteristics of actual trees, and differentiating trees from butterflies and toadstools. And so for Zhu Xi, *li* are eternal, immaterial, abstract, and unchanging, existing apart from and independent of particular individual, physical things as we know them from sense experience.

But there is also a Buddhist-like element in Zhu Xi not found in Plato. Whereas for Plato (and Aristotle) there are as many Forms as there are characteristics in the world (the Form of Treeness, the Form of Leafness, the Form of Greenness, and so on), Zhu Xi borrows the late Hua Yen Buddhist notion that everything in the world shares the *same* principle, or *li*. Zhu Xi's *li-qi* distinction most likely derives, in other words, from the Hua Yen *li-ji* distinction discussed in the previous chapter.

The Chinese Buddhists had long argued that every thing in the world shares the same Buddha Nature. Everything in the world is already the Buddha, only most of them do not know it and therefore do not act accordingly. The key to Buddhist salvation was therefore simply to become conscious of one's own inherent Buddha Nature, the nature one was born with, but for various reasons denied or was not aware of. To explain how one's own nature could be hidden from us, these Buddhists argued that there were various factors that clouded or covered over and hence obscured this inner nature, which was left like a pearl in muddy water (to use one of their favorite analogies, which Zhu Xi borrows) that cannot be seen even though it is there all along, unsullied by the dirty water. Once the dirt settles out of the water, there is the pearl in all its pristine glory, just as it has been from the outset, indeed, forever. By the time of Zhu Xi (twelfth century) these Buddhist ideas had become incorporated into various forms of Taoism, and it is probably from these Buddhist-inspired Taoist ideas that the eleventh and twelfth century neo-Confucian precursors to Zhu Xi (Zhou Tunyi, Shao Yung, Chang Cai, and the Cheng brothers [Cheng Hao and Cheng Yi]) developed the idea of the supreme principle, the *Tai Qi*, or Supreme Ultimate.

Zhu Xi interprets this Supreme Ultimate as a metaprinciple, the super principle that governs the other principles just as they govern the formation of individual things, perhaps, as Fung Yulan suggests, like Plato's super form, the Form of the Good, which makes intelligible all the other Forms. So Zhu Xi argues not only that every distinct kind of thing has its own principle, but that everything in the world has the *same* nature or principle (the *Tai Qi*, or Supreme Ultimate, sometimes referred to as the *Tao*), the super principle of principles, governing other principles as they govern particular things in the world.

Unlike in Buddhism, however, this inner nature of everything, according to Zhu Xi, is not Buddhahood, but the central Confucian virtue of *ren* or human heartedness. The difference between human beings and plants, rocks or other animals, each of which has its own *li*, is that this nature (Supreme Ultimate, *Tai Qi*) is more clearly displayed, more prominent, and more accessible in human beings. Just as Empedocles held that abstract Love and Strife rule the world, determining everything in it from rainfall to solar eclipses, and as Plato argued that the Form of the Good made everything be the particular thing it was, and as some Christians argued that the Word (logos) is the basic reigning principle of the entire universe, so Zhu Xi reasoned that in a deep and profound sense the Supreme Ultimate (*Tai Qi*) meta-*li* of *ren* (human heartedness) was the central controlling force in the world. No longer, then, is *ren* merely one of the human virtues; it has now become a metaphysical principle governing the entire universe.

What is most interesting about Japanese followers of Zhu Xi (Shushi) is their complete rejection of his notion that the ultimate reality of the world is the abstract, immaterial, eternal, and unchanging *li*. Korean Confucianists, by contrast, took this "Platonic" element in Zhu quite seriously, actively debating for centuries whether both *li* and *qi* existed (that is, as in the debate between Plato and Aristotle, whether the abstract *li* could exist independently of the material *qi*) and if so, which of the two was primary. Korean scholars staked out every possible position in this complex debate, that *li* and *qi* both existed and were separate and that *li* was primary, that *li* and *qi* both existed and were separate and that *qi* was primary, that *li* and *qi* both existed but were not really separate (so the question of primacy did not arise), and so on.

Japanese Confucianists, on the other hand, rejected en masse Zhu Xi's leading idea that the ultimate reality is something abstract, immaterial, eternal, and unchanging, existing apart from material *qi* and individual things. If there is anything that is peculiarly Japanese in Japanese Confucianism, or indeed in Japanese philosophy in general, it is surely this preference for what is immediate, immanent, sensuous, changing, material, and naturalistic, along with the correlative suspicion and lack of sympathy for anything exclusively intellectual, transcendental, abstract, immaterial, unchanging, ethereal, and so on. Indeed, throughout their history whenever Japanese have embraced foreign culture, they have taken and interpreted only those parts that were compatible with this preference: despite many extensive borrowings from other cultures, Japanese have rarely if ever abandoned any of their own culture. They have simply used the new, foreign culture to buttress and more rationally justify their own uniquely Japanese ways.

Some three hundred years after Zhu Xi, Wang Yangming rejected Zhu's *"li xue"* (the philosophy of principle) in favor of a new branch of neo-Confucianism stressing mind *(xin)* instead of principle (called *xin xue* instead of *li xue*). And this, too, had its important counterpart in Japan *(Ō yōmei)*. As we have seen, Zhu Xi developed a position similar to Western Platonism in which real immaterial, abstract "universals" are differentiated from any material embodiment, including minds, and minds are regarded as part of the material embodiment of an actual, living, feeling, and thinking human being or animal, from which it follows that human nature, and indeed the nature of everything, was abstract, immaterial *li* separated from actual physical objects, including living, breathing, feeling, and thinking human beings and their minds.

On the other hand, Wang Yangming (whose given name was Wang Shouren, Yangming being the place he worked and was long associated with), identified the ultimate nature or essence of things with mind, adopting a position similar to Western idealism (to be is to be perceived; the ultimate reality is mind and ideas entertained by mind). For Wang human nature is mind, not *li*, and the Supreme Ultimate (the over-arching *Tao* of everything) is Mind *(Xin)*, not *Li*.

Other differences follow from Zhu's privileging of *li* and Wang's preference for *xin*. Whereas for Zhu we follow the *Da Xue* (the Han dynasty Confucian classic, *The Great Learning*) in "extending learning by investigating things," Wang contends that, following the other Han dynasty Confucian classic, *Zhong Yong (Doctrine of the Mean)*, one can best learn the ultimate principles of reality by simply reflecting within one's self. The ultimate *Tao* is Mind and where better to study Mind than our own mind? The other major difference between these leading neo-Confucianists is that while Zhu (somewhat like Aristotle) saw a gap between knowledge and action (that one can know the right thing to do and not do it [Aristotle's "weakness of will"]), Wang argues (somewhat like Socrates and Plato) that if one truly understands what is right, one will do it. Of course, part of the disagreement between Zhu and Wang on this point has to do with different notions they have of knowledge, Zhu stressing something akin to ordinary commonsense knowledge, and Wang, something closer to meditative quasi-Buddhist enlightenment. While it seems clear that Zhu Xi borrows from Hua Yen Buddhism the li-qi (Hua Yen li-ji) distinction, Wang Yangming's indebtedness to Yogācāra Buddhism is equally clear.

As we saw in chapter 2, a major contribution to Chinese Mahāyāna Buddhism was Yogācāra idealism, which held that everything is the Buddha Mind, that the phenomenal world is a mentally produced illusion. Yogācāra joins with Nāgārjuna's Mādhyamika, or "middle way" (which holds that reality is empty, not mental) to form most of the leading schools of Chinese Buddhism, especially Chan (Japanese Zen). For that reason Wang is often called a closet Chan Buddhist. As we saw in the previous chapter, most Japanese Buddhist philosophers rejected Yogācāra idealism as too remote from common sense realism and entirely too alien from the peculiarly Japanese celebration of the infinite aesthetic richness of the phenomenal world of everyday sense experience. For this reason most Japanese neo-Confucians rejected Wang's idealism, though many Japanese found great sympathy for the spiritual sincerity of Wang's emphasis on inner reflection and self-cultivation. Nonetheless, the fact is that Japanese followers of Wang rejected his main idea, just as followers of Zhu rejected *his* main idea. In both cases Japanese adopted Chinese neo-Confucianism in their own, Japanese way.

In the Qing dynasty (seventeenth through twentieth centuries) Confucianists rejected all the Taoist and especially Buddhist elements with which Song (Zhu Xi) and Ming (Wang Yangming) dynasty neo-Confucianism had become embedded, and urged a return to the original Confucianism of the Han and pre-Han period. In reaction to this Buddhistic (and hence Indian, ergo, non-Chinese) Confucianism the Qing dynasty Confucianists led a movement "back to the original (thoroughly Chinese) Confucianism," that is, a renewed study of the Confucian classics, including not only the four Confucian books, *Analects*, *Great Learning*, *Doctrine of the Mean*, and *Mencius*, but also the still more ancient nonphilosophical classics, *I Jing (Book of Changes)*, *Spring and Autumn Annals*, both of which Confucius himself had studied. And this too was closely followed by Japanese Confucianists.

More interesting was the Japanese adaptation of this "back to the (nationalistic) origins" as a "return" to *Japanese*, not Chinese, ancient writing. Of course, there is no Japanese writing of comparable antiquity to that of China, but there were the early "histories" commissioned in the seventh and eighth centuries by Japanese rulers—primarily collections of mythological prehistories of what later became known as Japanese Shintō. Like its Chinese counterpart, this represents the first dawning in Japan of a kind of "intellectual nationalism" that became increasingly important all over the world in the early twentieth century (1920–1940).

Let us turn now to a more detailed analysis of Tokugawa Confucianism. Although "neo-Confucianism" did not attain any prominence until the beginning of the Tokugawa period, it was known in Japan from the fourteenth century and even sporadically encouraged by several pre-Tokugawa Japanese emperors. There were arguments by young nobles at the court of Emperor Go-Daigo in 1333, for example, for and against adopting Zhu Xi's political philosophy for Japan's rulers. In this early period neo-Confucianism was propagated under the auspices of Buddhism, especially Zen Buddhism, which continued to be the dominant intellectual, educational, and cultural force in Japan.

This is somewhat ironic since neo-Confucianism arose in China specifically as a revolt against the dominance of what Chinese perceived was the alien (Indian) influence of Buddhism for approximately five hundred years, and a reassertion of an indigenous Chinese tradition of Confucianism. Zhu Xi, the leading figure in the neo-Confucian movement, explicitly rejected Buddhism and its alliance with Taoism, and, as we indicated earlier, sought to bring philosophy and the center of intellectual life back to social, political, and moral concerns of good government and away from the spiritual, religious, and personal concerns of Buddhism and Taoism. At the same time, however, neo-Confucians, including Zhu Xi, incorporated many elements of Buddhist-Taoist metaphysical and spiritual concerns, as we saw above, presented as a more sympathetic interpretation of Mengzi (Mencius). In China, therefore, the rise of neo-Confucianism meant the decline of Buddhism-Taoism as an intellectual and cultural force.

Because neo-Confucianism was first presented to Japanese by Buddhists within the context of Buddhism, the antagonism between Confucianism and Buddhism was not apparent at first and the two coexisted peacefully, side by side, for centuries. But the new political regime of Tokugawa *shōguns*, in their attempt to unite the many feudal principalities of Japan into one nation under the nominal head of the emperor but controlled by the shōgun, found the differences between Confucianism and Buddhism useful to themselves politically and therefore encouraged the development of a new Confucianism that was not only different from Buddhism but antagonistic to it. Where Buddhism was perceived as being otherworldly, spiritual, personal, and metaphysical, Confucianism came to be perceived as being this worldly, humanistic, rational, and focused on social and political concerns. As a result Buddhism declined as Confucianism rose, though not to such a great extent as in China. Buddhism was disparaged as being superstitious, emotional, useless for society, whereas Confucianism was praised for being humanistic, rationalistic, and pragmatic.

Nonetheless, Chinese culture was always adjusted to Japanese sensibilities and needs and neo-Confucianism is no exception. Almost immediately Japanese intellectuals accepted that part of neo-Confucianism that suited their needs and rejected those parts they considered un-Japanese. Basically, they accepted the humanism and rejected the rationalism. The main criticism of Zhu Xi was his stress on rationality at the expense of emotion; almost all Japanese neo-Confucianists rejected what they perceived as Zhu Xi's rationalistic conception of human nature (cf. Aristotle's "man is a rational animal"). It may seem strange to hear Chinese philosophy criticized as being too rational, since to many Western commentators it is just the opposite: Chinese philosophy is said to be too emotional, organic, vague, and not nearly logical, analytic, precise enough for Western philosophical tastes. But these things are relative; certainly Zhu Xi is more rational and analytical than many other Chinese philosophers, and while Chinese philosophers themselves complained that Indian (Buddhist) philosophy was too intellectual for their tastes, they were on the whole more analytical, intellectual, logical than their Japanese counterparts. It is also true that just as Europeans in the eighteenth and nineteenth centuries had access only to the more rational, orderly aspects of Greek culture and so, until Nietzsche's *Birth of Tragedy*, tended to exaggerate the cerebral rationality of the Greeks, so Japanese had access only to the more philosophical, intellectual, moralistic, and rational Chinese writings, and so tended to see the Chinese as more intellectual, moralistic, and pedantic than they actually were. But for whatever reasons, from the Japanese perspective, neo-Confucianism was too intellectual, analytical, rational to fit neatly into Japanese sensibilities.

It must be said, however, that while Japanese Confucianists tended to reject Confucian rationalism in favor of humanism, their embrace of Confucian humanism was itself qualified. On the whole, it was rejected politically but accepted morally; that is, Confucian humanism was rejected, at least initially (in the seventeenth century), as part of the political philosophy supporting the new Japanese Shōgunate *bakufu* government, while it was generally accepted as the foundation for a more general and widespread moral code throughout the country. As a military government Japanese leaders tended to be less paternalistic and more rigidly duty-bound. They demanded and expected absolute obedience from their citizens. Here again Chinese thought was used to support, justify, and defend existing Japanese traditions, rather than to modify or alter those traditions. The peculiarity of Japanese culture and history is that while the Japanese embraced foreign traditions where these were perceived as underlining superior cultures (and therefore useful to Japan's advancement), they stubbornly retained their most ancient beliefs and traditions. Even today the most advanced and sophisticated technological practices exist side by side with some of the most primitive religious beliefs in the world.

On the other hand, Confucianism was a very important factor in the development of Japan's early modern (seventeenth and eighteenth century) moral consciousness. The center of Chinese Confucianism has always been the family, from which political philosophy is to be derived, that is, the relation of the ruler to his subjects is to be understood ideally as that of a morally good father to his family (including both obedience-duty and also love-concern). Because all aspects of Chinese culture were introduced into Japan to serve and support the government, Japanese Confucianists tended to reverse this emphasis, being more concerned with the support that Chinese neo-Confucianism could be seen to provide for justifying Japanese feudal relations of emperor to military leader to samurai to ordinary citizens. Nonetheless, as Confucianism began to be disseminated more widely outside government circles, especially among the rising middle class of wealthy, educated merchants in the cities, the more humanistic side of Confucianism had a major impact on moral consciousness.

At first, Japanese Confucianists sought to find this more humanistic side of Confucianism in the earlier Han and pre-Han Confucianism of the *Analects* and the *Mengzi*. But eventually Japanese Confucianists turned away from Chinese sources altogether for this missing ingredient and began to look instead within their own ancient Japanese traditions. In the final analysis Japanese intellectuals tended to perceive this softer, more paternalistic, loving, and emotional side of Confucianism as a return to Japanese traditions, rather than as a more balanced reinterpretation of Chinese neo-Confucianism. Early Japanese Confucianists tended to exaggerate Zhu Xi's intellectualism and to ignore the softer humanistic strand in Zhu Xi and other Chinese neo-Confucianists. Therefore, when later Japanese Confucianists began to criticize this overly cerebral, rigidly intellectual side of Confucianism they did not see that the more loving side of filial piety was there all along in Song and Ming dynasty Chinese Confucianism. Instead, continuing a systematic misreading, they urged a return first to the older, original Confucianism and later to Japanese traditions privileging sentimental feelings of love and concern toward family members.

This criticism of Zhu Xi provided Japanese Confucianists a peculiarly Japanese justification for preferring the "Ancient Learning" phase of neo-Confucianism. Following the Buddhist-Taoist interpretations of Confucianism by Zhu Xi (thirteenth century, Song dynasty) and Wang Yangming (sixteenth century, Ming dynasty), Chinese scholars sought to purify Confucianism of these alien Buddhist and Taoist elements and return to the original Confucianism of Kongzi, himself, or at least the Confucianism of the Han dynasty. This had a special appeal for Japanese Confucianists because they saw this as a return to a more balanced view of human nature and the world. Mengzi certainly had stressed human feeling and emotion as the key to understanding human nature. The "beginning" of *ren* (human-heartedness), which is present in every human being from birth, is best illustrated by the immediate, spontaneous, emotional reaction of every person to save a child about to fall into a well. For Mengzi one's first impulse (feeling, emotion) is the impulse to do good; intellectual afterthoughts, he held, were more often clever calculations to substitute selfish motives for duty (my first impulse is to run to save the child, but as I wonder why I should endanger myself or ruin my clothes, or inconvenience myself, I decide to let someone else save the child).

This in turn opened the door for the still more religious, emotional, irrational move from the return to ancient Chinese learning to the return to ancient Japanese (i.e., Shintō) learning, that rejected the rationalism of neo-Confucianism as well as its humanism. Like Mozi's rejection of the human-centered orientation of Kongzi because it did not properly recognize the power of the gods to control human events, so Japanese ancient learning portrayed the secular humanism of neo-Confucianism as a weakness, not a strength; it was bad because it ignored the ancient Japanese belief in the mysterious power of the *kami*, a mysterious power that cannot be discovered by logical analysis or empirical investigation, but only by the authority of ancient texts.

Here we see quite clearly the clash between religious and philosophical styles of explanation. Sometimes what is divinely revealed in sacred scripture can also be demonstrated and explained by reason alone. But in other cases, religious doctrines can only be known from divinely inspired sacred scripture. Those who are more inclined toward philosophical explanations will tend to ignore those religious doctrines that cannot be explained rationally, while those more religiously inclined will tend to reject philosophical accounts precisely because they are unable to explain and defend much of what is revealed in divinely inspired scripture. In the nineteenth century European debate over "natural religion," for example, there are parts of the Judeo-Christian religion that secular, humanistic, rationalistic and even scientific thinkers thought could be discovered "naturalistically," simply by the power of human reason and sense perception, without the aid of divine revelation. But other aspects of biblical religion could *not* be so discovered: various miracles as recorded in the Bible, for example, which were neither rational nor scientific and could therefore only be learned through a study of the divinely inspired Holy Bible. All this raises a fundamental and still unresolved dilemma: is this a weakness in religious accounts (that they cannot explain everything rationally) or is it a weakness in philosophical accounts (that they cannot explain everything that has been revealed in sacred scripture)? Often, when push came to shove, Japanese, as we shall see, tended to choose the religious explanation where this conflicted with or was not supported by secular philosophy.

Now that we have taken a quick overview of the introduction of Chinese Confucianism into Japan, let us examine this chronology in more detail. The history of Tokugawa Confucianism begins with Fujiwara Seika (1561–1617). Trained as a Zen monk of the Rinzai sect, he was an advisor to the *daimyō* of Harima. Gradually, his studies carried him away from Buddhism toward Confucianism, though never to a complete conversion. Earlier we indicated as one of the reasons for the slow growth of Confucianism in Japan from the seventh to the seventeenth century the difficulty Japanese find in reading Chinese. Although the characters *(kanji)* are largely the same, the grammar of the two languages is very different. For centuries Japanese scholars had worked on ways to punctuate the Chinese texts for easier Japanese readability. But these editorial devices were, for the most part, kept secret within hereditary scholarly associations available only to a small elite among the aristocracy. Fujiwara Seika was largely instrumental not only in perfecting such a system of punctuation but in making that information widely available to a much larger number of moderately educated former samurai *(rōnin)* and even the modestly educated rising merchant middle class, thus ensuring the spread of neo-Confucianism. In a letter to his student, Hayashi Razan, Fujiwara Seika criticizes both Zhu Xi and Lu Xiangshan (the precursor of Wang Yangming):

> Zhu Xi was by nature conscientious and consistent; he had a taste for the profound and the precise. Those who followed him were therefore liable to suffer from the defect of hair-splitting. Lu Xiangshan was by nature superbly brilliant and craved unfettered simplicity. Those who followed him, therefore, were inclined to suffer from a lack of restraint. That is where they differed, and people took note of their differences without taking note of their agreement on fundamentals.
>
> Where did they agree? They agree on the approval of the sage kings, Yao and Shun, and on the disapproval of the tyrants,

Chieh and Zhou. Both also agreed on reverence for Confucius
and Mencius, and on the rejection of Śākyamuni Buddha and
Laozi. They also considered an action in accord with heaven's
law as public-spirited and an action that follows human desire
as selfish-minded. (341)

When Ieyasu offered him an official post in the new *bakufu* military
government, Fujiwara, wishing to remain independent and not fully con-
vinced of the neo-Confucianism of Zhu Xi, declined, recommending
instead his disciple, Hayashi Razan (1583–1657). The latter proved to be
an enthusiastic promoter of Zhu Xi philosophy. Having studied in the
Kenninji Zen Monastery in Kyōto, he had been employed as a kind of sec-
retary, along with Duden, a high Zen official, and Tenkai, Abbot of the
Tendai sect, for the Ieyasu Bakufu.

It is always tempting for philosophers to exaggerate their influence
on contemporary public affairs. In all honesty, Karl Marx was probably
closer to the mark when he said, "Philosophy bakes no bread." As Plato
said, borrowing a metaphor from Pythagoras, there are three kinds of
people in the world, like the three kinds of people at a sports event, participants, spectators, and vendors selling snacks. Philosophers, said Plato
and Pythagoras, are like the spectators, not the active participants or vendors. In both Western and non-Western philosophy philosophers have
often tried to influence political events, though usually ineffectually. Plato
tried unsuccessfully to train Dionysus of Syracuse to be a "philosopher
king," and Aristotle was equally unsuccessful with Alexander. Kongzi
gave up after many years trying to convince government rulers to adopt
his philosophical principles for the good of the country, retiring finally
toward the end of his life from active politics to a life of teaching.
Nonetheless, philosophers can serve governments by providing rational
justification and thereby intellectual support for their policies, and this
seems to have been the case with the Tokugawa Confucianists. They were
never called upon to advise government, and certainly none of the
shōguns attempted to adjust Japanese policy to better fit the neo-
Confucian model. But the neo-Confucianism of Zhu Xi was useful in justifying existing *bakufu* policy.

Ieyasu looked to neo-Confucianism to support the new military
authoritarian system of government. Zhu Xi's neo-Confucianism differs
from the older Confucianism of Kongzi, Mengzi, and Xunzi in projecting
Confucian moral virtues onto the vast nonhuman universe, as a grand
metaphysical principle governing the entire universe, and not just norma-
tive principles that ought to govern individual people and groups of people. Specifically, Zhu Xi elevates the principle of obedience of son to

father, and citizen to ruler, to the status of a fixed principle of the universe, like an eternal Law of Nature, and therefore a powerful legitimation of shōgunate authoritarian government. At the same time, Confucianism promised many advantages to the new government over Buddhism (which was never, however, completely abandoned by the Japanese government), especially in its rationalistic, humanistic slant as opposed to the otherworldly, transcendental principles of Buddhism. A military government ruling as feudal autocrats, *bakufu* policy tended to be conservative, authoritarian, concerned mainly with maintaining social order. Neo-Confucianism focuses on human relationships of loyalty, cooperation, and obedience to superiors, and this was easily adapted to the hierarchical feudalism of Tokugawa Japan, especially in the Japanese interpretation of the Chinese Confucian virtue of "conscientious sincerity" as "unwavering loyalty to the state."

Neo-Confucian morality was very influential, on the other hand, in helping to redefine a new role for the traditional warrior class of samurai. Before Tokugawa, Japan was not a unified country but a collection of small feudal principalities, each of which was ruled by a *daimyō* with a private army of professional hereditary soldiers, the samurai. Under feudal traditions, the samurai could not operate on their own, but only under a feudal lord. Once Ieyasu had unified the country, these private armies were disbanded and the samurai were out of work (and thereafter became known as *rōnin*). Gradually, the *rōnin* were reorganized as the civil service of the new *bakufu* government. Many of the old virtues of the samurai warrior class were easily transferable to their new role: loyalty to the government, selfless devotion to the needs of the state (rather than promoting their own private fortunes). But just as Zen Buddhism in the pre-Tokugawa period had been useful in providing a cultural rationale for samurai courage and selfless devotion in the face of death, so in the Tokugawa period neo-Confucianism provided a cultural rationale for a loyal and selfless class of civil servants derived from the former samurai. (A Western parallel might be the study of the Greek and Latin classics as a preparation for British colonial civil servants in the nineteenth century.)

Surely the greatest contribution that neo-Confucianism made to the new role for samurai, beyond defending and supporting the samurai virtues they already possessed, was in supplying the need for education among the newly emerging class of civil servants. In China, of course, there had been a long tradition of Confucianists comprising the educated class (the *ru*). Fung Yulan suggests that Confucianists, including Kongzi himself, originally came from the small group of educated advisors (the literati) to the feudal lords on ceremonial matters, and the tradition of education continued among the Confucianists. Throughout most of China's history since the Han dynasty (roughly 200 BCE – 200 CE) civil servants were selected on the basis of merit as determined by success in uniform examinations based on knowledge of the Confucian classics. So in China success in government service depended entirely on knowledge of Confucianism, and Confucianism therefore became the main, and almost the only, form of Chinese formal education. In Tokugawa Japan a new class of bureaucrats was needed in the unified *bakufu* government, and the easiest and best way to fill that need was to retrain the samurai. Neo-Confucianism was certainly very instrumental in that process.

Hayashi Razan was an enthusiastic follower of Zhu Xi and violently opposed to Buddhism as being otherworldly, transcendental, irrational, nonempirical, and foreign to Japanese traditions. Hayashi was a tireless scholar, writing many books on history, literature, Confucian philosophy, and Shintōism (including *Honchō jinja-kō, Honchō Tsugan*). He made his home (in the Ueno section of Yedo) into a Confucian college, called Shinobugaoka. Consistent with Japanese traditions, though, ironically, opposed to Chinese Confucianist principles of meritocracy, official Tokugawa Confucianism remained in Hayashi Razan's family, being passed down from father to son, from Hayashi to Gahō (1618–1680), and then to *his* son, Hōkō (1644–1732).

Hayashi Razan was outspoken not only in his criticism of Buddhism, but also of Taoism, especially the Taoist advocacy of a retreat from an active life of service to society in favor of a passive "return to nature." According to Hayashi, this is contrary to *human* nature, and human nature is what we ought to be pursuing: the Way of Man, not the Way of Nature or the Way of the Buddha. Human beings are active, thinking creators of culture, Hayashi argues; it is senseless to pretend that people can or should try to become like plants or lifeless objects.

> Laozi said, "The Way that can be told of is not an Unvarying Way." What he considered the Way was quiescence and non-striving, and what he spoke of was the original undifferentiated state of nature. But man is born into the world of today and cannot even achieve the untroubled state of high antiquity; how much less can he put himself in the original undifferentiated state of nature? If it is true in the case of nature that in the original state of unresolved chaos there was no thought, still while men live and breathe how can they avoid thinking? Man is essentially an active living thing. How can he be compared to desiccated bones? That old fool, Zhuangzi's arguments based on withered trees, dead ashes . . . are of the same sort: all weird, perverted talk. (*Confucian*, 348)

The Confucian "Way," that is, the "Way of the Sages," is entirely different from this, he argues. The Confucian way, Hayashi points out, following
Zhu Xi's theory of the *li* of human nature, is a moral and social Way.

> The Way of the Sages is altogether different from this. Their Way
> consists in nothing else than the moral obligations between sov-
> ereign and subject, father and child, husband and wife, elder
> and younger brother, and friend and friend [the five Confucian
> human relations]. One practices it with the five virtues. The five
> virtues are rooted in the mind, and the principle *[li]* which
> inheres in the mind is the nature of man. What all men partake
> of together is the Way, and attainment of the Way in one's mind
> is called virtue. Therefore, the Way, virtue, humanity, righteous-
> ness, decorum, and wisdom [the five virtues] are different in
> name but the same in essence. It is not what Laozi called the
> Way. If one casts aside the moral obligations of man and calls
> something else the Way, then it is not the Confucian Way, it is not
> the Way of the Sages. (*Confucian*, 348)

We showed earlier that Japanese Confucianists were never much
interested in the abstruse and abstract metaphysical issues that occupied
the Song and Ming dynasty Chinese neo-Confucianists, as well as their
Korean counterparts. This we see again in the following exchange
between Hayashi and three Korean envoys (interestingly, carried out in
written Chinese, the only medium shared by Chinese, Korean, and
Japanese Confucianists).

> The Bakufu asked me, "What did you discuss in writing with
> the three Korean envoys?" I told him that I asked whether prin-
> ciple *[ri,* Chinese *li]* and material force *[ki,* Chinese *qi]* are to be
> regarded as one or two. Their answer was, "Principle is just one;
> as to material force there is the pure and the impure. The four
> impulses [i.e., Mengzi, "the beginnings of the virtues"]," they
> said, "come from principle, but the seven emotions arise from
> material force." I asked what that meant. Their answer was,
> "When pleasure, anger, sorrow, and happiness are normal, they
> are called pure; when they are abnormal, they are called impure.
> However, material force itself also comes from principle."
> I then asked which is greater, Zhu Xi or Lu Xiangshan.
> Their answer was, "Zhu Xi achieved the supreme synthesis of
> the various philosophies. Xiangshan cannot be compared to
> him. . . . As to the foregoing opinions, they are set forth in many
> books already known to me and there was nothing to be
> learned by asking them." (*Conversations*, 351–352)

Despite its official governmental sanction, opposition to the Hayashi family Confucianism quickly grew. In some ways Hayashi's eager enthusiasm to establish the new Confucianism in government policy-making circles worked against him, convincing his critics that he was "insincere," that he didn't practice what he preached, in short, that he was a shallow opportunist. One such important critic was Nakae Tōju (1608–1648). Nakae was one of the first to gear neo-Confucianism toward the shifting bureaucratic role of the samurai in the Tokugawa government. Himself a member of the samurai class, Nakae had served a small fief in Iyo, performing his military duties during the day and studying the Confucian Four Books *(Analects, The Great Learning,* the *Doctrine of the Mean,* and *Mengzi)* at night. He began to speak out against the Hayashi school and eventually abandoned the objectivist and realist neo-Confucian theory of Zhu Xi in favor of the subjective and idealist Ming dynasty Confucianist, Wang Yangming (known in Japanese as Ō Yōmei).

Zhu Xi had argued that one could only learn the underlying *li* of the universe by studying the particular *li* of many different sorts of things in the physical world. Wang Yangming had argued against Zhu Xi, defending the subjectivist and idealistic theory (derived ultimately from Chan, or Zen Buddhism) that one could more directly grasp the universal *li* of the world by intuitively grasping the essentially human *li* within oneself. And whereas Zhu Xi held that human *li* (human nature) was an abstract principle, somewhat like a Platonic Form, Wang Yangming argued that human *li* (human nature) was *xin,* that is, mind and heart. Therefore, by meditating on one's own mind and heart, anyone could discover not only the *li* common to all human beings, but the essential *li,* or nature of the universe. Also, as we indicated earlier, Wang Yangming argued, against Zhu Xi (and somewhat like Socrates's "knowledge is virtue"), that genuine intuitive knowledge of one's inner *li* was sufficient to lead one to right action.

When Nakae was thirty-three he wrote a dialogue called *Ōkina Mondō* arguing similarly, and contrary to Zhu Xi, that every person has within them an innate moral sense, an intuitive knowledge of which is all that is required for right action. Written in simple language and stressing action over theory, practice over words, Nakae's book, and his exemplary life, had a great appeal to serious members of the samurai. All men have within them this "divine light," or moral conscience that tells them what is right and urges them to do it. Thus, Nakae was able to appropriate Wang's Xin Xue as a kind of "intuitionist" moral theory for internalizing moral principles from external social sanctions to an inner moral sense of conscience.

The superior man will be watchful over those inmost thoughts
known to him alone. In his everyday thinking, he will not think
anything for which he would have to fear if brought into the
presence of the Divine. In his everyday actions he will not per-
form an act of which he might be ashamed if it were known to
others. By mistake an evil idea may arise, a wrong deed may
present itself; but since there is within the mind a divine awareness illuminating it, what we call "enlightenment" will come.
Once this realization occurs, rectification will follow, the evil
idea and wrong deed will disappear, and the mind will revert to
its normal state of purity and divine enlightenment. The ordinary man, unfortunately, continues to think such evil thoughts
and goes on doing what he knows is wrong. Nevertheless, since
the divine light in the mind makes the man aware (that he is
doing wrong), he tries to hide it. In everybody's mind there is
this divine light, which is one with the Divinity of Heaven, and
before which one stands as if in a mirror, with nothing hidden
either good or bad. (*Divine*, 372–373)

By paying attention to this inner conscience and learning to follow it,
Nakae writes, the ordinary person can become a sage.

There is no distinction among men, be they sages or ordinary
persons, so far as their Heaven-bestowed nature is concerned.
They are all gifted with the divine light that tells good from bad.
All men hate injustice and are ashamed of evil because they are
born with this intuitive knowledge. It is only from the self-
watchfulness of the one and the self-deceit of the other that the
vast distinction arises between the superior man and the inferi-
or man. If, however, the inferior man realizes where he has
erred and becomes watchful over himself, correcting his mis-
takes and turning to the good, he may then become a superior
man. (*Divine*, 373)

Two hundred years after Nakae Tōju's voice had ceased resounding
in the school in Ōmi where he taught, a pilgrim was to arrive who
became, if not Japan's most famous *Ō Yōmei* philosopher, at least arguably
its best-known devotee. This was the tumultuous figure of Ōshio
Heihachirō (1793–1837), whose thought and action is the subject of an illuminating account in Ivan Morris's *The Nobility of Failure*. Ōshio, Morris
informs us, was the eldest son of a samurai family and in his youth
"evinced a special fascination with philosophy" (188). He was also
endowed with resolute integrity, as he showed during his fourteen years
as a police inspector in Ōsaka, consistently refusing bribes and combating

corruption until he resigned at the age of thirty-seven. It was after this that he made the fateful pilgrimage to Ōmi, which was to result in a spiritual awakening. On his return to Ōsaka, Ōshio began writing and lecturing on *Yōmeigaku* and founded a private school, exhibiting as a teacher, we are told, a "strong will and idealism . . . combined with a wild hot-tempered nature that bordered on the frenetic" (Morris, 192).

Ōshio's metaphysics, Morris writes, "was based on Wang Yangming's concept of *taikyō* (Absolute Spirit)," understood as the "fundamental creative force and the source of all things in the universe." It is to the Absolute Spirit that we must return if we wish to overcome "false, conventional categories of distinction" in an attitude characterized by "true nature" and "sincere action," as well as by a noble disregard of death.

> By reidentifying oneself with the Absolute, one attains purity of spirit and sincerity of motive; and then life, in the classical samurai phrase, becomes "lighter than a bird." (Morris, 196)

Morris notes, interestingly, the consonance of Wang Yangming thought here with the ancient Japanese concept of *makoto*.

> Ōshio applied the concept of Absolute Spirit to the realm of ethics by stressing that one of its main aspects was sincerity (*makoto*), and thus he provided a philosophical basis for the concept that was always central to the Japanese heroic ideal. (196)

Ōshio adopted Wang Yangming's notion of "sincerity" (*makoto*), but gave it a highly personal, Japanese interpretation. As we indicated earlier, the neo-Confucianism of Zhu Xi, and more so of Wang Yangming, borrowed heavily from Buddhism, despite their protestations to the contrary. One of these borrowings was a more internalized and personal interpretation of the Confucian virtues. Normally, we think of the virtues as habitual forms of public behavior (being courageous, polite, etc.). The superior person acts according to *ren, yi, li,* as a matter of course, without thinking. Buddhists, on the other hand, had stressed the cultivation of inner tranquility, and neo-Confucians, especially Wang Yangming, reinterpreted the Confucian virtues, especially as developed in the *Doctrine of the Mean*, as an inner quality of "sincerity." For Ōshio, combining Wang's Buddhist-like notion of "sincerity" with the traditional samurai ideal of fearless action in the face of death, our actions must spring from this inner quality of "sincerity."

The Wang Yangming imperative of sincere action was, in Ōshio's case, to take a spectacular form. Angered by official failure to assist starving townsfolk in a time of famine, he sold off his entire library and distributed most of the considerable proceeds among the needy. With the rest, he secretly purchased firearms, which were put to use, in March 1837, in an open revolt. This was an act with little practical chance of success, and culminated in Ōshio's committing suicide on the verge of capture. His gesture of sincere self-sacrifice can be seen, however, as a successful *philosophic* closure. Morris quotes Abe Shinkin's observation that *Yōmeigaku* is "not so much a philosophy of action as a philosophy of failure in action" (Morris, 215). Certainly it is Ōshio's revolt and suicide, manifesting and completing the coherence of his philosophy, that ensured his continuing renown.

Ōshio's death was to have an anachronistic ripple of consequence some 133 years later when writer Mishima Yukio, an ardent admirer of Ōshio, engineered his own spectacular finale in similar fashion. Mishima's suicidal revolt against what he perceived as the insipidity of postwar Japanese society may at first seem merely eccentric histrionics, a bizarre, quixotic gesture. We can only begin to understand it if we place it in the context of his deep commitment to Wang Yangming thought. He had, Morris informs us, lamented that since the suicide of General Nogi in 1912, Wang Yangming's philosophy had all but been ignored.

Another early critic of the Hayashi brand of neo-Confucianism was Yamazaki Ansai (1618–1682). Born in Kyōto, he studied first in a Zen monastery, but left in order to study Confucianism. He returned to Kyōto in 1648 criticizing both Buddhism and the Hayashi school of Confucianism, primarily for failing to practice the teachings of Zhu Xi that they preached. Yamazaki was particularly inspired by Zhu Xi's theory of education.

> The philosopher Zhu Xi was conspicuously endowed with intellectual leadership. Following in the line of Zhou Tunyi and the Cheng brothers, he advanced the cause of Confucianism in both elementary and higher education. For the guidance of his students he established these regulations [for the School of the White Deer Cave], but they failed to gain wide acceptance in his own time because of opposition from vile quarters. (*Regulations*, 355)

Applying Zhu Xi's philosophy of education to Japan, Yamazaki argued that the primary emphasis should be on Zhu Xi's ideas on how to cultivate the Confucian "Five Human Relations."

> It would seem to me that the aim of education . . . is to clarify human relationships. . . . Zhu Xi's school regulations list the Five Human Relationships as the curriculum, following an order of presentation which complements the curriculum of the

Great Learning. Study, questioning, deliberating and analyzing: these four correspond to the "investigation of things" and "extension of knowledge" in the *Great Learning.* The article deal- ing with conscientious action goes with the "cultivation of one's person." From the emperor to the common people, the cultiva- tion of one's person is essential, including both "making the thoughts sincere" and "rectifying the mind." The "managing of affairs" and "social intercourse" [mentioned in Zhu Xi's Regulations], refer to "regulating the family," "governing the state" and "establishing peace." (*Regulations,* 355–356)

Thus, for Yamazaki, the core of good education is moral training, particu- larly in the cultivation of the Confucian virtues.

In speech be loyal and true; in action be conscientious and rev- erent. Subdue ire and stifle passion. Change yourself for the bet- ter; do not hesitate to correct your errors. These things are essential to personal culture.

Do not do to others what you do not care for yourself. When action fails to get results, seek the reason for failure in yourself. . . .

The aim of teaching and guidance given by ancient sages and scholars, it seems to me, is nothing more than to set forth moral principles, in order, first, to cultivate them in one's own person, and then to extend them to others. Simply to accumu- late knowledge and learn to write well in order to gain fame and a well-paid position, is far from being the true function of education. (*Regulations,* 356–357)

Of course, behind this moral education lay a great deal of scholarly hermeneutical and exegetical study of the development of Confucianism, as we see in this example of Yamazaki's interpretation of Zhu Xi's inter- pretation of Cheng Yi's interpretation of Kongzi's interpretation of "rever- ent care" (in which Zhu Xi's balance of "inner" and "outer" worlds is tac- itly preferred over Wang Yangming's stress on the "inner").

"By Devotion we straighten ourselves within; by Righteousness we square away the world without." The significance of these eight characters cannot be exhausted by even a lifetime of appli- cation [Zhu Xi's comment on a statement by Cheng Yi]. Indeed, the Master Zhu was not exaggerating at all in saying this.

In the *Analects* of Confucius when it says "the superior man cultivates himself with reverent care [*kei*, Chinese *qing*]," it sim- ply means "By Devotion [*kei*] we straighten ourselves within." What is said further in the *Analects,* "To put others at ease by

cultivating oneself, and thus to put all men at ease" is the same
as "By Righteousness we square away the world without . . ."

The virtue of Sincerity is not merely for perfecting oneself
alone; it is also for perfecting things around us. Perfection of self
is Humanity [ren]; perfection of things is Knowledge [zhi].
These are virtues which manifest our nature; this is the Way
which joins the inner and the outer worlds [The Doctrine of the
Mean]. Cheng Yi also said, "Devotion and Righteousness hold
each other together and ascend straightway to attain the Virtue
of Heaven." Thus when Zhu Xi said that these eight characters
of Cheng Yi are inexhaustible in their application, he was not
exaggerating at all. (Devotion, 357–358)

We can see the influence of Confucian thought on the newly emerging
class of samurai-bureaucrats in several bakufu decrees issued between
1615 and 1650. The first, Buke sho-hatto (Rules for the Military Houses), states
explicitly that "the study of literature and the practice of the military arts
must be pursued side by side," a clear reference to the transformation of
the military class of samurai from a fighting force to something more on
the model of the Chinese Confucian scholar (ru).

Another area of selective adaptation of Chinese neo-Confucianism to
Japanese culture is in the interpretation of the Confucian Five Human
Relations. In Chinese Confucianism these have always been primarily
relations within the family, the relation of husband to wife, father to child,
oldest son to other siblings, and so on. But in Japan the Five Relations
were interpreted more broadly to prescribe the correct social relations in
the Japanese feudal hierarchy, that is, relations among ruler and samurai,
farmer, artisan, and trader.

Although the Hayashi college in Yedo was considered to embody the
approved, official, orthodox Confucianism, there was little serious
attempt to stifle opposed views. Besides Nakae Tōju and Yamazaki Ansai,
more severe objections were offered by Yamaga Sokō (1622–1685) and
Kumazawa Banzan (1619–1691), who openly denounced the orthodox
version but were punished by the government with little more than official reprimands and warnings. (Criticism of the bakufu government,
including its official educational policy, on the other hand, was more
severely punished by exile and banishment from the capital Yedo).

Yamaga Sokō of Aizu had been a student of Hayashi Razan and had
made a careful study of Buddhism and neo-Confucianism. His main concern, however, was the relation of Confucianism to military affairs and the
role of the samurai in the new Tokugawa bakufu unified Japan. Yamaga
lectured in Yedo, then spent a brief spell from 1652 to 1661 as military
instructor of the daimyō of Akō, before returning to Yedo. In 1661 he wrote

a book, *Seikyō yōroku* (*The Essentials of Confucianism*), in which he joined earlier Chinese and Korean scholars in rejecting the Song and Ming dynasty interpretations of Confucianism (i.e., Zhu Xi and Wang Yangming) in favor of a return to the original Han and pre-Han dynasty Confucianism of Kongzi and Mengzi.

As we indicated earlier, between the pre-Han and the Song and Ming Confucianism is a gap of more than a thousand years during which all sorts of other non-Confucian elements (mainly Taoist and Buddhist) had been absorbed into and claimed by later Confucianists. Pre-Han Confucianism is mainly concerned with moral and social, that is, broadly humanistic, matters, whereas the neo-Confucianism of Zhu Xi and Wang Yangming emphasized metaphysics and epistemology, and is much more intellectual, systematic, complex, scholarly (not to say scholastic) than the Confucianism of Kongzi himself. In addition to these hermeneutical problems, there were also problems in simply being no longer able to read the ancient pre-Han Chinese. As this linguistic facility faded, it became all the more difficult to see the differences between pre-Han Confucianism and Song/Ming Confucianist interpretations of the pre-Han texts.

Qing dynasty Chinese scholars rejected Song and Ming neo-Confucianism because it was not pure Confucianism and because it was not pure Chinese. They wanted to weed out especially Taoist metaphysics and Indian Buddhism, and they developed the linguistic ability to read the ancient pre-Han texts freed from all these anachronistic influences. Japanese scholars joined in these intense linguistic and exegetical studies of ancient Chinese writing (which eventually led, as we will see, to parallel attempts to recover ancient Shintō texts), but they tended to prefer the older Confucianism for reasons of their own, mainly, because it was less intellectual, less complex, and better able to establish a personal morality for the expanding role of the new samurai bureaucrats.

Because Yamaga Sokō's attack on the orthodox Hayashi school involved criticism of the government's official educational policy, the government forced him to leave Yedo and return to Akō, where he continued to study in exile. His book, *Shidō, The Way of the Warrior*, became a Japanese classic explaining the role of the former samurai (*rōnin*) in the new unified society, and was a precursor of the tradition later known as "Bushidō." In the Preface to *The Essentials of Confucianism* (literally, *The Essential Teachings of the Sages*), Yamaga's students explain the dangers they faced in publishing an account of Confucianism so at variance with the state-supported Hayashi brand of Song and Ming neo-Confucianism.

> The Sages lived far in the past and their precise teachings have gradually sunk into oblivion. The scholars of the Han, Tang,

Song, and Ming dynasties have misled the world, piling confusion upon confusion. And if this has been true in China, how
much the more has it been true in Japan.

Our teacher [Yamaga Sokō] has made his appearance in
this country when it is already 2,000 years since the time of the
Sages. He has held high the way of the Duke of Zhou and
Confucius, and been the first to set forth their essential teachings. . . . We, his disciples, made a collection of his sayings and
then made this request of our master: "These writings should be
kept secret. . . . Your criticisms of Confucian scholarship in the
Han, Tang, Song, and Ming dynasties run contrary to the prevailing view among scholars. Some readers might complain to
the authorities about it."

The master answered, "Ah, you young men should know
better. The Way is the Way of all the world; it cannot be kept to
oneself. Instead, it should be made to permeate the whole world
and to be practiced in all ages. If this book can help even a single man to stand on his own convictions, that will be a contribution to the moral uplift of our times. The noble man must sometimes give his life in the fulfillment of Humanity. Why should
my writings be kept secret? . . . The Sages' scriptures are self-
evident to all the world; there is no need for lengthy comment."
(*Confucianism*, 391–392)

One of the obstacles that Yamaga felt the Hayashi family had erected,
which prevented the full implementation of Confucianism in the moral
education of Japan, was the elitist image Hayashi (following Zhu Xi, following Taoist and Buddhist models of the quiescent, transcendent sage)
had encouraged of the Sage as a superhuman person.

> In order to know what the real master of the Way is like, you
> should first have a very clear understanding of what the sage is
> like. The sage, according to the prevailing notion among con-
> ventional scholars, is one who has a mien of moral superiority, a
> distinctive personality, remarkably conspicuous in a crowd of
> men. (*Sage*, 393)

But this image, Yamaga points out, is completely contrary to Confucius
himself and what he taught. Confucius taught that the superior person
is not someone of unusual ability or superior birth, but rather someone
who cultivates the innate human potential of every human being. By
doing this, the sages do, of course, become better than the average person, but that is only because they have worked hard to develop and perfect themselves. In principle every person can become a sage.

> Now this indicates a lack of real knowledge concerning the
> sages. Upon studying the utterances, the actions, and the politi-
> cal ordinances of the Duke of Zhou and Confucius we find that
> they were not at all like this. The sage represents only the best of
> humankind and is not a bit different from other men. He is fully
> accomplished in those things which make a man a Man, is well-
> informed of things and affairs, and is not perplexed by them at
> all. As to his personality and character, he is warm, amicable,
> humble, frugal, and self-sacrificing. . . . Contented with his own
> lot, he never deviates from the course of duty. . . . Thus, in all
> that he does, there is nothing strikingly different from what oth-
> ers do. (*Sage*, 394–395)

During his forced exile Yamaga wrote *Haisho zampitsu (An
Autobiography in Exile)*, in which he extends the search for the Chinese
roots of Confucianism to the search for the roots of Japanese culture
before contact with China. If we study the situation carefully, Yamaga
writes, we will see that far from being inferior to China or Korea,
Japan has from its earliest beginnings actually practiced and exemplified the virtues of humanity *(ren)* and righteousness *(yi)*, as well as
martial valor, far more than those who simply talked and wrote about
them.

> I once thought that Japan was small and thus inferior in every
> way to China, that "only in China could a sage arise". . . . Only
> recently have I become aware of the serious errors in this view.
> . . . In Japan the one true imperial line, legitimate descendants
> of the Sun Goddess, has ruled from the divine ages down to
> the present time without the interruption of a single genera-
> tion. . . . Has not this been due to the wide prevalence in Japan
> of the cardinal virtues of humanity and righteousness? . . . No
> less deserving of mention is Japan's pursuit of the way of mar-
> tial valor. The three kingdoms of Han were conquered and
> made to bring tribute to the court. Korea was subjugated and
> its royal castle made to surrender. Japanese military headquar-
> ters was established on foreign soil and Japanese military
> prestige was supreme over the four seas from the earliest
> times down to the present day. Our valor in war inspired fear
> in foreigners. As for invasion from abroad, foreigners never
> conquered us or even occupied or forced cession of our land.
> (*Autobiography*, 395–396)

Thus, if you look at the actual history of the people, what they do and not
what they say, Yamaga argues, it is clear that in actual practice the
Japanese are superior in every way.

> Wisdom, humanity, and valor are the three cardinal virtues of a
> sage. When even one of these three is lacking, a man falls short
> of being a sage. When we compare China and Japan with these
> virtues as criteria, we see that Japan greatly excels China in each
> of them and undoubtedly merits the name of Middle Kingdom
> far more than does China. (*Autobiography*, 397)

From this point of view, Yamaga developed a critique not only of the
practice of the Chinese but also of their theories. Basically, Yamaga
argues, these theories are too far removed from everyday life. The reason
Chinese have been unable to practice their own teachings is that their
teachings are too abstract, abstruse, complex, technical, and, in short, too
impractical.

> Many paths to learning have existed in the past and present.
> Confucianism, Buddhism, and Taoism each has its own basic
> principles (all of which I studied). . . . Nevertheless, when it
> came to everyday matters, there was still much that I did not
> comprehend. . . . Some say that if the perfection of virtue [*ren*,
> Japanese *jin*] could be fully realized in one's mind, all the things
> of this world and all the affairs of men would be taken care of;
> others say that if the compassion of Buddha were made the
> basic principle, all would work out for good in the . . . past, pre-
> sent and future. All these ideas, however, serve only to keep
> learning apart from the real world. Whatever others may think,
> I myself cannot believe otherwise or accept that kind of learning
> as satisfactory. I have consulted both Confucianists and
> Buddhists. . . . Their teaching goes one way and life another.
> (*Autobiography*, 397–398)

Following the logic of this line of thought to its ultimate conclusion,
Yamaga realizes that the theoretical teaching best suited to the practice of
Japan is Japan's own teaching, that is, Shintō. The best way to bring practice in line with theory, then, is for Japanese people to study, not the Way
of the Sages or the Way of the Buddha, but the Way of the Gods, that is,
Shintō. The problem with Shintō, as Yamaga points out, is the fragmen-
tary and obscure nature of its most ancient writings, the *Kojiki* and
Nihongi. But this is probably due, Yamaga comes to realize, to the present
inadequacy in Japanese education in the study of very ancient languages
and cultures. The neo-Confucian practice of reading Han and pre-Han
culture through the eyes (and the language) of much later Song and Ming
culture had obviously distorted and regrettably obscured the meaning
of the ancient texts. What is now urgently needed, Yamaga insists, is a
thorough study of the ancient culture and texts. From there, he argues,

we should be able to find our way back into ancient Shintō texts, and through these texts, back into ancient Japanese life and culture before contact with outside influences.

> Shintō is the way of our own country but the early records of it are lost: what we know is fragmentary and incomplete. . . . I began to . . . read more widely and to ponder on what earlier scholars had left behind them; but on many points my doubts were not clarified. . . . Then . . . it occurred to me that my failure to comprehend might be due to the fact that I had been reading the scholars of the Han, Tang, Song, and Ming. By going directly to the writings of the Duke of Zhou and Confucius, and taking them as my model, the guiding lines of thought and study should be correctly ascertained. (*Autobiography*, 398–399)

Yamaga Sokō became known as one of the Three Great Rōnin. Along with Kumazawa Banzan and Yui Shōsetsu, he gained this distinction on account of his interest in relating Confucianism to military affairs and his concern for the welfare of the samurai in the new society.

Kumazawa Banzan (1619–1691) was military advisor to the *daimyō* of Okayama and, after a period of study in the capital under Nakae Tōju, returned to administrative duties. In many ways Kumazawa was a model of the new samurai bureaucrat. His most important work lay in several successful economic reforms: controlling water by riparian works, forestry development, educational reform, among others. His reformist thinking also included a recommendation to the *bakufu* government to relieve the *daimyō* of having to keep two households at all times, one in their local fiefdoms and the other in the Yedo capital. His reform efforts, especially this last criticism of the central government, were inconsistent with the conservative policies of government officials he worked under, and much of his later life was spent in virtual exile. Nonetheless, Kumazawa's policies were widely adopted, especially the transformation of the former samurai *(rōnin)* into a well-educated, hard-working, and devoted class of civil servants.

Kumazawa argues that times have changed and that today's problems demand new solutions. While in the past economic suffering and deprivation could be alleviated by a more equitable distribution of the national wealth, there is simply not enough wealth in the nation today to significantly remedy the financial hardships that many, including the *rōnin*, face.

> Benevolent rule cannot be extended throughout the land without first developing our material wealth. In recent times there

have been a great many people with no one to turn to: that is, with no one to depend upon, no place to go for help, and no work by which to support their parents, wives, and children. The benevolent rulers of the past attended first to the needs of such persons with no one to turn to. Today the worst off of these people are the *rōnin*. There are innumerable cases of their starving to death during the frequent famines. (379)

The problem is that in the new Tokugawa regime the old feudal rulers have themselves been left impoverished and there is no new source of wealth to distribute among the needy.

This is due to the impoverished condition of the feudal lords who are thus forced to stop giving allowances to some of their retainers. The retainers in turn cut off their dependents. . . . The public treasure of the shōgunate would not suffice to pay so much as one percent of the people's debts, even if all the stored up money and grain were devoted to the purpose. (379–380)

What most urgently needs to be done, therefore, he argues, is to apply the great Confucian principles of the past to the problems of today. This is a task for humble, civic-minded Confucian scholars (i.e., the *rōnin* on the model of the Confucian *ru*).

Nevertheless it would be quite easy to relieve the situation if benevolent rule were adopted, for there is a Great Principle [from the *Li Yuan,* the *Record of Rites*] which can be applied in the present better than ever in the remote or recent past. . . . The ideal can only be comprehended by those who, while of lowly extraction, still have deep insight into events and into the workings of the human heart, and who at the same time have learning, administrative talent, and true loyalty. Only men of such character are qualified to be the teachers of kings. (380–381)

Along with Yamaga Sokō, discussed above, the strongest opposition to the Hayashi school of Zhu Xi neo-Confucianism came from Itō Jinsai (1627–1705), who rejected Song and Ming dynasty Confucianism altogether in favor of a return to the original Confucianism *(kogaku-ha)* of Confucius himself and his pre-Han followers. Not a samurai but a member of the newly emerging middle class of wealthy, educated merchants, Itō Jinsai opened a school in Kyōto for the study of major Confucian classics which attracted a large number of students.

The perceived need in Japan was not for endless scholastic disputations over metaphysical principles, but a simple, personally inspiring code of ethics for the ordinary person. And from this perspective Kongzi (Confucius) and Mengzi (Mencius) were far more useful than either Zhu Xi or Wang Yangming. In addition, as pointed out above, it had become clear by the late seventeenth century how much non-Confucian elements, especially late Taoist and Buddhist elements, had crept into Song and Ming Confucianism. Finally, as we indicated earlier in this chapter, even in the Han dynasty (in Dong Zhongshu, for example) many superstitious elements alien to the original Confucianism of Kongzi, Mengzi, and Xunzi had attached themselves to Confucianism. For all these reasons, Itō raised high the banner, "Back to Confucius!"

> Only with the appearance of Confucius was true learning based on the Way and virtue fully brought into the light of day. . . . Only then were the many kinds of superstitious and supernatural beliefs dealt with in the light of reason in order to avoid confusion with the Way and virtue. . . . Since the Han and Tang dynasties, however, scholars have looked up to the Six Classics (including *The Great Learning* and *The Doctrine of the Mean*) as the highest authority, without knowing that the *Analects* was the foremost book of all, rising high above the Six Classics. (*Primacy*, 410)

We have traced the shifting priority among the Confucian virtues (*ren, yi, li, zhi*, etc.) over the centuries, settling in the Song and Ming Confucianism of Zhi Xi and Wang Yangming on the Buddhist-like inner virtues of "tranquility" and "sincerity." Itō is firm in his preference for the primacy of *ren* (Japanese, *jin*) as the chief virtue and the foundation for all the other virtues, just as Confucius himself had argued in the *Analects*. *Ren (jin)* is an extremely hard term to translate accurately, its meaning varying from affection to mutual respect for other persons. Itō interprets *ren (jin)* as a kind of sincerely felt affectionate love.

> Humanity *[ren, jin]* is the virtue! It is great! But to extol it in one word, it is called love. For what is called righteousness or duty between sovereign and subject, paternal affection between father and son, distinction between husband and wife, precedence between elder and younger brothers, faith between friends (the Confucian Five Human Relations), this all comes from love!
>
> Because love originates from a genuine heart, these five feelings, when they come forth from love, are true; when not from love, they are feigned. Therefore, in the eyes of the gentleman, there is no virtue above compassionate love, and nothing more pitiable than a vicious, hardened, and shallow heart. In

Confucianism, humanity is considered the fountain-head of the
virtues. That is the reason for it. (*Love*, 411–412)

Once more we see the Japanese preference for genuine emotion over
abstruse intellectual and moral formalism. We have also shown several
times above that Japanese intellectuals tended to reject any idealist or
nihilist denial of the ordinary world of everyday sense experience. As we
can see from the following passage, this was for Itō yet another reason to
prefer the earlier Confucianism of Kongzi to the Buddhistic Confucianism
of Zhu Xi and more so, Wang Yangming. (One wonders, however, if Itō
realized that the Zen Buddhist, Dōgen, had also equally rejected the
denial of the reality of the phenomenal world.)

> The Buddhist takes emptiness [*śūnyatā*] as the Way, while Laozi
> considers vacuity [*wu*] the Way. The Buddhist thinks that moun-
> tains, rivers, and the great earth are all illusions, and Laozi says
> all things are produced out of nothing. Still heaven overspreads
> us and earth upholds us throughout eternity; the sun and moon
> shine and shed their light on us throughout eternity. The four
> seasons come and go in order, while mountains stand and rivers
> flow for eternity. Feathered creatures, furry creatures, scaly crea-
> tures, and naked creatures, as well as plants and vines, continue
> as they are for eternity. . . . Life follows life endlessly. Where do
> you find this so-called emptiness and vacuity? (*Life*, 412)

Itō Jinsai did not write a great deal, and for the most part his theories
are known to us through the writing of his son, Itō Tōgai (1670–1736). Itō
Tōgai was a critical scholar, well aware of the many changes that had
occurred in Confucian teachings from the time of Kongzi to that of Wang
Yangming.

> The change from the Way of the Sages in the Three Dynasties to
> the Confucian teaching of today has been a gradual one and not
> something that happened overnight. There was one great
> change during the Han dynasty and a second during the Song
> dynasty. Quietly and surreptitiously the teaching has been
> altered or done away with throughout ten centuries or more,
> with the result that present-day teaching is no longer identical
> with early Confucianism. (*Devolution*, 403)

Confucianism begins with the fall of the old feudal order of the Zhou
dynasty, a time when Confucianism struggled uneasily with other competing schools of philosophy, suffering a major but temporary setback
during the book burning of the Qin dynasty.

> The decline of the Zhou dynasty was followed by the Warring
> States period. Rites and music were allowed to deteriorate and
> were then abandoned. Warfare raged day after day. Steady
> decline led to the rise of the ruthless Qin dynasty, who burned
> the classics and had Confucian scholars killed. The Way of the
> early kings vanished from the earth completely. (*Devolution*, 404)

In the Han dynasty Confucianism rose in prominence, promoted by a professional class of scholars (the *ru*), but also during this period many
superstitious elements crept into Confucianism, which was further undermined by Buddhist and Taoist theories.

> With the rise of the Han dynasty the *Book of Odes* and *History*
> came into a certain vogue, and Confucian scholarship was
> favorably regarded. Still at that time the government adopted
> its own political system and its own regulations, while the sur-
> viving documents of the early kings were relegated to learned
> men dealing with the past. Thereupon the Confucianists of that
> day made the transmission of this heritage the private and
> exclusive business of their own schools. Thus the conduct of
> government and the teaching of the Way took separate paths.
>   In addition, the interpretation of portents in terms of the
> five elements theory became fashionable. Everything in heaven
> and earth was reckoned in fives. In this way the virtue of faith
> was joined to the four virtues of humanity, righteousness, deco-
> rum, and wisdom, to make up the five norms corresponding to
> the five elements. . . . Thus the first great change took place in
> the ancient teaching. Thereafter Confucian scholarship was
> turned into the study of textual commentaries, the mastery of
> literary style and the art of making rhetorical allusions. Thus
> the Way of the Sages was left in darkness and obscurity for
> more than a thousand years. . . . [Later] the teachings of
> Gautama Buddha and Laozi threw the world into a commotion.
> (*Devolution*, 404–405)

Finally Song and Ming neo-Confucianism, in their efforts to revive
Confucianism, ironically introduced many alien elements.

> In the Song dynasty true Confucianists appeared to champion
> the Way of the Sages and denounce heretics. The profundity of
> their scholarship and the thoroughness of their research went
> far beyond that of the Han and Tang Confucianists. Never-the-
> less, they considered man's true nature to be principle [*li, ri*] in
> its disembodied and unmanifested state, and believed that the
> eradication of physical desires was the method for attaining
> sagehood. . . . They insisted that man's true nature must be

sought in an original unformed and undetermined state. So
humanity, righteousness, decorum, and wisdom (the original
Confucian virtues) could not be seen or heard any more than
sound within a bell or fire within a stone before they are struck.
Names they were, but not real things. Thus Confucianism
underwent a second change. Since then, because neo-
Confucianism has been accepted in the schools for so long and
become so completely systematized, entwining and entangling
everything, patching here and thatching there, its bonds could
not be broken. (*Devolution*, 405–406)

As we indicated earlier, one of the major differences between earlier
and later forms of Confucianism lies in the precise sense in which the
virtues of *ren, yi, li,* and so on can be said to be part of our original human
nature. Mengzi had said that all men were born with the "beginnings," or
"impulses" of the four virtues, but that these beginnings had to be nour-
ished and strengthened by education, socialization, and training before
maturing into fully developed virtues. Dong Zhongshu had emphasized
still more the need for socialization by calling the virtues within us at
birth "seeds" that did not themselves possess goodness (or even the
beginnings of goodness) but only the potential for goodness. And, of
course, Xunzi had gone even farther in arguing that human nature was in
itself evil but nonetheless had the potential of becoming good through
social intervention.

The difference between Mengzi on the one hand and Dong Zhongshu
and Xunzi on the other is a matter of degree, though an important one.
For Mengzi the "beginning impulses" of the virtues are themselves good,
though only in a small way that requires further development and
strengthening, whereas for Dong and Xunzi the "seeds" of virtue are only
potentially good and are not good in themselves. In the following passage
we can see that Itō Tōgai supports Mengzi against Dong Zhongshu and
Xunzi.

Now if we go to the root of things, it may be seen that any individual, insofar as he is a man, possesses four impulses [or
"beginnings," from *Mencius*], just as he possesses four limbs.
The sense of sympathy is the impulse from which humanity
[ren] develops; the sense of shame and aversion is the impulse
from which righteousness *[yi]* develops; the sense of humility
and reverence is the impulse from which decorum *[li]* develops;
the sense of right and wrong is the impulse from which wisdom
[zhi] develops. These impulses are what constitute the goodness
of human nature and what distinguish man from all other
things. If brought to fulfillment, they become the virtues of

humanity, righteousness, decorum, and wisdom. If, however, nothing is done to cultivate the impulses with which we are born, then they will remain weak rather than develop their full power, and when put to a test may be lost together with that into which they were born. The Sage was concerned about this, so he established moral training in order to let people expand and fulfill that which they were born with. Men cannot endure the suffering of others, so he brings them to where they can endure them; they do not dare to act, so he brings them to where they dare to act. Thus gradually but steadily they move towards good and reject evil, so as to attain the fulfillment of virtue. (*Erroneous*, 408–409)

(The last part of this quotation is rather odd. Certainly the Sage was concerned to expand and fulfill the original "impulses" to virtue, but *not* to *harden* men to be able to bear the sufferings of others, or to *overcome* their reluctance to aggression!)

At the opposite extreme from Dong Zhongshu, Song and Ming neo-Confucianists, borrowing from Buddhist doctrines, argued that all men were born with the virtues fully formed within them, though "obscured" by ignorance. Again, the difference between Mengzi and the neo-Confucianists is a matter of degree, though an important one. Although Mengzi allows that the "beginning impulses" toward virtue are themselves good (that is, are immature forms of virtue), he insists that to achieve their full development these beginnings must be socially nurtured through education and training. For the Buddhists and, later, the neo-Confucianists, on the other hand, the Buddha Nature and later the Confucian virtues are fully formed within each person, although they are obscured just as a perfectly formed pearl in muddy water is not clearly visible (or, in another often used analogy, as dust might obscure the image in a perfectly formed mirror). Itō Tōgai firmly rejects this Buddhistic neo-Confucian interpretation.

In later times, however, neo-Confucian teaching has not been in accord with the original aim of the Sages. Humanity, righteousness, decorum, and wisdom are considered to be complete in man's original nature. Only the waywardness of the life force and the beclouding effect of matter, they say, cause this natural brilliance to be obscured; so we must try to get rid of the beclouding screen and sweep away the dust in order to restore the original, as a mirror cleansed of dust regains its brightness, or as water when kept still becomes clear again. Therefore the virtues of humanity and righteousness do not need to be acquired through cultivation; they are there already. (*Erroneous*, 409)

Ogyū Sorai (1666–1728) offered a far more radical criticism of neo-Confucianism in all its forms. Neo-Confucianism, he argued, concentrated too much on complex metaphysics and idealistic self-cultivation, pursuits open only to a tiny, highly educated elite, and failed to provide answers to pressing social questions, which he thought should be the primary responsibility of philosophers. If we look at the historical context of Confucianism, Ogyū argued, we can see that most of the orthodox texts are basically commentaries on the pre-Confucian classics (*The Book of Changes, Spring and Autumn Annals, The Book of Odes*, etc.). It is from this scholastic perspective that the traditional canon of orthodox Confucianism arose, that is, *Analects, Mencius, The Doctrine of the Mean, The Great Learning*, and later the Song and Ming neo-Confucianist texts. But from the point of view of its contribution to what is socially useful, Ogyū held, we would construct a very different canon of ancient Chinese philosophical texts. Unlike Itō Tōgai, who regards all pre-Han Confucianism as the pure, original Confucianism, Ogyū sees the distortion and degeneration of the original Confucian texts occurring as early as the pre-Han *Mencius* and *The Doctrine of the Mean*.

> The Way is difficult to know and difficult to express because of its magnitude. What the Confucianists of later times saw of the Way was only one aspect of it. The true Way is the Way of the early kings of China, but after the appearance to Tzu Ssu [Confucius's grandson and the supposed author of *The Doctrine of the Mean*] and Mencius it degenerated into the Confucianist school which began to contend for supremacy among the "hundred philosophers" of the late Zhou, and by so doing, itself demeaned the Way. (417)

We have already seen the criticism leveled against the Song and Ming neo-Confucian elevation of the virtue of "sincerity" over the original Confucian virtues of *ren, yi, li, zhi*, and so forth. Ogyū has a very interesting historical explanation of how this came about at a much earlier period, in which he claims that Tzu Ssu wrote *The Doctrine of the Mean* (or simply *Mean*) as a refutation of the Taoist Laozi. Instead of allowing Confucius to remain a humble moral and social reformer (emphasizing the virtue of *ren*), as he saw himself, Ogyū argues, Tzu Ssu tried to interpret Confucius to fit the more metaphysical, transcendental, and spiritual Taoist notion of a "sage" (and so, emphasizing the virtue of "sincerity"), thereby distorting Confucius's message and deflecting for two thousand years the primary moral and social thrust of his teachings. By defending, enlarging, and systematizing the traditional feudal virtues (*ren, yi, li, zhi*, etc.) of the Zhou dynasty, Kongzi was accused by the Taoists of stressing the "artificial," that is, the *conventional* values of a particular society (the Zhou dynasty) at a particular point in time, instead of looking to the "natural," that is, the *eternal* ways of Nature, as Laozi had done. To refute this criticism, Ogyū argues, Tzu Ssu interprets Kongzi to look and sound more like a Taoist sage, especially in his shift from the more historically contextual virtue of *ren* to the more universal and "natural" virtue of "sincerity."

> Take the case of Tzu Ssu who wrote the *Mean* in opposition to Laozi. Laozi had called the Way of the Sages artificial. Tzu Ssu therefore said the Way was in conformity with nature, in order to show that the Confucian Way was not artificial. This brought him in the end to his theory of absolute sincerity. . . . In ancient times an originator was considered a sage, but as Confucius was no originator, absolute sincerity was spoken of in the *Mean* as the virtue of the Sage, and the . . . explanation of the virtue of the Sage was put forward in order to rescue Confucius from embarrassing criticism. Sincerity, however, is only one virtue of the Sage. How could it be thought of as all-sufficing and all-inclusive? (417–418)

(One problem with Ogyū's hypothesis is that scholars today regard Laozi as having lived much later than Tzu Ssu. Nonetheless, regardless of who actually wrote the *Mean* and the *Tao De Jing*, and when, Ogyū may be right that the *Mean* is a Confucian response to just such an early "Taoist" critique.)

Ogyū Sorai is one of the first in Japan to appreciate the contribution of the realist Confucianist Xunzi in his opposition to the idealist Mengzi. As we pointed out above, although both Mengzi and Xunzi hold that all human beings equally possess the potential to be virtuous (and therefore to be sages), Mengzi sees this potential as the beginning of virtue, which is itself good, whereas Xunzi sees this merely as a potentiality that could become good but is not itself good. Indeed, on this basis Xunzi argues in direct opposition to Mengzi that when people are first born they are not good as Mengzi had said, but evil, that is, selfish, aggressive, and appetitive, and can only be made virtuous by rigorous social education and training.

In Mencius's debates with Gaozi in *Mencius*, Gaozi argues, in effect, that there is no human nature, that human beings have the potential to become almost anything and that how they turn out depends entirely on their socialization. In his analogy with the willow tree, Gaozi argues that people are infinitely malleable like the wood of the willow tree which can be bent and shaped into many different forms, from cups to baskets. Mengzi counters Gaozi by pointing out that this can only occur by violating the nature of the willow, whose nature is to continue growing as a willow tree and not to become a cup or basket. But this implies that moral training and socialization is a violation of human nature, or at least that any socialization that attempts to radically transform people violates their basic nature.

Again, the difference between Mengzi and Gaozi here is a matter of degree, though an important one. Mengzi prefers to look at education as encouraging and nourishing a tendency already present in young children, whereas Gaozi prefers to see education as a process of thwarting and inhibiting many selfish, antisocial tendencies in children and building their character more or less from scratch. Mengzi went too far, Ogyū argues, in stating in his debate with Gaozi that shaping the willow tree into various utensils is distorting and therefore a violation of its nature. The willow, unlike other, harder trees, has the potential to be variously shaped, but this shaping requires an opposing, outside force, which Mengzi did not want to admit. Human nature has the potential to become virtuous but only if shaped by society through education and training.

As Ogyū points out, between the claim that virtue is consistent with human nature and the claim that virtue is contrary to human nature lie many quite different philosophical positions which Chinese Confucianists confused. After all, from Dong Zhongshu, at one extreme, through Xunzi and Mengzi to the neo-Confucianists at the other extreme, all admitted that human beings possessed the potential from birth to become virtuous, that is, to become sages. But, Ogyū asks, at what precise point along this continuum lies the truth? Do we want to say with Xunzi that human beings are capable of becoming virtuous but that they are not born virtuous, or do we want to say with Mengzi that human beings are actually born not only with the potential to become virtuous but with the innate tendency (the "beginning impulse") to virtue and therefore already are in a sense virtuous, though only in a small way? In the following passage Ogyū argues, against the main trend in neo-Confucianism, that on the whole Xunzi is closer to the truth on this point than Mengzi.

> Mencius's conception of human nature as good is an example of the same sort as Tzu Ssu. By likening human nature to the willow which can be bent into any form, Gaozi had said all that could be said about it. Mencius's attempt at refutation went too far. Now what Tzu Ssu had really meant to say was that when the Sages established the Way, they did so in conformity with nature; he did not mean to say that every human being is in conformity with nature and that therefore all men are naturally in conformity with the Way. It is true that while other trees cannot be bent or twisted, the willow is by nature bendable and twistable; but this does not mean that to be bent and twisted is

the natural state of the willow. The sense of sympathy and
shame point to the fact that humanity [ren, jin] and righteousness [yi] have their origin in nature, but the sense of sympathy
is not all there is to humanity, and the sense of shame and aversion may not necessarily constitute righteousness. It is a case of
a slight misstatement that leads to a tremendous error. The
latter-day School of the Mind [Wang Yangming's *Xin Xue*] had
its inception in this. Xunzi's criticism of it was correct. So I say
that Tzu Ssu and Mencius were defenders of the Confucian
school while Xunzi was a "loyal minister" [i.e., a frank critic] to
Tzu Ssu and Mencius. (418)

Ogyū was also one of the first to recognize the importance of the
Legalist movement (of Han Feizi) of political realism so despised by
Confucianists since the Qin dynasty when the Legalists briefly succeeded
in outlawing all schools of philosophy except their own (the famous book
burning of 213 BCE). In general, Ogyū took a pragmatic and utilitarian
approach to social problems. Moral training advocated by the official
Confucian canon just will not work, he argued; and idealistic theories of
encouraging a basically good human nature are of little help in the actual
governance of a country. What is required is a system of strict controls (the
system of rewards and punishments advocated by the Legalists) and a
greater public display of state ritual and ceremony to instill feelings of
loyalty and social cohesion among the people (as advocated by Kongzi
and Xunzi). The fact that Ogyū was able to openly teach such unorthodox
views is due both to the limited hold the Hayashi school really had on the
bakufu and also to Ogyū's enormous credentials as a Chinese scholar. In
the following excerpt we can see Ogyū's rare understanding of the problem of reading ancient (pre-Han) Chinese texts, whose style is quite different from modern Chinese. Again, Ogyū traces the beginning of the distortion of the original Confucianism back much farther than other *kogaku*
scholars, such as Itō Jinsai, indeed back to the pre-Han *Doctrine of the Mean*
and *Mencius.*

By the time Han Yu made his appearance in the Tang, however,
writing had undergone a great change. Thereafter came the two
Cheng brothers and Zhu Xi, admittedly scholars of great
stature, yet nonetheless unacquainted with the ancient language. Unable to read and understand the Six Classics properly,
they showed a preference for the *Mean* and *Mencius* because
these texts were easy to read. Thus, . . . they read the ancient
style of writing as if it were the modern style and, since they
were ignorant of what was actually referred to, a discrepancy

arose between reality and discourse, whereupon sense and reasoning took separate paths. Thus the teaching of the early kings
and Confucius was seen no more.

In recent years Itō Jinsai . . . has become aware of this general state of things. Nevertheless, in the interpretation of the
Analects he has depended on *Mencius* and has read the ancient
style of writing as if it were the modern. . . . Moreover, he has . . .
put the Six Classics aside in favor of the *Analects* alone. (419)

Through his careful examination of the ancient texts Ogyū could see that
the *Analects* was already an interpretation of the pre-Confucian classics.
By ignoring these pre-Confucian texts, which Kongzi interprets, and
indeed by failing to see that Kongzi's writing is primarily an interpretation of other works, Ogyū claims Song and Ming Confucianists completely missed the point of much of Kongzi's analyses.

I painstakingly went through the Six Classics for a great many
years. Gradually I arrived at an understanding of the terms and
their corresponding realities, and thereupon the interpretation of
the texts became clear. . . . The Six Classics contain facts while the
Book of Rites and *Analects* offer interpretations. Interpretations
must be supported by facts, however, before they can be accepted
as definitive explanations of the Way. If facts are disregarded and
interpretations are accepted of themselves, it will scarcely be possible to avoid generalization, exaggeration, and arbitrary judgment. These are the faults found among scholars following . . . the
Cheng brothers and Zhu Xi. (419–420)

Despite his prominence as a scholar, Ogyū Sorai wrote a great deal of
very practical advise to the government of his time, urging greater integration and synthesis of the law and adoption of the Chinese system of
meritocracy in the civil service (this was especially directed against the
hereditary monopoly of the Hayashi family over Japanese education).

In response to Ogyū's call for a thorough reexamination of the ancient
Chinese classics, Shintō religious leaders, such as Kada Azumamaro
(1669–1736) called on the government to support a similar reexamination
of ancient Japanese classics, such as the anthology of poetry known as the
Manyōshū, as well as the historical chronicles, especially the *Kojiki.* This
was the beginning of the National Learning movement to discover the
purely Japanese cultural roots unsullied by contact with outside, primarily Chinese, influences.

The most important of the National Learning philosophers was
Motoori Norinaga (1730–1801). For more than thirty years Motoori

struggled to have the *Kojiki* made the basis of accepted Shintō scripture. The problem was that the *Kojiki* is mainly a loose collection of ancient myths, legends, and genealogical records of the imperial family. It contains little abstract or profound philosophical thought. Motoori, nonetheless, tried to show that this was a strength and not a weakness. He argued that, like other sacred texts, religious truths in the *Kojiki* were beyond ordinary sense perception, common sense, or reason. He also interpreted certain elements in the *Kojiki* as a purely Japanese sensibility of spontaneous sentiment privileging the emotional and aesthetic side of human nature over its more rational and moral side as favored by the Chinese.

Instead of attacking ancient Shintō myths as primitive and childlike, Motoori praises them for being close to the roots, the origins of a Golden Age of sympathetic religious understanding of the world, which was subsequently corrupted and lost all over the world except in Japan. Turning the "evolutionist" argument on its head, Motoori argues that the later doctrines are not better because they are more developed or more sophisticated; on the contrary, he argues, the more ancient the doctrines, the closer to the origins, and therefore the better, that is, the closer to the truth.

> The True Way is one and the same, in every country and throughout heaven and earth. This Way, however, has been correctly transmitted only in our Imperial Land. Its transmission in all foreign countries was lost long ago in early antiquity, and many and varied ways have been expounded, each country representing its own way as the Right Way. But the ways of foreign countries are no more the original Right Way than end-branches of a tree are the same as its root. (*Sun*, 15–16)

For Motoori the truth has been revealed in the sacred texts of the *Kojiki*. They cannot be independently figured out rationally, even by the most intelligent persons. The details of any revealed religion, about Noah, for example, or Lazarus, can only be discovered by reading the revealed sacred texts. Thus, no one would know about the creator gods, Takami-musubi and Kami-musubi, without reading the *Kojiki*.

> Let me state briefly what that one original Way is. One must understand, first of all, the universal principle of the world. The principle is that Heaven and earth, all the gods and all phenomena, were brought into existence by the creative spirits of two deities, Takami-musubi and Kami-musubi. . . . [T]his spirit of creativity is a miraculously divine act the reason for which is beyond the comprehension of the human intellect. (*Sun*, 16)

What about people in other parts of the world who have not had the opportunity to read the *Kojiki* and so do not know about Takami-musubi and Kami-musubi? Since people outside Japan did not know about the Way of the Gods, Motoori argues, they could only use their own human reason to construct plausible but fallacious, philosophical theories about the origin and purpose of the world.

> But in the foreign countries where the Right Way has not been transmitted this act of divine creativity is not known. Men there have tried to explain the principle of Heaven and earth and all phenomena by such theories as the *yin* and *yang*, the hexagrams of the *Book of Changes*, and the Five Elements. But all of these are fallacious theories stemming from the assumptions of the human intellect and they in no wise represent the true principle. (*Sun*, 16)

Since the chief divinity, the Sun Goddess, is actually the sun itself, all peoples everywhere have been familiar with the Sun Goddess and have realized their dependence on her. But gradually other countries have lost the religious understanding of the Sun Goddess and substituted in its place all sorts of humanly constructed philosophical, cosmological speculations having nothing to do with reality. Only in Japan, Motoori argues, has this original insight been preserved in the ancient, sacred Shintō texts.

> The Sun Goddess is the goddess who reigns in Heaven (i.e., the sun). Thus, she is without a peer in the whole universe, casting her light to the very ends of heaven and earth and for all time. There is not a single country in the world which does not receive her beneficent illuminations, and no country can exist even for a day or an hour bereft of her grace. . . . However, foreign countries, having lost the ancient tradition of the Divine Age, do not know the meaning of revering this goddess. Only through the speculations of the human intelligence have they come to call the sun and the moon the spirit of *yang* and *yin*. . . . However, because of the special dispensation of our Imperial Land, the ancient tradition of the Divine Age has been correctly and clearly transmitted in our country, telling us of the genesis of the great goddess and the reason for her adoration. (*Sun*, 17–18)

Not surprisingly, Motoori was severely criticized by the neo-Confucian philosophers of his day for his naive and irrational theories. But Motoori's defense is always to go on the offensive. He does not try to prove that his view is intellectually clever or sophisticated or even rational; he agrees that it is simple and that it is not rational. But he defends

this point of view as the truth of revealed religion versus humanly constructed speculations of mere human reason (i.e., philosophy). It is not
rational, but he claims there is something beyond and higher than rationality. Motoori, we might say, is a Shintō fundamentalist. If someone
questions him why he thinks the sun we see in the sky is actually a god,
he replies that this is what the Shintō "Bible" tells us, and that this must be
true because it is the word of God.

> **Objection:**   You are obstinate in insisting that the Sun Goddess
> is the sun in heaven. If this is so, perpetual
> darkness must have reigned everywhere before her
> birth. The sun must have been in heaven since the
> beginning of the universe.
>
> **Motoori:**   First of all, I cannot understand why you say that I
> am obstinate. That the Sun Goddess is the sun in
> heaven is clear from the records of the *Kojiki* and the
> *Nihongi*. . . . The acts of the gods cannot be   •
> measured by ordinary human reasoning. Man's
> intellect, however wise, has its limits. It is small, and
> what is beyond its confines it cannot know. The acts
> of the gods are straightforward. That they appear to
> be shallow and untrue is due to the limitation of
> what man can know. To the human mind these acts
> appear to be remote, inaccessible, and difficult of
> comprehension and belief. (*Wonder*, 19–20)

And, of course, this is precisely why Motoori thinks Japanese Shintō is
superior to Chinese philosophy.

> Chinese teachings, on the other hand, were established within
> the reach of human intelligence; thus, to the mind of the listen-
> er, they are familiar and intimate and easy of comprehension
> and belief. The Chinese . . . refuse to believe in the inscrutability
> of the truth, for this, they conclude, is irrational. This sounds
> clever, but on the contrary, it betrays the pettiness of their intel-
> ligence. (*Wonder*, 20)

Another objection Motoori tackles head on is the criticism that instead
of appealing to a universal human reason that could be appreciated by all
people everywhere, as most philosophers try to do, Motoori isolates the
Japanese people from everyone else in the world. According to Motoori's
explanations, only the Japanese who follow the *Kojiki* know the truth and
follow the true Way; only they are the chosen people. But that is just the

way it is, Motoori responds. The gods favored Japan and more clearly revealed the Way of the Gods to them, and the Japanese people have preserved this ancient, sacred tradition better than other people who have abandoned what religious understanding they once had in favor of new, man-made philosophical explanations.

> **Objection:** Motoori treats this country as if it were different from other countries.

> **Motoori:** The objector also says at the end of the book that I want "to put our country outside the universe." I cannot understand what he means, but I surmise from what he says before and after that he is criticizing me for my statement that the Sun Goddess, who is the sun in heaven, was born in our country. . . .
>
> Our Imperial Land . . . is superior to the rest of the world in its possession of the correct transmission of the ancient Way, which is that of the great Goddess who casts her light all over the world. (*Error*, 22–23)

Again, from this point of view Japanese Shintō is superior to Chinese philosophy. Within Chinese philosophy those philosophers, such as Kongzi, who tried to preserve the ancient ways are superior to those, such as Mencius, who tried to introduce new ways (especially in setting limits on the divine right of kings) through their own personal reasonings and speculations.

> [Chinese] sages are superior to other people only in their cleverness. The fact is that they were all impostors. Among them the least blameworthy was Confucius. He was respectful of the Zhou dynasty. . . . That he deplored the impositions and irregularities of the feudal lords is a thing deserving of praise. But Mencius . . . was quite different. While professing the kingly way, he encouraged revolt wherever he went. (*Error*, 24)

In his explanations Motoori tends to be theistically fatalistic: everything is decreed by the gods, whether for good or evil. Why do things happen as they do? Why is there so much suffering in the world? How can we explain the existence of evil? How can this be fair, especially as the most honest and noble individuals often suffer the most while the most evil men often seem to be blessed by fortune and to enjoy life the most? Instead of looking for

rational reasons to justify the fact of undeserved evil, Motoori simply says
that we know from the *Kojiki* that this is what the gods decided and the way
they acted. If you go on to ask why the gods did things in this way, you are
asking a question that simply cannot be answered. The Way of the Gods is
not the Way of Man. From a human point of view the Way of the Gods is not
understandable, not rational. But this does not make it bad; it only shows
that gods are different from people.

> All things in life . . . are due to the spirits of the gods and their
> disposition of things. In general, there are various kinds of
> gods, noble, mean, good, bad, right, and wrong. So it is that
> things in life are not always lucky and good: they are mixed
> with the bad and the unfortunate. . . . Not infrequently, good or
> bad fortune befalls a man contrary to the principles of justice.
> Such things are the acts of the evil deities. . . .
>   Why is it that life does not consist solely of the good and
> the right . . . ? Here again there is a basic reason, fixed in the
> Divine Age and recorded in the *Kojiki* and the *Nihongi*. It is . . . a
> long story, difficult to relate here in detail, . . . about the pollu-
> tion of the land of death . . . situated beneath the ground at the
> bottom of the earth. (*Evil*, 24–25)

One of the most glaring problems with man-made rational explanations, according to Motoori, is their pitiful attempts to rationalize away
human suffering. Ordinary people regard life as containing much that is
good and enjoyable and they see death as something unmitigatedly bad.
So ordinary people try to pack as many of the good things into life as
they can before death overtakes them. Philosophers, on the other hand,
try to explain all that away, sometimes arguing that because life contains
some pain mixed with pleasure, therefore all of life is suffering, or that,
appearances to the contrary, death is actually good because it takes us
away from the body, into Nirvāna, or into some sort of unearthly heav-
en, and so on. But this is nonsense, says Motoori, the good things of life
should be enjoyed and the bad things, including death, should be
frankly and honestly acknowledged as bad. Here Motoori seems to
strike a particularly responsive chord in the Japanese psyche, privileging the honest acceptance of our direct experience of the ordinary
phenomenal world over any and all transcendental rationalizations.
What should we revere? The sun itself, the one we can see with our own
eyes. How do we know what is ultimately good and bad in life? By
means of our own immediate feelings, that pleasure is good and pain
is bad, that health is good and sickness is bad, that life is good and death
is bad.

Upon his death man must leave everything behind . . . and depart forever from the world he has known. He must of necessity go to that foul land of death, a fact which makes death the most sorrowful of all events. . . . Some foreign doctrines, however, teach that death should not be regarded as profoundly sorrowful. . . . These are all gross deceptions contrary to human sentiment and fundamental truths. Not to be happy over happy events, not to be saddened by sorrowful events, not to show surprise at astonishing events, in a word, to consider it proper not to be moved by whatever happens, are all foreign types of deception and falsehood. They are contrary to human nature and extremely repugnant to me. (*Evil*, 26)

In his discussions of poetry Motoori continues this line of thought, celebrating our honest and straightforward emotional response to the everyday things we directly experience. Here Motoori expresses a view very similar to the Western notion of aesthetic disinterestedness, that unlike "passion," which seeks to gain something, "emotion" is a pure sensitivity to feeling for its own sake and that this is what poets objectively, nonjudgmentally report. Unlike Chinese poetry, which is often didactic and moralistic, Motoori praises the frank, unashamed celebration in Japanese poetry of human emotion, of love, sorrow, longing, and regret.

There is a distinction between emotion and passion. All the varied feelings of the human heart are emotions, but those among them which seek for something in one way or another are passions. . . . Only such feelings as sympathy for others, sadness, sorrow, and regret are specifically called emotions. But as far as poetry is concerned, it comes only from emotion. This is because emotion is more sensitive to things and more deeply compassionate. Passion is absorbed only in the acquisition of things. . . . Thus, it has no capacity for tears at the sight of flowers or the song of birds. (*Poetry*, 30)

Instead of constantly trying to control or restrain our emotions, as the rationalistic philosophers are always telling us, Motoori insists on a more frank acknowledgment of the power of emotion in our lives. Sometimes, it is true, emotion leads us into indiscretions that we later regret. But we cannot help ourselves. Here we are reminded of the constant conflict in Chikamatsu's plays between Confucian duty (*giri*) and Japanese feelings (*ninjō*), the latter, of course, always winning out in the end, and always tragically. We should not be so judgmentally harsh on ourselves or on other people, Motoori urges us, but rather sympathetically recognize (with fatalistic resignation) the power of emotion to occasionally lead us astray.

> The human heart is susceptible to love; no one can avoid it. Once involved in and disturbed by it, the wise and foolish alike frequently behave illogically, in spite of themselves, and they end by losing control . . . and ruining their bodies and their reputations. . . . And this occurs despite the fact that everyone fully realizes that such behavior is evil and that one must guard against becoming wildly infatuated. But not all men are sages. Not only in love but also in their daily thought and conduct the good does not always prevail. . . . And Man, even with the realization that conduct contrary to the dictates of his own mind is evil, is helpless to control it. (*Poetry*, 31–32)

Once more, Motoori tells us, this indicates the superiority of Japanese thinking to Chinese philosophy. Like Pascal, Kierkegaard, Nietzsche, and Wittgenstein in the Western tradition, and Nāgārjuna in the Indian tradition, Motoori uses philosophy to overcome philosophy. That is, he philosophically critiques the limits of reason in traditional philosophy. As we will see in the next two chapters, Japanese thinkers in the twentieth century have once again been highly engaged philosophically, along with their Western "postmodern" colleagues, in rejecting the logocentrism of mainstream philosophy. Motoori helps us to see more clearly that this perennial debate between the head and the heart is not a debate between East and West, but within philosophy, both Eastern and Western. It is perhaps good to end this chapter with Motoori, who more than anyone in the Tokugawa period finds a true, authentic Japanese voice, no longer repeating and defending Chinese ways of thinking but expressing finally a thoroughly Japanese sensibility.

> The Chinese . . . customarily subject all things to long, tedious moralistic judgments. . . . In general our countrymen are generous and not particularly discerning or critical. . . . This is particularly true of our poetry and novels, which have as their aim the expression of a sensibility to human existence; they are calm, straightforward revelations of the varied feelings of men in love. (*Poetry*, 33)

CHAPTER 4

ENCOUNTERING MODERNITY

For long years we have been imitating them [the Chinese], senselessly delighting in their ways without thinking of anything else. This has led to our excessive stupidity with respect to geography, and to a limitation on the knowledge we have gained with our eyes and ears.

—Ōtsuki Gentaku, *Rangaku kaitei*

If there is one salient feature of our previous two chapters, it is the almost constant reference to China, reflecting Japan's cultural indebtedness to the Middle Kingdom. If Japan fashioned its own specific forms of Buddhism and Confucianism, these were consistently defined in the manner of distinctions from corresponding mainland forms, and principally those of China. As we have seen, even the National Learning movement was inspired by a Chinese precedent, and the neo-Shintōism that developed from it rested firmly on Confucian ethics.

In the eighteenth century all this began to change, largely owing to a spreading awareness of rational discoveries made in the West. Japan had already had experience of Western technical ingenuity during the encroachment of the Portuguese and Spanish in the sixteenth century; along with tobacco, bread, and the sponge cake, these "southern barbarians" had, in 1543, introduced firearms. This development failed to generate any systematic scientific inquiry among the Japanese, and during the years of the shōgunate's *sakoku* (closed door) policy, firearms themselves largely fell into disuse. However, the Japanese could not, henceforth, be complacent. Information and objects trickling in at the one Dutch trading post allowed to operate at Dejima was evidence enough of barbarian technical prowess, some of which it might be in Japan's interest to adopt.

In 1720, the shōgun Yoshimune, wishing to promote *jitsugaku* (study of real things), ordered the book-banning policy in place since 1630 to be partially lifted. There was an immediate influx of Western learning from China, where translations had been encouraged under the late Ming and Qing dynasties. All this impelled what has been called Japan's eighteenth-century rationalism, a trend that was to spill over from the purely scientific to have philosophical implications, and engender a newly awakened sense of cultural independence with regard to China.

The eighteenth-century Japanese rationalist philosophers were inspired not yet by individual Western philosophers so much as by the discreet intellectual trend of the time; politically they were ahead of their time, often uncomfortably so, as is clear in the case of Tominaga Nakamoto (1715–1746), persecuted for his uncompromising objective approach to the study of history and religion. The shift in vision going on in this period, especially its rejection of anthropological, teleological explanations of natural phenomena, is summed up in the following lines from Miura Baien (1723–1789):

> Those whom the world acclaims as leaders in thought and action take humanity and human motives as the basis of their thinking and speculation in order to set up standards for what is to be believed and done. But human minds are like human faces; their preferences differ one from another. Each considers what he has arrived at to be right, a revelation from Heaven or a deposit of truth from antiquity, and thinks those who do not accept his standards should be exterminated. It is my conviction, therefore, that there is no systematic truth or logic [*jōri*] except that which enables man to comprehend the universe without setting up standards conceived in terms of humanity or human motives. (487–488)

Where the moral and political authorities were still purveying "received wisdom" by way of neo-Confucianism, Miura sets out to shine his own light on reality. The *jōrigaku* that he proposes is characterized by the twin notion of *hankan-goitsu*, representing opposition and unity in a process strikingly reminiscent of Hegel's dialectics.

The most intriguing thinker of this period is one who led an obscure existence in his own lifetime and was unrecognized for more than a century afterward. Only with the rediscovery of his writings in 1899 did Andō Shōeki begin arousing scattered curiosity, and although his reputation has been established by critical attention from well-known scholars such as Maruyama Masao there are still those who question whether he deserved his "resurrection."

Active in the mid-eighteenth century as a doctor in a very poor area of northeastern Honshū, Andō must have observed firsthand some of the very worst misery occasioned by the feudal system. Amid a disastrous economy, the peasantry was being burdened with increasingly heavy taxes and rice levies, with famine and a sharp rise in infanticides among the consequences. Uprisings against this inequity were severely repressed.

In Andō's eyes, such injustice had arisen because the "world of nature" had been subverted by the "world of law" set in place by would-be saints and sages, especially Confucians who sought to justify a political hierarchy of social superiors and inferiors on the model of the cosmic ordering of Heaven and Earth. Among those singled out for criticism is Zhu Xi.

> It was a serious mistake of Fu Hsi [Zhu Xi] to maintain that a circle symbolizes the Great Ultimate of the universe, and that its very abstractness contains all theories. A circle represents fullness and positiveness. To regard it as representing the universe prior to the coming into existence of Heaven and Earth, to call that which moves as Heaven and that which remains stable as Earth, thus dividing the universe into two, and to regard Heaven as superior to Earth, are root causes for the enacting of selfish laws and regulations all created in order that a few might rule the multitudes by interfering with the operation of Nature's laws. (202)

To hold that Zhu Xi was in error was directly contrary to the official orthodoxy of the time. But Andō goes much farther. He would claim that the teachings of *all* the so-called sages are really a hypocritical means to secure social privilege. Hence, Confucius perpetuated the "evil" of Zhou rulers who "in imitation of the earlier saints, stole Heaven's way and exploited the direct cultivation of the masses in order to live in luxury" (136–137). Likewise, Śākyamuni, who

> obscured the Way, became a beggar, spoke glibly, induced men of similar interest to be his disciples, made them collect alms in his place, seated himself on the high platform and ate greedily by virtue of his sweet eloquence. (146)

Fired up by his indignation over social injustice, Andō scoffs at saintly "benevolence":

> Saints, . . . if they fail to collect such taxes as they desire, even resort to arms to extort tribute, and when rejected, go to the

extremity of killing the innocent masses of people. Really it is the saints who are obliged by the benevolence of the common people. (120)

One of Andō's most admiring champions, E. Herbert Norman, finds this comparable to Kant's assertion in *Metaphysik der Sitten* that self-styled benevolent government, treating its subjects paternalistically like minors, incapable of mature judgment, is in fact the "greatest despotism" (120). Genuine benevolence, Andō declares, "lies with the masses, who conform with Heaven in virtue, because they are inspired by nature herself" (120). Nature, stripped of all human, teleological masks, is, indeed, Andō's own primary inspiration and his constant reference point. Thus he can write:

> The universe has no beginning or end, there is no up or down, there are no exalted or lowly, no precedence in rank. There is only nature. Heaven and Earth are inseparable. (201)

Here is how Norman himself restates Andō Shōeki's vision of nature.

> Nature is in flux and constant change; it is incorrect to regard the outside world as static or unchangeable. Qualities which appear to be opposites are but the changing aspects of Nature and not permanently opposed to each other. Thus good and bad, true and false, suffering and ease, heaven and earth, man and woman, are all concepts which must be understood in the light of *gosei* (relativity or reciprocity). These contrasting ideas, while distinct *(nibetsu)*, are yet identical *(isshin)* like a figure and its shadow. The everchanging movements of objects, at once distinct and identical, Shōeki termed the living facts *(kasshin)* of Nature. (203)

Nature being the "unique principle of practical virtue," Andō felt it vital to return to the "world of nature" that he implies as having preceded the sages' theft of the "Way." It is a world inhabited by the old gods of Japan, before they themselves were coerced into "Shintōism." In this world, all citizens would engage once more in "direct cultivation," released from hierarchical and hypocritical creeds that allow exploitation of the weak by the strong.

Such a philosophy as this provides ample opportunities for criticism: one wonders how he could fail to perceive the similarities in his views to those of Laozi, and it would be easy to mock Andō's portrayal of the saints and sages as simplistic, or his ideal society as utopian. But there is much here that invites prudent comparison with other thinkers of greater renown, from Marx to Nietzsche and Foucault. Even if such comparisons were found excessive, Andō would still have a major *symbolic* importance. He is that shadowy figure who approaches from behind to tap philosophy on the shoulder in the name of the millions condemned to silence by illiteracy, poverty, and oppression, and to offer a caustic reminder that Japan's official philosophy spoke only for the few. The entire intellectual canon of the time is in an instant radically challenged.

As a doctor and a freethinker who took much interest in the Dutch learning then seeping into Japan through Nagasaki, Andō Shōeki would have much approved Dutch-inspired developments in medicine in the late eighteenth century and their implications for Japan's intellectual evolution. A quintessential moment occurred in April 1771, when two Japanese physicians, Sugita Gempaku (1733–1817) and Maeno Ryōtaku (1723–1803), who had both acquired a 1731 Dutch book of anatomy, *Tafel Anatomia*, by the German, Johann Adam Kulmus, observed the dissection of a human corpse and were able to compare what they saw both with Kulmus's descriptions and with traditional Chinese teaching. Sugita later recalled:

> When Ryōtaku and I compared what we saw with the illustrations in the Dutch book, we discovered that everything was exactly as depicted. The six lobes and two ears of the lungs, and the three lobes on the right and four lobes on the left of the kidneys, such as were always described in the old Chinese books of medicine, were not found. The position and the shape of the intestines and stomach were also quite unlike the old descriptions. (in Keene, 22)

The significance of this moment has been highlighted by Donald Keene, who notes that when the two doctors (with the aid of a third) had completed their laborious translation of Kulmus's work, it "started a great wave of interest in Dutch learning of every description, although medicine continued to be the chief subject of study" (24).

As we saw in the declaration of Ōtsuki Gentaku, a student of Maeno Ryōtaku, at the head of this chapter, the discrediting of Chinese medicine also hastened the end of thoughtless imitation of the Chinese and led more and more Japanese to question the very "wisdom" of Japan's great neighbor. The skepticism of the rationalists ceased to be an eccentric position. As Keene says, "Japanese scholars began to doubt the value of all that had been believed for more than a thousand years" (27).

So firmly was the orthodox ideology enforced by those in power that this rationalist revolution remained in large part under wraps, with little immediate philosophical flow into society at large, although any discrediting of China did lend ammunition to the Scholars of National Learning in their crusade to reformulate Japanese culture and thus emancipate it from the Chinese sphere. It was primarily to combat this and Wang Yangming heresies that the shōgunate enacted in 1790 its decree prohibiting "heterodox studies," although Western learning was increasingly repressed as well. However, skepticism regarding Chinese knowledge and corresponding interest in the West were growing ineluctably. It was a movement that was to lead to profound consequences in Japan's political, social, and cultural life. Insofar as the "Western phase" of Japan's philosophical developments will occur against a political background taking shape in this period, it is important here to outline broadly the evolution of Japan's response to the Western arrival.

Events abroad were to make clear the perils of seclusive conservatism. It was evident early that at least militarily the Western powers held the upper hand, and as midcentury approached, it also became obvious that they intended to use their superior power to colonize much of the non-Western world. This was brought home to the Japanese with chilling clarity by the defeat in the Opium Wars of 1839–1842 of China, the great neighbor, the Middle Kingdom, the source of so much of their own world view. By this defeat China's prestige diminished sharply in Japanese eyes. By 1860, European flags were flying too over government houses in most of Africa, Central and South America, India, and much of Southeast Asia. It was Japan's effort to avoid being similarly colonized that led to the building up and exploitation of nationalist sentiment and concepts, the evolution of which ultimately legitimized its own imperialism.

For the immediate future, Japanese intellectuals and government leaders increasingly faced a dilemma. On the one hand, any non-Western nation wishing to avoid colonization had no choice but to adopt Western science and technology in modernizing its military, industry, and economy. On the other hand, no non-Western country wished to give up entirely its own national culture. The problem was therefore how to "have one's cake and eat it too," that is, how to adopt enough Western science and technology to avoid being colonized without in the process losing one's own national identity. One solution commonly adopted, and still being employed, was to combine Western science and technology with one's own indigenous moral and social ethos.

Hirata Atsutane (1776–1843), and Sakuma Shōzan (1811–1864) are two of the many writers active from the late eighteenth century onward in whose works we find support for such a position, and their examples show how very different attitudes could find fellowship in its support. In Hirata Atsutane, we find a nationalist of the deepest hue for whom, in Keene's words, the "supposed natural claims of the Japanese to superiority over all other mortals came to be the object and justification of all recourse to Western learning" (172). One notes a paradox here. If Japan needed Western learning, did not that indicate the inferiority of Japanese ways vis-à-vis Western ways? In resolving this paradox, we find a partial answer to the key question we posed in chapter 1 concerning the failure of

Japanese intellectuals to argue that they had their own indigenous philosophy. Characteristic of Japanese such as Hirata is the belief that ethnic superiority does not depend on scientific, technological, or philosophical accomplishments. These latter are seen as important only in maintaining one's military and economic independence and advantage relative to other nations. They are irrelevant to the ethnic superiority of the Japanese as a uniquely favored people.

> Japanese differ completely from and are superior to the peoples of China, India, Russia, Holland, Siam, Cambodia, and all the other countries of the world. . . . It was the gods who formed all the lands of the world at the Creation, and these gods were without exception born in Japan. (39)

In other words, while Japan was spiritually superior to the Western powers, it nonetheless required Western practical techniques to safeguard its divinely endowed national polity in the face of barbarian force. To improve Japanese learning, Hirata accordingly advocated incorporating the best features of Chinese, Indian, Dutch, indeed, "all the different kinds of learning" (39).

Much more measured in his expression, Sakuma Shōzan was a samurai who studied the Confucian classics of the orthodox Hayashi school at Edo. Appointed advisor in 1841 on the defense of Japan's coasts, Sakuma demonstrated practical realism in recommending a buildup of coastal defenses with Western-style military equipment. As this contradicted Japan's official seclusion policy, his proposals met fierce resistance and he was forced to resign. He then devoted himself to Dutch studies, which he considered especially urgent after the Opium Wars, mastering the language and much practical information and skills in chemistry and metallurgy. When in 1854 Sakuma's disciple, Yoshida Torajirō (better known by his pen name, Shōin), was caught trying to stow away on one of Perry's ships, Sakuma was himself imprisoned for allegedly encouraging a breach of Japan's Seclusion Laws. When the treaty with the United States was signed in 1858, he became known as a strong advocate of *kaikoku-ron*, "opening the country" to the West. This is how he advocated combining Western learning and traditional Japanese culture.

> The gentleman has five pleasures, but wealth and rank are not among them. That his house understands decorum and righteousness and remains free from family rifts: this is one pleasure. That exercising care in giving to and taking from others, he provides for himself honestly, free, internally, from shame before his wife and children, and externally, from disgrace before the

public: this is the second pleasure. That he expounds and glori-
fies the learning of the sages, knows in his heart the great Way,
and in all situations contents himself with his duty, in adversity
as well as in prosperity: this is the third pleasure. That he is
born after the opening of the vistas of science by the Westerners,
and can therefore understand principles not known to the sages
and wise men of old: this is the fourth pleasure. That he
employs the ethics of the East and the scientific technique of the
West, neglecting neither the spiritual nor material aspects of
life, combining subjective and objective, and thus bringing benefit to the people and serving the nation: this is the fifth pleasure. (103)

That "employing the ethics of the East and the scientific technique of
the West" became the core of government policy is well demonstrated in
the Charter Oath of June 1868.

Knowledge shall be sought for all over the world, and thus shall
be strengthened the foundations of the Imperial Polity (kokutai).
(in Brown, 103)

In the preceding section, we have seen how the Western learning
being promoted or supported in the interests of Japan's technological
progress engendered an indigenous trend of rationalist thought. This set
in motion the revolution by which the West was eventually to dominate
Japan's intellectual milieu at the expense of complacent Chinese wisdom.
For philosophy it was, as we have seen, at first primarily influence by
implication. But when the shōgunate at last lifted restrictions on the
importation and study of Western thought as such, a new era began.

How, then, did Western philosophy finally make itself felt in Japan?
With what precedents of Western philosophy in Japan did Japanese philosophy of Western style, in the narrow, technical sense we earlier
defined, finally emerge? Meanwhile, what developments were there in
Buddhism and Confucianism? And what relationship did the philosophy
of each tradition have with Japan's intellectual evolution? How did they
shape, and take shape within, the country's Weltanschauung and its social
and political life? These are the issues to which we must now turn.

Whatever efforts the Japanese authorities made to censor Dutch
learning of any but a technological nature, we know that some knowledge
of European philosophy did find its way into Japan at this time through
Dejima. Gino K. Piovesana, in his excellent survey of Western-style philosophy in Japan, cites as a precursory figure, Takano Chōei (1804–1850), a
fervent supporter of opening up Japan to the West (and promptly persecuted for this by the government), whose pioneer work Bunken manroku

(Casual Records of Things Heard and Seen) outlines the history of Western philosophy all the way from Thales to Kant. To refer to this form of learning, Takano used the term *gakushi* (formed from the characters *gaku*, meaning "learning," and *shi*, meaning "history"), which, as Piovesana notes, means in context "general or most important learning" (*Recent*, 11).

It was not until the more clement political climate of the latter half of the nineteenth century, however, that the dissemination of Western philosophy began to flourish. In 1862, Nishi Amane (1829–1897), a scholar attached to the *Bansho Shirabe-sho (Center for the Investigation of Barbarian Books)*, prepared the draft for the first lectures on Greek and European philosophy to be delivered in Japan, and in order to distinguish this novel discipline from Asian thought, he devised the term *kitetsugaku* (abbreviated from *kikyū tetsuchi*, meaning "science of seeking wisdom"). Along with his colleague Tsuda Mamichi (1829–1903), Amane set off that same year to study in Europe and while there the two acquired a fresh batch of books (including "many works by Comte and Mill, Cousin, Montesquieu and Hegel's *Phänomenologie des Geistes*"). Both men thereafter wrote philosophical works colored by their new reading, though with a fundamentally divergent outlook, Tsuda as a positivist materialist much influenced by Comte, and Nishi more as an idealist, though with "Comte-Mill empiricism and positivism . . . evident in many of his works" (Piovesana, *Recent*, 18).

The philosophical value of this output may have declined, but it is difficult to exaggerate the historical significance of these two key figures in the introduction of Western philosophy to Japan, and its subsequent propagation. On their return to Japan, both became scholars within the *Kaisei-sho* (derived from the old *Bansho Shirabe-sho*), which was to evolve by stages into Tokyo University (founded in 1877). Nishi, in particular, continued to be greatly influential, not only through his prolific output of writing on diverse fields of philosophy, including logic, aesthetics, and ethics, but also as tutor to the Emperor Meiji (in 1871–1872) and as a member, along with Tsuda, of the progressive Meiji Six Society, which found much inspiration in Western liberal ideas. Significantly for our subject, it is Nishi too who devised many terms to denote philosophical concepts for which there had hitherto been no word in the Japanese language. In 1874, he also further abbreviated his coined word for Western philosophy itself from *kitetsugaku* to the now standard *tetsugaku*.

In chapter 1 we stated that philosophy in the broad sense and philosophy in the narrow sense are rarely unrelated, in that with the exceptions of such domains as pure logic, philosophy in the narrow, technical sense reflects on and absorbs (whether deliberately or unconsciously) elements of philosophy as broadly and popularly understood, that is, the *Weltanschauung*, which is then philosophically rationalized, elaborated, clarified, and systematized and thus perpetuated. Needless to say, this popular *Weltanschauung* is often formulated in a way that supports and legitimates existing social and political structures. In other words, even the philosopher bent on exploring technical questions of identity, value, and so on is much affected by the cultural, social, and political climate of the times. Whether we are referring to long-term trends or to passing moods, the *Weltanschauung* is, above all, dynamic. (If we can refer to "cultural climate" and also to "political storms," we might also be justified in coining the intermediate metaphor and talking too of "social weather," to take account of the fact that elements within any *Weltanschauung* range all the way from those enduring from ancient times to those whose transience is closely associated with immediate events.)

That said, it is important for our understanding of the development of Japanese philosophy in the turbulent Meiji and post-Meiji years to attempt to sketch the country's *Weltanschauung* in a manner faithful to its complex movement. Fundamentally, as in any modern society, but in a very dramatic way in a society in transition from premodern to modern, this movement involves two main elements: tradition and transformation (appropriately highlighted by Reischauer and Craig in the title of their book on this era), where the latter entails not only change brought on by iconoclastic radicals or moderate reformers but also that wrought within the tradition by its defenders.

In a society as tightly knit as that of Japan, the political and the social form a significant part of the *Weltanschauung* which the philosopher tries to thematize. This is all the more true in an era as filled with social fervor and political frenzy as the one we are examining. Granting this, we shall now give attention to these factors, but with the reminder that our concern here is not to recount as such the history of Japanese politics and social evolution (with which we assume the reader to be familiar) or to set down in detail the successive stages in Japan's self-image. Rather, it is to emphasize the continuity and importance of these concerns within the intellectual climate that Japanese philosophy (in our narrow, technical sense) set out to rationalize, justify, thematize, synthesize, systematize, and in short, to defend and make sense of.

In the period under discussion, the history of Japanese philosophy is a history of intellectual activity primarily concerned with national identity and the development of ideology and specific policies that are the concrete manifestations of that preoccupation. As in our two previous chapters, we find that philosophies, in order to flourish, require the support, or at the very least the indulgence, of state authority. Among the forces of tradition we have outlined in our previous chapters, it is Shintō, reformulated and reinvigorated, that will play the major role. Among its elements we should note especially the long-standing inclination to believe in, and on occasion to contrive evidence for, a special national destiny that was divinely guaranteed. Combined with an equally contrived fiction of the Japanese nation's racial homogeneity, this guarantee carried with it the corollary of a divinely privileged racial purity, and hence the potent implication of national supremacy.

The durability of this outlook is striking. Even prior to the Nara period (710–784 CE), we find this commentary on Korean and Chinese immigrants to Japan:

> The immigrants were clearly superior to the Japanese in their knowledge of the techniques of civilization. The advantage that the Japanese claimed was their descent from the Gods, and to this heritage they jealously clung. (in Tsunoda et al., 86)

Augmented and maintained through history by a lineage of nationalist exponents (Nichiren, Kitabatake Chikafusa, Kumazawa Banzan, Motoori Norinaga, to name a few) and enshrined in state Shintō at the dawn of the Meiji Era, the notion of a divinely appointed Japan endured as the single most powerful force on the side of tradition in the nineteenth and twentieth centuries.

With the Western arrival, and the increasing inflow of Western ideas, this orthodoxy now faced its greatest challenge, all the more so in that many Japanese, eager for change, welcomed novel foreign perspectives on social and political issues. The *Meirokusha* (Meiji Six Society), founded in 1874 but proposed as the name implies in the sixth year of Meiji (1873), is evidence of this enthusiasm. The thirty-three members announced as their goals the promotion of Western learning and the establishment of new ethical standards for the Japanese people, although the precise means by which they envisaged reaching these objectives reflected their own diverse backgrounds. Some recent scholars, such as David Huish, consider the society's influence to have been exaggerated. Along with Nishi Amane and Tsuda Mamichi, prominent members included the Confucian, Nishimura Shigeki, and the then still liberal Katō Hiroyuki.

In 1875 the Meiji Six Society fell victim of new censorship laws directed at the more politically active Freedom and People's Rights Movement. Originally campaigning for samurai rights, the latter formation had evolved into a genuinely democratic movement and, despite its own struggles with the censors, it came to provide the genesis of the Liberal Party, founded in 1881. Through all these struggles, the dissemination of Western learning continued apace. Many long-held and largely unquestioned beliefs were jolted in those who encountered, one after the other, Comte, Mill, Spencer, Macaulay, de Tocqueville, Buckle, Guizot, Carlyle,

Disraeli, and Bentham, as well as Rousseau, whose *The Social Contract* had been translated in 1871 by philosopher, and by then leading light in the Liberal Party, Nakae Chōmin.

More influential because more widely read was the pragmatist Fukuzawa Yukichi (1834–1901), another prominent Meiji Six figure. Inspired by Western social and political theory, Fukuzawa astonished average Japanese by his statement (reminiscent of Andō Shōeki) that the upper class had no absolute right to rule. "It is said," he wrote, "that Heaven does not create one man above another man, nor does it create one man below another" (in Irokawa, 59). Condemning absolutism, he declared elsewhere: "We have inherited a disease from our distant ancestors" (151). These words evidence the exigency of personal autonomy that was to make of their author, in retrospect, a pioneer in the career of assertive *shutaisei* (subjectivity), although the term *shutai*, as translation of *subject*, would gain currency only in the 1920s. Fukuzawa's perspectives were eagerly adopted by the proponents of a liberal transformation, although Fukuzawa came to disagree with certain among them, notably the radical extremists of the Freedom and People's Rights Movement, whom he condemned as irresponsible. Their insubordinate stance might, he felt, provoke a conservative reflex that would hinder Japan's modernization.

The hopes of foreign-inspired reformers began to evaporate, however, in the 1880s, as the Japanese became more and more indignant over the "unequal treaties" forced on the country by the Western powers, as well as the frequently arrogant and racist attitudes shown by Westerners both in Japan and abroad. To counter the liberal intellectuals, the government fired off a few philosophical shots of its own, by commissioning translations of such politically conservative works as Edmund Burke's *Reflection on the French Revolution* and *Appeal from the New to the Old Whigs*, as well as part of Thomas Hobbes's *Leviathan*. Impelled in part by such adept opinion molding, the political and social mood of the country shifted markedly to the right, the old slogan "Revere the Emperor; Expel the Barbarians" being sounded with new conviction, and the intellectual climate shading back toward tradition. Those who, like Fukuzawa, had advocated compromise lapsed into conservatism; others, who had enjoyed the stimulus of Western ideas more as a fad, reverted squarely to an anti-Western stance. This reactionary trend was accompanied by an upsurge of popular hostility toward Western thought and by a revival of Confucianism, which had largely been out in the cold since the Meiji Restoration on account of its collaboration with the feudal regime.

In 1889, the nationalistic mood proved favorable to a new constitution that finally secured the ascendancy of imperial over popular sovereignty. A new individualistic trend that emerged around 1900 and outlasted the nationalistic flurry of the Russo-Japanese war did lead again toward liberalism, in what has been called the "Taishō democracy" (from about 1905 to 1932). However, the forces of the Right could henceforth justify themselves by reference to an immovable orthodoxy. We observe here the triumph of arguments the Mito school scholar Aizawa Seishisai (1782–1863) had advanced in his clandestine 1825 work *Shinron (New Discourse).* Aizawa had affirmed that Japan's *kokutai* (national polity), with the central place it accorded the Shintō gods and the emperor, was evidence of the nation's superiority. With such ideas now mainstream, the *kokutai* became a key concept of the 1889 Meiji Constitution. Reischauer and Craig have detailed how the nationalist orthodoxy thus set in place overcame opposition to evolve into an autocratic ideology.

An 1888 statement by Itō Hirobumi, quoted by Reischauer and Craig, is noteworthy:

> In Europe, religion as a common principle penetrates and unites the hearts of the people. . . . In our country, as a common principle, there is only the Imperial House. (211)

Reflecting the conviction of many that the imperial powers should be limited, Minobe Tatsukichi, a Tokyo University professor from 1900 to 1932, added the provision whereby the state became a legal person with both sovereignty and authority to rule. According to this interpretation, the emperor had the right to carry out extensive functions of state, but was nonetheless subordinate to its rules. This was an attempt by a democratic constitutionalist to separate out from politics the more irrational elements of Shintō mythology.

Minobe's provision can in hindsight be seen as a fragile safeguard in the face of the more nationalistic currents within Japanese society. In education, as Reischauer and Craig note, *kokutai* already had a less liberal sense, deriving from a blend of Japanese tradition and "less rational elements of nineteenth century German thought":

> The *kokutai* had been viewed in Confucian terms as an immanent and eternal order, and the imperial house as "coeval with Heaven and Earth." Hozumi Yatsuka, another professor at Tokyo University (between 1888 and 1912), added the notion that Japan was a "family-state" since all Japanese were descended from a common folk ancestor, identical with the imperial ancestor. (Reischauer and Craig, 213)

From this, the political Right then went on, incrementally, to secure its identity with the moral and religious right. We have noted before the Japanese preference for the phenomenal over the transcendental, the literal over the metaphorical. Thus, in the next step, history was merged into

Shintō myth so that the emperor became sacred "not simply as the embodiment of a moral order, but also as a lineal descendent of the Sun Goddess." Then, in a final touch that brought the *kokutai* ideology to the form in which it prevailed in the 1930s, "Uesugi Shinkichi, still another Tokyo University professor (between 1903 and 1929), appended a theory of absolute monarchy in which the emperor was identified with the body of the state" (Reischauer and Craig, 213).

A first consequence of all this for the philosopher is the issue of identity. "Where the Meiji thinkers were morally, socially, and even politically akin to the Restoration leaders, intellectuals after the turn of the century became increasingly alienated both from society and from the late Meiji political order" (Reischauer and Craig, 210). Those who wholeheartedly adopted Western ideas and values, and in so doing radically rejected the Japanese heritage, could not but find themselves alienated amid the official late Meiji neotraditionalism, both because in their rhetoric at least they had renounced the ties that bound them to the nation, and because the ideas and values they now professed to hold had roots in a vastly different culture, of which they had no lived experience.

Given that the Japanese communal identity was deeply bound to the fiction of divine election we outlined above, and that one's identity in Japanese society derived (and still derives) from successive levels of group allegiance, it must have been extremely difficult for all but the most gifted and courageous individuals to achieve a margin of genuine independence (including independent thinking). For most, imitating Western ways, lending voice to Western ideas, without sharing in the cultural roots of Western values, could have only transient or cosmetic consequences. Even now, in this age of more cosmopolitan exchange, cultural assimilation takes time, even if one lives within the culture one aspires to assimilate. How much harder it must have been in that period, when those Japanese who prescribed assimilation of Western perspectives and social systems did so against a contrary psychological and social grounding, not to mention adverse political pressure! Unless there was deep conviction, such a position could only be tenuous. In most cases, was it not just a fashionable posture?

This was evident to a young student of the time named Nishida Kitarō, who will figure large later in our account. Nishida recalls his observations of 1893 (also the year Raphael von Köbel began lecturing on philosophy at Tokyo Imperial University):

> Japan's attitude in adopting European culture was problematic
> in every respect. The Japanese did not try to transplant the roots
> of the plant, but simply cut off eye-catching flowers. As a result

the people who brought the flowers were respected enormously, but the plants that could have produced such blossoms did
not come to grow in our country. Despite this, Japanese scholars
and prodigies strutted about displaying their knowledge of
Western things noisily and proudly. (in Irokawa, 72)

Where alien inspiration did lead to a genuine social commitment, the outcome was, we repeat, necessarily a psychological, even spiritual, struggle.
The Christian leader and writer Uchimura Kanzō (1861–1930) serves as an
illustration. Quitting a teaching job on account of the Imperial Rescript on
Education and a position on a newspaper on account of its jingoistic line
toward the Russians, Uchimura went on to devote himself tirelessly to
reconciling the teachings of Christ with what he saw as the true interests
of the Japanese individual (serving the two "Js", as he famously put it,
Jesus and Japan). It was a crusade that was in direct contradiction to the
historical trend. In keeping with the successive redefining of the *kokutai*,
the identity of the individual not only was becoming dissolved in the destiny of the empire, but was at risk of being insidiously tinctured by each
new nationalistic overtone.

All that we have discussed here foreshadows the *tenkō* phenomenon
of the 1930s, which saw thousands of "thought criminals" *(shisōhan)*
recant their leftist ideals (usually under pressure), pledge allegiance to the
emperor, and accept the *kokutai*. "The most powerful tactic was to instill a
sense of guilt and obligation toward other family members, and toward
the emperor and nation" *(Japan, 1552)*.

So far, in describing Western philosophy's impact on Japan, we have
emphasized that which most challenged Japanese orthodox thinking, that
is, the liberal, enlightened ideas of such men as Locke and Hume. Clearly,
however, not all Western thought is or ever has been liberal, democratic
individualism. From Plato to Rousseau to post-Kantians, such as Hegel,
the right of the State has been championed over the freedom of the individual, communitarianism stressed over individualism, and spiritual feelings of communal belonging to the larger social *Geist* privileged over an
enlightened and rational utilitarian and pragmatic approach to social problems. Where the Left in Japan drew inspiration from the Enlightenment,
the Right found kinship in the more spiritually and emotionally holistic
communitarian ideas we have just described, and above all in Hegel.

Just what this struggle between Left and Right meant for the definition (and fate) of the Japanese self is illustrated by the strange case of
Thomas Hill Green (1836–1882). The Japanese reception and diverse interpretations of Green's thought have been well analyzed by Hirai Atsuko,
who recounts how Green was introduced to Japan in the early 1890s by a

Tokyo Imperial University professor, Nakajima Rikizō. Nakajima "adopted *Prolegomena to Ethics* as a classroom textbook and trained a number of
representative exponents of Green, including such well-known thinkers
as Ōnishi Hajime, Takayama Rinjirō, and Nishida Kitarō" (Hirai, 108).
Thereafter, Green's moral philosophy became the subject of prolific scholarly attention and had a doubly distinctive impact: it "influenced people
from diverse walks of life who subscribed to conflicting political and
philosophical positions," and "was not merely a fashion among the
Westernized intellectual elite but also a lively concern near the grass-roots
level" (Hirai, 109). According to Hirai, the appeal of Green for the intellectual elite lay in three things. First was the possibility of a rehabilitation of
metaphysics, held in contempt by the positivism that had constituted the
first wave of Western philosophy in Japan. On encountering Green, many
thinkers unsatisfied with positivism felt vindicated, and notably those
with religious convictions. "To them, Green's metaphysics offered a
means of survival of traditional religion in an age of science and reason"
(Hirai, 113). Correspondingly, the second element of Green's appeal was
his notion of a priori ethical values, welcomed all the more by Japanese in
that "samurai asceticism" led them to look on the Utilitarians' pleasure
principle with great reserve (Hirai, 113–114). Finally, Green's belief that
virtue consists in realizing a priori moral ideals leads us directly to that
feature of his thought most admired in Japan: "his affirmation of the self
and personality in relation to the common good" (Hirai, 110).

Hirai underlines the immense impact this had:

> For the Japanese, who had been made to believe for centuries
> that absolute effacement of the self was the true virtue, it was a
> revelation to be assured that fulfillment of the self was good-
> ness itself. (116)

However, this was not to lead to a decisive contestation of nationalism.
On the contrary, Green's concept of self-realization was mobilized in support of the National Morality by the professor of education and government moral mouthpiece Yoshida Seichi, for whom each self must seek fulfillment in the "common good" constituted by the "virtues enunciated in
the Imperial Rescript on Education" (Hirai, 118). Thus, there developed a
pseudo-Green philosophy—significantly the *only* Green known to most
scholars of the day—tailored for the needs of propaganda. In this, the
metaphysical resonance of the genuine Green had no place, and as Hirai
further points out, his conception of "social realization," in the sense of
the realization of metaphysical ideals within a society always subject to
the judgment of "all persons possessing reason and conscience," was
transformed into that of promoting a society immune from such judg-

ment and claiming to know best how to "realize" the individual. The genuine Green's ideas on social resistance had no place in this and simply vanished (see Hirai, 116–126).

So it was that where the real Green had been first introduced to the Japanese in Nakajima's *Eikoku shin Kanto-gakuha ni tsuite (The English Neo-Kantian School)*, and had an impact as such on those who recognized his commitment to the worth of the person as an end, the pseudo-Green favoring state absolutism had a greater immediate impact as an influential figure in Japan's neo-Hegelianism.

If Japanese intellectuals were ever to achieve a veritable autonomy in keeping with the ideals the real Green espoused, their best chance occurred in the relatively liberal atmosphere of the Taishō "democracy," which saw a growth of party politics and the 1925 enactment of a universal suffrage law that increased the electorate to 20 percent of the population (as against 1 percent in 1889). We should not be misled by the term *democracy;* the nationalist ideology was in place and if the government acted on occasion to curb leftist sentiment, it did little to restrain nationalist groups, who had the convenient argument that in their actions they were more imperially loyal than the government. The extent of intellectual freedom is tellingly noted by Piovesana when he writes of the newly introduced pragmatism of Dewey and James.

> Even then, pragmatism was called *zaya* philosophy, or philosophy of the "opposition" taught most in private universities, while state institutions followed the more official German philosophy. (*Contemporary*, 239)

Nonetheless, this was a time when Western philosophy, previously studied mostly with utilitarian motives, became the object of a more dispassionate and genuine research. And there was at least in this period a mood, or an illusion, of emancipation; a sense of freedom, even if, on the whole, the freedom felt was on an individual level; a state of mind, whose continuance was never secured by corresponding changes in social structures. It was with this limitation that we find individual rights once more upheld and the personal nature of morality and religion once again affirmed by the likes of Abe Jirō (1883–1959), best known for his *Santarō no nikki (Santarō's Diary)* of 1914–1918.

The intellectual climate of the time can be inferred from the trends that appeared within it: "personalism," "self-culturalism," and, perhaps most significantly, "culturalism," in all of which, but especially this last, we see the strong influence of neo-Kantianism, in which the individual was free to define him or herself, but only in isolation from any democratic interaction with other free individuals. With regard to the problem of

identity we outlined above, the culturalism of philosophers such as
Tomonaga Sanjurō and Kuwaki Genyoku and—most originally—Hatano
Seiichi, like Abe's exploration of his own self, can be seen as an attempt to
create a middle way, or a sort of safeguarding of independence by withdrawal from social interaction and engagement (some may say less kind-
ly an escapism). Naturally enough, when the national mood again slid
right, culturalism failed to have any lasting consequences. The following
lines describe well the culturalist project:

> The emphasis on the capacity of the self to create universalistic
> values turned writers and intellectuals away from questions of
> social responsibility and political action. In the final analysis,
> their philosophical aim was to construct a domain of pure cre-
> ative spirit independent of the world of existing structures.
> (Najita and Harootunian, 736)

Paradoxically, however, this "self" that was to "create universalistic
values" was a Japanese non-self that had not learned to define itself vis-à-
vis the ideology that laid claim to it. Hence, again, its vulnerability.

> Although the impulse toward culture as the manifestation of
> universal value was initially informed by cosmopolitanism,
> thus dramatizing the possibility of a unique Japanese contribu-
> tion to a universal human culture that recognized no national
> boundaries, the affirmative role of a particular cultural inheri-
> tance could easily dissolve into cultural exceptionalism. (Najita
> and Harootunian, 736)

As a symptomatic case, we shall shortly examine in some detail
Watsuji Tetsurō's 1935 *Fūdo (Climate and Culture)*, an intriguing piece of
writing that begins on a neutral tone of philosophical inquiry, progresses
to an affirmation of Japan's "particular cultural inheritance," and concludes with an appeal for loyalty to the Imperial House. Before turning to
Watsuji's work, however, we should make the important observation that
while Germany remained the "Mecca" of Japanese thinkers, from the
1920s their focus shifted away from neo-Kantianism toward the phenomenology of Husserl and, above all, the existentialism of Martin Heidegger,
which has been supremely important for Japanese philosophy ever since.
In the dissemination of Heidegger's ideas the early role was played by
visiting Japanese scholars and students. A notable example is Kuki Shūzō
(1888–1941), who spent eight years in Europe from 1921 and during this
sojourn was already elaborating his famed *Iki no kōzō (The Structure of Iki)*,
to be published in 1930. This is a study of the Japanese aesthetic sense
whose approach is clearly inspired by Husserl and Heidegger. Kuki was

reportedly on warm personal terms with Heidegger, and did much to propagate the latter's ideas. Not only did he publish *Haidegga no tetsugaku* (*The Philosophy of Heidegger*) in 1933, but there are convincing claims that it was Kuki who introduced Heidegger's philosophy to Sartre, when the latter was still a student.

Intellectuals in Japan quickly developed an intense interest in Heidegger that is unparalleled in any other country. We learn from Graham Parkes that the first substantive commentary on his philosophy (aside from a few brief reviews) was published in Japan in 1924, and that Kuki's 1933 study was the first book-length study of Heidegger to appear (ix). Not only this, but *Being and Time* was translated some six times into Japanese before ever appearing in English (Parkes, 9).

This enthusiasm for Heidegger has proved enduring. Even today, he remains the Western philosopher of choice among Japanese intellectuals. The reason, no doubt, is that for the Japanese there is something familiar to them in his work. A self-recognition. Specifically, one might point to affinities centered on Heidegger's redefinition of Being: "Being, Nothing, Same," as he himself wrote (in May, 21). This was radical for Europeans, but in no way novel to a people lacking the tradition of a metaphysics of substance.

This does not mean that Heidegger's thought was accepted without reserve. Indeed, often it was deemed by Japanese to be too concerned with the individual at the expense of the social. In this respect, Watsuji Tetsurō's response was typical. Why, he wondered, did Heidegger in *Being and Time* emphasize time so much, while giving relatively little attention to space? In Watsuji's view, the neglect of space prevented a description of human existence sufficiently concrete to allow for a true depiction of history, and (to cite Watsuji's chosen focus), of climate's role within it. Again, we see the Japanese predilection for the empirical and phenomenal over the abstract and transcendental.

In order to overcome the "limitations of Heidegger's work," Watsuji first establishes what he sees as "the basic principles of climate," using experience of the cold as an example, and concludes:

> That we feel the cold is an intentional experience, in which we discover ourselves in the state of *"ex-sistere,"* or our selves already out in the cold. (*Fūdo*, 4)

Or rather, as Watsuji goes on, "out among other 'I's,'" for this is a shared experience, in which "we," in a "mutual relationship," discover our selves in the cold.

Having set down this Heideggerian schema, Watsuji can undertake to show how humans apprehend themselves in climate and how climate has affected not only clothing styles, building design, and diets, but also "all the expressions of human activity, such as literature, art, religion, and manners and customs" (*Fūdo*, 7–8). Broadly speaking, he continues, there are three kinds of climate: monsoon, desert, and meadow. Cultures of monsoon climates are characterized by "receptivity" and "resignation," but in the case of the Japanese character, these traits are both "tropical" and "frigid": "tenacity" (from the cold zones) underlies "emotional changes" (from the tropics).

> It is neither unresisting acquiescence of the tropical zone nor persistent and patient doggedness of the frigid zone. For, although essentially resignation, through resistance it becomes mutable and quick-tempered endurance. Violent winds and deluge rains in the end enforce resignation on man, but their typhoon nature provokes in him a fighting mood. (*Fūdo*, 136)

Resignation is similarly ambivalent. Thus,

> Resistance, lurking behind this mask of resignation, can erupt with the unexpected savagery of a typhoon, yet once this storm of emotion has died down, there remains an equally abrupt and calm acquiescence. (*Fūdo*, 137)

Watsuji comes here to a striking explanation of the samurai ethos that enables us to discover "the national spirit of Japan." From the point of view of the sort of resignation "symbolized by the cherry blossom" or by the "open-hearted throwing away of life,"

> Anything that is grounded on resistance or fight is a clinging to life. For all that, when this attachment to life was exhibited in its most intense and objective aspect, the most prominent and central feature of this attachment was the attitude that was the very opposite, a complete contradiction of this tenacity. This is shown to perfection in war. The spirit of Japanese swordsmanship is the harmony of sword and calm meditation. (*Fūdo*, 137)

This, then, for Watsuji is the paradox of Japan's "typhoon resignation." We see it also, he claims, in ancient Japanese love poems. Loves there "have a typhoon savagery," yet often manifest in suicides a "calm and selfless resignation." The monsoon climate is also linked to a "community of family life" different to the emphasis on the couple (in meadow climates) or the tribe (in desert climates). And this family life exhibits the same dichotomy observed above. The family is characterized by a calm affection. However, if thwarted, "this quiet affection turns into ardent passion, forceful enough even to overwhelm the individual for the sake of the whole family." Indeed, "the family relationship takes the form of a heroic and martial attitude, unsparing even of life itself." The samurai, for example, was willing to die for his house.

Watsuji discusses at length the way in which contrasting Japanese and European house design and use reflect corresponding contrasts in national characteristics. The European house is compartmentalized, in accord with individualism; the Japanese house is "open, unpartitioned," with family members linked indissolubly. "It was," he says, "by way of the concept of the house as a whole unit that the Japanese came to be aware of themselves as a whole" (*Fūdo*, 147). Hence the religious unity of this "land of the *kami*." It was as if the Japanese people as a whole constituted "one great family which regarded the Imperial House as the home of its deity." The individual's duty becomes the protection of the state:

> Within the borders of this state as a whole, there should be the same unreserved and inseparable union that is achieved within the household. The virtue that is called filial piety from the aspect of the household becomes loyalty from the standpoint of the state. (*Fūdo*, 148)

If we have reproduced Watsuji's line of thought here at some length it is not so much because of its original attempt at cultural comparison, but rather because his book is symptomatic of the perspective of Japanese philosophers of the time. As we saw in the observation of Nishida Kitarō, the philosophy imported from the West, informed as it was with individualistic values and rationalist concepts, had no roots in Japan and was therefore contrary to what most Japanese, in their hearts, were comfortable with and felt their country stood for.

Yet, on the other hand, since the Japanese people were conceived as belonging to a family-state identified with the emperor, any philosophy for the Japanese was susceptible of becoming too a philosophy for the empire. On this point, as we shall see, the schemas of other philosophers who sought to rehabilitate traditional values in contradistinction to those of the West tended, whatever their intermediate pathways, to converge on a broad consensus.

The only radical challenge to the social structure came from the Marxists, and even their discourse was oddly inhibited by the Japanese identification with the national polity. Japanese trade-unionism, we are told, had to appeal to the proletariat both as "Japanese" and as "workers." It had to somehow resolve or gloss over the conflict between loyalty to the nation and action (perceived as "disloyal") for social gains (see Tsunoda et al., vol. 2, 806–807). Prewar Japanese Marxism was to yield some significant philosophers, notably Miki Kiyoshi and Tosaka Jun. But politically, as embodied in the Japan Communist Party (founded in 1922), it was never greatly effective. The JCP, beset from the outset by internal divisions, was increasingly hampered by official harassment culminating in mass trials of Communists in 1931–1932. By the mid-1930s it was exhausted as a political force amid a crisis of morale and a multitude of defections. The final curtain for the prewar Left came down on February 26, 1936, when about 1,400 soldiers, eager for Japan to be more militarily active in China, mounted a coup d'etat, during which they occupied central Tokyo and murdered three Cabinet ministers. Martial law was declared, and the incoming prime minister, Hirota Kōki, was little more than a tool of the military. Thereafter, new laws restricted freedom of speech and movement, and Western culture was viewed with disfavor. The darkest period of Japan's nationalism had begun.

In order to cast light on the influences on and choices made by Japanese philosophy, we have outlined at some length Japan's evolving *Weltanschauung*, focusing, inevitably, on the intellectual fallout of social and political vicissitudes in the first sixty years or so after the Meiji Restoration. As we have seen, this background posed severe dilemmas for Japan's thinkers, and we can not appreciate all the implications of their individual philosophies without taking it into account. However, it would be mistaken to suppose that everything they said was political. We shall now turn to examining some of Nishi Amane and Tsuda Mamichi's principal successors, practitioners of Western philosophy in Japan, whom we have yet to mention or who deserve further attention. In so doing, we shall note their historical and/or philosophical significance irrespective of the degree to which their writings had sociopolitical import.

The philosophical influence of many of these figures has much declined, for various reasons: philosophers who owed their status to a privileged position in the regime, and primarily produced material that underpinned nationalist ideology, have generally been discredited by history and deemed as having little more than historical significance. In cases where a thinker borrowed heavily from a foreign source, enjoying a brief period of glory while, as Nakae Chōmin has said, monopolizing that knowledge, later readers have gone straight to the source. In all cases, of course, there has been a greater or lesser degree of supersession: the philosophers themselves, or the entire streams to which they belonged, have ceased to be in or near the mainstream, and have lost common respect.

Among those who have fared relatively well amid this slide to obscurity is Nakae Chōmin himself (1847–1901), translator, as we have mentioned, of Rousseau's *Social Contract*. If his early liberal aspirations came to nought amid the reactionary trend of the 1880s and his later socialist hopes were stillborn amid government repression, Nakae's reputation endures nonetheless, particularly through the literary merits of his 1887

Sansujin keirin mondō (A Dialogue on Statecraft by Three Drunkards) and the astute reflections of the 1901 *Ichinen yūhan (A Year and a Half)*.

Also starting out as a liberal, Katō Hiroyuki (1836–1916) soon came to prefer German political thought and was instrumental among others in the reactionary transformation of Tokyo University, of which he twice served as president. Katō was a major figure in the propagation of Social Darwinism in Japan, notably in his 1893 *Kyōja no kenri no kyōsō (The Struggle for the Rights of the Strongest)*.

That Confucianists and Buddhists were also caught in the ideological turmoil is well demonstrated respectively by the cases of prominent Meiji Six figure Nishimura Shigeki (1828–1902) and Kiyozawa Mitsuyuki (1863–1903), who both endeavored to make improvements on tradition by incorporating Western elements. Better known is Inoue Enryō (1859–1919), a Buddhist priest who toed the government line and sought in his 1873 *Bukkyō katsuron (Introduction to the Revitalization of Buddhism)* and the 1886–1887 *Tetsugaku isseki-wa (Brief Talks on Philosophy)* to give new vitality to Buddhism with the aid of Hegel. Quoting Inoue's assertion that "[t]he position of Buddhism, as manifested in Kegon-Tendai, does not differ in the slightest from that of Hegel" because "matter and mind both become the one reason, the Tathagata," Gino K. Piovesana adds the following summary:

> The logic of identity is applied to solve the opposition between the absolute and the relative, the Great Ultimate and the myriad of things. Moreover, the identity and the inseparability of Reason and the material-substance is indicative of the indestructibility of matter, as modern science postulates. (*Contemporary*, 230)

In chapter 2 we noted the striking similarity of late Mahāyāna Buddhism, especially Kegon and Tendai, with Hegelian "organicism." Later, as Japanese began reading Hegel for themselves, they, too, recognized this similarity and capitalized on it as a bridge between East and West. The Hegel-Buddhism "cross" proved a potent one and reappears, as we shall see later, in some of twentieth-century Japan's most profound and influential thought.

We should not forget that from the mid-nineteenth century until the early decades of the twentieth century the dominant philosophy in Europe was Hegelianism and other forms of post-Kantianism. Kant may be regarded as the last of the "Enlightenment" figures. Kant explicitly restricts knowledge to what can be empirically verified and the universal conditions of such empirical knowledge as they apply to all human beings. The "critical philosophy" of Kant thereby refused to grant the possibility of any theoretical knowledge of some ultimate Reality beyond all sense experience. We could wonder about such a reality and morally interact with it, but we could never intellectually know it. This proved a bitter pill for Europeans as the Romantic movement inaugurated the beginning of the nineteenth century, and as Goethe remarks, those who followed Kant tore down the critical barriers Kant had erected and proceeded to lay claim to spiritual and aesthetic knowledge of Absolute Reality despite Kant's enlightened "critical" modesty.

For Hegel, especially, Absolute Reality is the supersensible whole in which everything forms an integral and organic part, and indeed is defined by its place in this vast Whole, a whole that is historically evolving toward greater and greater perfection. Since the fundamental nature of this Absolute Whole is spiritual, the ever-evolving *Geist*, or World Soul, is understood to be historically moving toward greater and greater self-awareness, that is, human consciousness, whose most evolved manifestation is therefore the Spirit of the modern State, and above all, the most evolved of the modern nation-states, Germany.

Before World War II Hegelianism was not only a respectable European philosophy; it was the dominant philosophy in Europe and North America, dominating even British philosophy in the 1920s. It was only after the war that Hegelianism was widely discredited for the use the fascists had made of it. But before the war the spiritual vision of an all-encompassing State in which the individual could identify as a functioning part had tremendous appeal for many people in Japan, as well as in Europe and elsewhere. Even today we should not forget the wide appeal of contemporary "communitarianism" in its opposition to "liberal individualism."

All that said, it is worth noting that in the Meiji period, the significance of Hegelianism and other post-Kantian thought that we underline here, together with the preponderance of German philosophy in the state curriculum, and Germany's lead in philological studies (including those of Buddhism) established Germany as the destination of choice for Japanese students of philosophy.

Returning to our account of Japanese thinkers, we find Miyake Yūjirō (1860–1945) another who melded the country's traditional thought with Hegelian themes, especially in his *Uchū* (*The Universe*), written in 1906–1908. If Miyake sees each human existence as being played out between pre-life nonexistence and nothingness after death, there is nonetheless an optimism in his vision focusing on a future international federation and on a universe where beauty, goodness, and truth afford meaning. It is perhaps not fanciful to see in Miyake's romantically naive historicism a forerunner of similar schemes of things that developed later, also with Hegelian or with Marxist inspiration, and of which the outline paralleled, if not actually merged with, military strategy.

Inoue Tetsujirō (1855–1944) is historically important for his commentary on the Imperial Rescript on Education and the 1912 *Kokumin dōtoku gairon (Outline of Japanese Morality)*, in both of which he melded Confucianism and Shintōism in modern imperial ideology. Most significantly, he outlined a separation between mere ethics (including those of the Christians, who opposed the Rescript) and the "national morality," characterized by loyalty to the emperor. The latter's rule, being based on heavenly mandate, he saw as preempting the law. Inoue should not, however, be dismissed simply as a government pawn; not only did he make an interesting, though ultimately dissatisfying attempt, to fuse European and Oriental thought; he also co-authored with Arima Nagao Japan's first philosophical dictionary (*Tetsugaku jii*, published in 1884).

A determined opponent of Inoue Tetsujirō and of the "national morality" was Ōnishi Hajime (1864–1900), who gave primacy to doubt rather than dogma, and to the individual rather than the state. Piovesana expresses neatly the essence of Ōnishi's retort:

> It was not a collision between education as such and Christianity, as Inoue pretended, but between a state-defined education and religion. If Christianity was not pro-state, it was not anti-state either. (*Contemporary*, 236)

Moderate views such as Ōnishi's had no chance to prevail amid the *Nihonshugi* (Japanism) following the Sino-Japanese War of 1894–1895. This was a more assertive expression of the already well-established *kokusui hozon* (preservation of national essence) movement, and was defined by one of its main spokesmen, Takayama Rinjirō, as "the ethical principle stemming from the spirit of self-independence as the national characteristic. Its first aim was to enhance the aspiration for establishing an empire" (in Piovesana, *Contemporary*, 238).

Takayama later renounced such ideas and retreated into an aesthetic individualism, but Japanism as a movement remained enduringly influential in the nationalistic shaping of the Japanese psyche. It also, again, emphasized the enormous influence of Hegel: as Takayama saw it, "The individual had to reach his fulfillment through the state," where there was a "Hegelian conception of the ethical state" (Piovesana, *Contemporary*, 238–239).

Watsuji Tetsurō (1889–1960), whose *Fūdo (Climate and Culture)* we have already examined, made his mark very young with deeply original studies of Nietzsche and Kierkegaard, but soon turned to the study of Buddhism and its origins, and it is he who is credited with having rescued Dōgen from near-oblivion. The significance accorded to Dōgen reflects

Watsuji's emphasis on aesthetics rather than social aspects in his exploration and re-presentation of Buddhist history. In this, and the form his thought was to take thereafter, he manifests the influence of his reading of Okakura Tenshin (real name Okakura Kakuzō, 1862–1913). A much-traveled and highly cultured art curator and critic, Okakura began his *The Ideals of the East* (1903) with the catchphrase "Asia is one," and traced Indian and Chinese cultural ideals through successive stages to a culmination that guarantees Japan a special significance:

> Japan is a museum of Asian civilization; and yet more than a museum, because the singular genius of the race leads it to dwell on all phases of the ideals of the past, in that spirit of living Advaitism which welcomes the new without losing the old. (The Awakening of Japan, *Collected*, vol. 1, 16)

Yet increasing Westernization of Japan had come to threaten this legacy, a development that clearly left Okakura saddened, appalled, and indignant. Hence, when he treats of the Meiji period, both here and in the 1904 *The Awakening of Japan*, his writing modulates from erudite exposition to passionate militancy. Asian countries, he affirms, must join forces to oppose Western imperialism. As he wrote epigrammatically elsewhere: "Our recovery is Consciousness. Our remedy is the Sword." (The *Awakening of the East*, in *Collected*, vol. 1, 156)

Okakura Tenshin's vision of cultural history—whether Advaitistic or, as some have said, Hegelian—was to be echoed not only by Watsuji Tetsurō but by many of his famous contemporaries who also, moreover, re-edited Okakura's militant stance. In Watsuji's case, following an attempt to portray the Japanese spirit in his 1926 *Nihon seishin-shi kenkyū (Studies of the Japanese Spirit)*, the effort to revive the sense of a common Asian identity based on concrete phenomena and experience resulted in *Fūdo*. As we have seen, this work justified the Japaneseness of the Japanese in and on their own terms, regardless of Western representations, and exalted the symbolic importance of the Imperial House.

A more substantial opus was to follow in the form of *Rinrigaku (Ethics)*, the culmination of a number of works Watsuji produced on ethics. Written largely in opposition to Western notions of individuality, subjectivity, and temporality, it is at once the description, defense, and prescription of a social ethic and manner of being that follow from a conjunction of Confucian and Buddhist elements. Although this work was published in three volumes, with the last not appearing until 1949 (the first two in 1937 and 1942), its thematic consistency with both *Fūdo* and certain of Watsuji's political statements lead us to examine it here.

In *Rinrigaku* as in *Fūdo*, Watsuji taxes Heidegger with having neglected the relative importance of space with regard to time, and of the social with regard to the individual. But here he is more thoroughgoing and more profound. When he engages the ideas of *Being and Time* on spatiality and temporality in a sustained critical analysis, he ends up turning Heidegger on his head. The German philosopher, he complains, "stuck fast to an atomistic individuality" (*Rinrigaku*, 224), and "[kept] his eye focused on the total possibility of the 'self' only as comprehended with the aid of the phenomenon of death" (*Rinrigaku*, 224–225). This individual self was seen as "that authenticity inherent in a human being" (*Rinrigaku*, 225). Yet this Cartesian, Hobbesian notion of self, Watsuji declares, is artificial. In the following excerpt, where he offers a corrective view of authenticity, *ningen* is the Japanese word for human being, either in the singular or plural, with *nin* meaning person and *gen*, significantly, having the sense of between, thus already implying a relationship.

> One can contend that I becomes aware of itself only through the medium of non-I, by making a detour of nothingness only on the ground of the subject in which the self and the other are not yet disrupted. In holding this view, we must assert that the self and the other come to be opposed through negation only on the ground of *ningen*'s authenticity. This authenticity is the source of the "self," and at the same time, the "self" comes to be established only as the negation of this authenticity.
>
> The negation of authenticity is inauthenticity. What Heidegger calls authenticity is, in reality, inauthenticity. And when this in-authenticity becomes further negated through the nondual relation of self and other, that is to say, when the "self" becomes annihilated, only then is authenticity realized. (*Rinrigaku*, 225)

Enough of abstractions. Put more simply, Watsuji's ontology (like his ethics) is centered on the notion of *aidagara* (betweenness). As Yuasa Yasuo states it,

> Watsuji argues that man's life can exist only in the "between-ness" that is its foundation. . . . This view of man . . . inherits the East Asian tradition of Confucian ethics. Insofar as his mode of behavior is concerned, a person *(ningen)* is determined a priori by his position within the social hierarchy. (170)

Thus, not only does Watsuji undertake to correct Heidegger by giving due attention to space alongside time, but he emphasizes "subjective spatiality," space pervaded by the cultural and social. Rejecting the primacy of the individual, Watsuji stresses the supraindividual. A human being belongs from the outset to a society, and his or her social position is defined at various levels (by the couple, the family, the community, and ultimately the state). Moreover, since the individual is inseparable from a cultural and social context the individual/society relationship constitutes, to use Nishida Kitarō's terminology, a "self-contradiction," insofar as he or she is at once an individual and a member of a society, and cannot be exclusively one or the other. This, we already know from Watsuji's critique of *Being and Time*, is why assertion of the self as an "atomistic" individual is misguided and inauthentic. Such assertion, in effect, negates the "absolute negativity" (read "emptiness") that is the authentic nature of selves and society. The return to authenticity and absolutely wholeness, and the move to the "law of human beings, that is, basic ethics" (*Rinrigaku*, 124), can arise only by negating this "revolt."

> A person who has turned his back on his own foundation in revolting against one community or another may then try to return to his own foundation by negating this revolt once more. This return may also be achieved by recognizing another community. The acts constituting this movement signify the sublimation of individuality, the realization of socio-ethical unity, or the return to one's own foundation. (*Rinrigaku*, 134)

The conclusion is Buddhist: the emptiness at this foundation, or "home ground," is the condition whereby selflessness, and hence compassion, may arise. However, here as in *Fūdo*, Watsuji faces objections that his "authentic individual" can easily be submerged in totalitarianism, in that the community of which he or she is a selfless member is in practical terms inseparable from the state.

The historical record shows that at the very moment Watsuji was writing *Rinrigaku*, his intentions and philosophical discourse were already themselves being submerged in totalitarian ideology. In 1937 he participated in the drafting of the *Kokutai no hongi (Fundamentals of Our National Polity)*, a text published by the Ministry of Education with the goal of strengthening the nation's ideological uniformity. In it we read, for example, these lines that call to mind both *Fūdo* and *Rinrigaku*:

> An individual is an existence belonging to a state and her history which forms the basis of his origin, and is fundamentally one body with it. (in Tsunoda et al., vol. 2, 281)

The relationship between sovereign and subject, we are reminded, is a "dying to self and returning to [the] One" (in Tsunoda et al., vol. 2, 281).

> The spirit that sacrifices self and seeks life at the very fountain-head of things manifests itself eventually as patriotism and as a heart that casts self aside in order to serve the state. (in Tsunoda et al., vol. 2, 288)

The idealism occasionally shines through:

> Our present mission . . . is to build up a new Japanese culture by adopting and sublimating Western cultures with our national polity as a basis, and to contribute spontaneously to the advancement of world culture. (in Tsunoda et al., vol. 2, 288)

One can imagine the satisfaction felt by hardliners to have such gifted scribes at their service. Eventually, Watsuji was swept into the military maelstrom he had gullibly helped to precipitate. As Sakai Naoki reflects, in a highly quotable quote, "Watsuji's ethics of *nakayoshi* (being on good terms) transformed itself into the ethics of *ichioku gyōkusai* (the total suicidal death of one hundred million)" (90). As we shall see, such, alas, was the naivety of many a Taishō intellectual.

Many of the philosophers we have hitherto looked at in this chapter were to some degree practitioners of Western-style philosophy. Exactly when this evolved into a full-fledged "Japanese philosophy of Western style" is difficult to say, but if there is a single point of transition, most specialists would probably place it at the 1911 publication of *Zen no kenkyū (An Inquiry into the Good)*, by Nishida Kitarō (1870–1945). In retrospect, Nishida can be seen as the initiating figure of the *Kyōto-ha*, the Kyōto school of philosophers, of which other members with enduring reputations are Tanabe Hajime and Nishitani Keiji. Such was the domination of Nishida and his influence within the Kyōto school that the school's thought as a whole is sometimes referred to as "Nishida philosophy." The term *Kyōto-ha* has mixed connotations in Japan. On the one hand, all the school's major members were condemned in some quarters for collaborating with, or at the very least naively approving of, ultranationalist objectives; on the other hand, there has been widespread admiration for the quality of their purely philosophical activity, the best of which has been deemed of worldwide significance.

The originality of *Zen no kenkyū (An Inquiry into the Good)* lay in its author's attempt to express the Zen ideal of "unity of thought" within a densely argued philosophical system applying Western methods and concepts. This attempt represents a personal quest for coherence that reflected that of the Japanese people as a whole, a factor that no doubt explains the book's immediate and extraordinary success. Like his contemporary readers, Nishida faced, in a very concentrated way, being a practitioner of Zen and a student of Western thought, the problem of reconciling Japan's traditional values and those implicit in the technological revolution. At the same time Nishida saw Zen insight as a possible solution for the impasse in which Western philosophy found itself.

To understand this, we should recall the philosophical context of the time. In the West, the demise of Hegel's absolute idealism had signaled for many the ultimate downfall of the old essentialist metaphysics, confirming at last Kant's denial of the possibility of any theoretical knowledge of Absolute Reality. Finding in the latter only fallacious imaginings and constructs, adversary trends such as the realism of Feuerbach and Marx, the positivism of Comte, Spencer, and Mill, the utilitarianism of Bentham, had each in its own way inaugurated rigorous but often narrowly materialistic directives concerning what might henceforth be admissibly considered scientific "truth," a bitter pill for many, as Kant's denial of knowledge of Reality had been earlier.

As we have seen, for Nishi Amane and his immediate successors, the appeal of Western philosophy lay most of all in this rejection of metaphysics and in the claim to be scientific. Such an influential preference, or prejudice, resulted in the relative neglect of Western thinkers who, averse to Hegel's Idea, could accept no more easily the preeminence of Reason. Just as we indicated earlier the deep and long-standing tension within Western thought between liberal individualism and holistic communitarianism, so we should be alert to a similar tension in Western thought between a positivist denial of any spiritual, aesthetic, or moral dimension to reality and a continuing spiritual reaction against such a truncated view of the world.

As Amane journeyed to Europe in 1862, Kierkegaard had been dead for seven years, and a youthful Nietzsche was embarking on his own career of restoring due attention to the subjective experience and concerns of the individual. By the time mainstream Japanese philosophy veered back toward interest in the metaphysical, a later Western school, much inspired by psychology, was seeking a satisfactory middle course, at once reaffirming the commitment to scientific rigor characteristic of positivism, yet equally pledged to a thoroughgoing exploration of the subjective. Among prominent thinkers of this new trend we may cite Ernst Mach (1838–1916), Wilhelm Wundt (1832–1920), and William James (1842–1910).

It was Nishida's encounter with these thinkers, combined with other influences, that provided him with the suggestive sketch of a novel local solution to the Western impasse. This crystallized, as we shall see, around their notion of "pure experience," though significantly redefined. Since Nishida was a prolific writer not always easy to read, whose thought moreover evolved through several distinct stages, we shall limit ourselves here to treating this key notion of "pure experience," as well as his later equally notable "logic of place." In so doing, we shall draw on the writings of Nishida himself and on the authoritative commentaries of later practitioners of Nishida philosophy, Abe Masao and Nishitani Keiji.

In *Zen no kenkyū (An Inquiry into the Good)*, Nishida defines his task as follows: to "investigate what we ought to do and where we ought to find peace of mind," noting that "this calls first for clarification of the nature of the universe, human life and true reality" (37–38). Within this project, the term *pure experience* becomes the fusion point of Western and Eastern inspirations. Western writers had used the term *pure experience* but in a way that seemed to him factitious.

> For many years I wanted to explain all things on the basis of pure experience as the sole reality. At first I read such thinkers as Ernst Mach, but this did not satisfy me. (xxx)

What dissatisfied him in Mach, James, and the others was primarily that they engaged in a dualistic analysis of pure experience, which could not but ultimately betray it. Nishida held that abstract representation of pure experience, relying on whatever would-be explanatory vocabulary borrowed from psychology, inevitably introduces falsification. Sense datum psychologists and philosophers had tried to describe our experience prior to perceptual syntheses and conceptual classifications, but had nonetheless presupposed a subject-object dichotomy in which the perceiver is aware of himself looking at a world beyond himself. (A typical sense datum analysis of this period is the following: "What is this I see before me? At first I am tempted to say it is a tomato, but upon reflection I realize that this is a, possibly false, conceptual judgment of my pure experience. Rather, therefore, I should say that what I see immediately before me is simply a round, reddish patch of color.") What Nishida sought to describe was a still more elementary, "pure" experience prior to any subject-object distinction, the experience of a newborn child.

Such is the importance Nishida gives to his own corrective definition of pure experience that he undertakes it at the very outset of his book:

> To experience means to know facts just as they are, to know in accordance with facts by completely relinquishing one's own fabrications. What we usually refer to as experience is adulterated with some sort of thought, so by *pure* I am referring to experience just as it is without the least addition of deliberative discrimination. For example, the moment of seeing a color or hearing a sound is prior not only to the thought that the color or sound is the activity of an external object or that one is sensing it but also to the judgment of what the color or sound might be.

> In this regard, pure experience is identical with direct experi-
> ence. When one experiences one's own state of consciousness,
> there is not yet a subject or an object, and knowing and its object
> are completely unified. This is the most refined type of experi-
> ence. (3–4)

Here is the notion of pure experience, before and beyond all representation (even the representation of it as "my subjective experience"), that
Nishida rendered the referential core of a fresh philosophy. At one level,
Nishida's analysis of pure experience is a logical extension of sense datum
philosophy and psychology. Where the European analysis recognizes that
the judgment, "what I am seeing is a tomato," is not a part of pure experience but a later conceptual element added on to and not a part of the original experience, the European analysis nonetheless fails to recognize that
the distinction between subject and object ("I am seeing something; what
is it?") equally incorporates a later division not present in pure experience
(as we might imagine that of a child at birth, before differentiating self
from outer sensations and before beginning to conceptually classify those
outer sensations into objects). Nishida's corrective view we can trace to
his Zen training, yet, as Abe writes, while Nishida drew on Zen experience in undertaking his project, he needed to effect a double transformation of this experience in order to provide a truly philosophical answer.

> The practice of philosophy requires a logical expression of Zen
> experience that breaks through Zen's trans-intellectual charac-
> ter. At the same time, Zen practice requires that philosophy be
> transformed by breaking through its intellectual rationality in
> order to awaken to the living ultimate reality. (xii)

As Nishitani says, it involves "standing firm in the living, concrete reality
of experience itself as it is right now, from moment to moment" (82). This is
at once the standpoint of the instant and that of eternity. The future and the
past are both born in the now. Time comes into being through the unifying
activity of the consciousness, which enables us to "line up the contents [of
consciousness] in terms of a before and an after, and hence to think in temporal terms" (85). In Nishida's own celebrated words:

> Over time I came to realize that it is not that experience exists
> because there is an individual, but that an individual exists
> because there is experience. (xxx)

We can understand clearly from this that pure experience according to
Nishida's notion of it is not something passive, but is, rather, an intention-

ality, a participation. From the moment of birth a child begins to sort experiences into "me" and "world," where sensations from the "world" become desirable or undesirable to "me" and therefore ones that "I" can act on (now) to get or avoid (in the future), thus developing gradually a sense of temporal relations (seeing [now] something I want to eat, I know that by reaching for it [in the next moment] I can take it and put it in my mouth and enjoy a wonderful future sensation). Therefore, both self and time are human constructions developed from pure experience.

From a practitioner of Zen Buddhism, in which the self is perceived as an artificial construction inhibiting the Buddha vision and therefore best "dissolved," such a position does not surprise, but expressed thus, philosophically, it acquires the power of subversive dialogue with established Western beliefs. Only David Hume, among Western philosophers, challenged the fundamental reality of the conscious self, which Hume characterized as a bundle of sensations. The notion that the individual exists because there is experience is a reversal of conventional Western thinking and has consequences no less significant than those of Sartre's famous later statement that "existence precedes essence."

If self precedes experience, universal principles posited on the basis of individual experience are suspect. How can I know that my experience corresponds with reality or with that of other people? This is the danger of solipsism. In an effort to posit principles of unchallengeable universal import, Western thinkers have traditionally had to make assertions beyond experience. "Higher" realms and "hidden" essences have become chimeric foci in the hopeful quest of a human commonality. If, however, pure experience precedes self, and, as Nishida thereby concludes, "is more fundamental than individual differences," then such experience itself can be declared a universal principle. The problem for modern Western philosophy, how do I get my private individual self to a reality beyond, understood in terms of universal principles accessible to everyone, is not a problem for "pure experience," as conceived by Nishida, where there is no division between "me" and "reality" nor between "me" and others. No longer need we strive for a transcendence arbitrarily affirmed; to use the term of Takeuchi Yoshinori, we find instead self-evident fellowship in a "trans-descendence."

Nishitani Keiji explains it this way:

> The unifying power—the life—of nature is . . . intuited as the noumenon, the thing-in-itself, the self within a single plant or animal. The unifying self behind the whole of nature, the very power that unifies nature, appears as the self, the noumenon, of each and every living being. Our true self is a self able to perceive itself in the unifying self behind the whole of nature, in the

self with which nature is provided. It is a self capable of grasping the life or unifying power of nature immediately and intuitively. (*Nishida Kitarō*, 119)

By articulately taking a stand at the heart of the Western philosophical
tradition and challenging that tradition on the basis of convictions and
values drawn from Zen Buddhism, Nishida marks a double achievement:
he ensures philosophical respectability for the reception of Japanese
Buddhist thought in the West, and inaugurates a significant Japanese philosophy of Western style. He also does much to alleviate the disquiet over
values that had arisen amid the positivist rejection of tradition that came
to be seen as a sign of particularist Western influence. Those who felt
alienated by this or that aspect of Western thought, whether Westerners or
non-Westerners, could find solace in Nishida; as Nishitani points out,
Nishida's thought overcomes the divisive preconceptions of previous
metaphysics: thinking of "the conscious acts of knowing, feeling and willing as separate and distinct"; maintaining a "differentiation of subject
from object"; taking "the framework of the 'individual' to be absolute, so
that experience is always the experience of a given individual" (109).

The dissolving of the dualities of subject-object and phenomena-
noumena leads to a reaffirmation of holistic participation. As Nishitani
writes, the standpoint of *Zen no kenkyū (An Inquiry into the Good)* "restores
unity at a deeper and more basic level to the standpoints of speculation,
experience, and Existenz that have become cut off from one another in
Western philosophy" (34). Nishida, who much admired Paul's declaration
that "[i]t is no longer I who live, but Christ who lives in me," was not
averse to expressing his vision in Christian terms:

> Because the self and things are one, there is no truth to be
> sought and no desire to be satisfied. People exist together with
> God, and this is what is referred to as the Garden of Eden. As
> consciousness differentiates and develops, subject and object
> oppose each other and the self and other things go against each
> other. In this process, life brings us demands and anguish; we
> are separated from God, and the Garden is forever closed to
> Adam's descendants. (151)

It is in this sense that "[t]he unity of the world of nature ultimately
amounts to a kind of unity of consciousness" (160). Nishitani puts it this
way: pure experience for Nishida is "what Hegel called the spontaneous
self-unfolding of the concrete universal, at the root of whose self-awareness it became one with the reason of the universe" (33–34).

All this leads to the ethic Nishida states explicitly in his final chapters.
"The good," he asserts, "is the actualization of personality."

> Viewed internally, this actualization is the satisfaction of a
> solemn demand—that is, the unification of consciousness—and
> its ultimate form is achieved in the mutual forgetting of self and
> other and the merging of subject and object. Viewed externally
> as an emergent fact, this actualization advances from the small-
> scale development of individuality to a culmination in the
> large-scale unified development of all humankind. (142)

However, Nishida asserts too that "the pinnacle of learning and
morality can . . . be reached only by entering the realm of religion" (152).
"God," he writes a little later, "can be seen as one great intellectual intuition at the foundation of the universe, as the unifier of pure experience
that envelops the universe" (164). The collective fulfillment he prescribes
occurs therefore within a panentheistic world view:

> Our true self is the ultimate reality of the universe, and if we
> know the true self we not only unite with the good of
> humankind in general but also fuse with the essence of the uni-
> verse and unite with the will of God—and in this religion and
> morality are culminated. (145)

The work was not, however, without its flaws, as its author
acknowledged. Responding to the view that "the standpoint of [*An
Inquiry into the Good*] is that of consciousness, and it might be thought of
as a kind of psychologism," Nishida aimed next to demonstrate that
"what lay deep in my thought when I wrote it was not something that is
merely psychological" (xxxi–xxxii). Hence the 1917 *Jinkaku ni okeru
chokkan to hansei (Intuition and Reflection in Self-consciousness)*. Here, says
Nishida, "through the mediation of Fichte's *Tathandlung*, I developed the
standpoint of pure experience into the standpoint of absolute will"
(xxxii).

This was the standpoint of *jikaku*, which Abe feels is better translated
as "self-awakening" than "self-consciousness" and needs to be understood as "an ontological and religious concept in which true reality awakens to itself and is awakened by us" (xxi). Intuition is seen as the basis of
will. From this position, a number of transitional texts led to the 1927
Hataraku mono kara miru mono e (From the Actor to the Seer), where the
standpoint of pure experience was significantly re-expressed.

> In the second half of *From the Actor to the Seer*, through the medi-
> ation of Greek philosophy, I further developed it, this time into
> the idea of *place*. In this way I began to lay a logical base for my
> ideas. (xxxii)

The motivation behind the elaboration of an original logic of place is most clearly set out in the 1938 *Nihon bunka no mondai (Problems of Japanese Culture)* where Nishida asks:

> Must we assume Occidental logic to be the only logic, and must the Oriental way of thinking be considered simply a less-developed form [of the same way of thinking]? (Tsunoda et al., vol. 2, 355)

Nishida's "logic of place *(basho)*," or "logic of nothingness" (where "nothingness" corresponds to the Buddhist *śūnyatā* which should not be understood as a negation of Being but only as a negation of determinate, or classifiable Being) was to be quite unlike what he called the "objective" logic that subtended the West's rationalism. Just as he had criticized the dualistic opposition that he saw as falsifying the Western representation of pure experience, so he calls here for a regress from the standpoint of reason (ensconced in the constructed subject) to the more fundamental "standpoint of nothingness," set farther back in the "place of absolute nothingness," that is, at the very depths of our awareness, where experience is wholly pure of the later construction of self (with its constructions of categories of determinate being) and, still later, of the rational self. Only after pure experience has been differentiated into self and world and thereafter world has been classified into categories of conceptual thought can reason and cognition begin its work. Prior to that there is, in traditional Western logic, literally nothing to say. Nishida has developed a logic prior to the confrontation of a knower confronting an object. Hence, the notion of "seeing without a seer."

Abe writes : "Nishida defined the most concrete universal as 'the predicate that cannot become subject' and undertook to establish a logic of unobjectifiable reality" (xxiii). Just how this challenged conventions of Western metaphysics Abe makes clear in his following appraisal:

> Nishida was convinced that for the individual as the grammatical subject—viewed by Aristotle as Substance—to be known, there must exist that which envelops it, the place in which it lies, and that this place in which the individual lies must be sought in the plane of "transcendent predicates," not in the direction of the logical subject. . . . What is referred to here as the direction of predicates is the direction of consciousness, and what is referred to as the plane of transcendent predicates subsuming the individual as grammatical subject is nothing other than "place" or nothingness as the so-called field of consciousness. In his grasping of the *plane of consciousness* as the *plane of predicates*, with Aristotle's *hypokeimenon* as medium Nishida

> gave a logical foundation to immediate and direct conscious-
> ness and seeing without a seer which otherwise could not
> escape subjectivism and mysticism. By so doing, he also laid a
> logical foundation for Reality. (370–371)

Nishida's "logic of place" has been the most influential invention of post-Meiji Japanese thought; Nakamura Yūjirō has called it a "great historical discovery" (*Nishida Kitarō*, 96). As a cogent and radical justification of the Japanese "sense of things" so threatened by Western rationalism, it became a central reference point in the Japanese "comeback" and confirmed Nishida as the country's philosophical *chef de file*.

For all the originality and luster of Nishida's thought, aspects of it nevertheless met with doubt and objections in certain quarters. A notable detractor was his own erstwhile disciple Tanabe Hajime (1885–1962). Educated in part at Freiburg under Husserl, Tanabe later gravitated toward Hegelian dialectics, but strove to ground his own dialectical system realistically by incorporating Nishida's notion of absolute nothingness. Nishida's philosophy as it stood, Tanabe came to consistently criticize as being reclusively aesthetical; he contended that Nishida, in his emphasis on self-knowledge attainable within the realm of absolute nothingness, was neglecting immediate historical and ethical issues. Moreover, for Tanabe history's very irrationality seemed to preclude the self's attainment of awareness through its own power. Where was the evidence that the dominant will within the world tended toward the world's own self-awareness, as affirmed by Nishida? If that was so, how was it that humankind was so caught up in contrary aims and activities?

In chapter 2 we indicated the need within Chan (Zen) Buddhism to acknowledge the doctrine of a "double truth." In the absolute sense no things exist, but in the relative sense of day to day existence, distinct things do exist (the Chan [Zen] novice has been sent to the market to get cabbages and not bamboo shoots). Prior to the distinction between self and world there are no distinct things *(śūnyatā)*, but thereafter there are. And when that occurs, these distinct objects in a world apart from myself have an existence and life of their own often contrary to my purposes and desires. Even if this is a relative truth and reality, and not the absolute, it must nonetheless be dealt with.

In his effort to elaborate a more concrete philosophy, Tanabe came out in 1934 with what he called his "logic of species." Nishida, he concluded, had remained abstract and ahistorical because he had taken account only of the individual on the one hand and of the genus (humankind as a whole) on the other. Believing that, as in logic, a philosophy of history must give due attention to the middle term, Tanabe in his own dialectical vision saw a central role for the species. Of course, Tanabe is not here referring to the "species" in the biological sense of the human species (homo sapiens), but in the logical sense of the middle term of a syllogism lying between the particular and the genus, in this case, between the individual person, on the one hand, and humankind, on the other. Between the individual person, then, and the "genus" of humankind, stood the state as the middle term, or logical "species." The condition for the success of the human quest for freedom and fulfillment, he says, is the overcoming of alienation. The species, he adds, is the "self-alienation of the genus." Individuals have the rational power to negate this, and thus to bring the dialectic to fruition in the form of the species (i.e., the state). Each individual's participation in this enterprise is the way to his or her own fulfillment.

Such is the reasoning that led Tanabe to write, in 1939, the following:

> The act of self-denial in which individuals sacrifice themselves for the sake of a nation turns out to be an affirmation of existence. Because the nation to which the individual has been sacrificed bears within itself the source of life of the individual, it is not merely a matter of sacrificing oneself for the other. Quite the contrary, *it is a restoration of the self to the true self.* This is why self-negation is turned to self-affirmation and the whole unites with the individual. The free autonomy of ethics is not extinguished in service to the nation and in submission to its orders, but rather made possible thereby. (*The Logic of National Existence*, in Heisig, 283)

Clearly, such a would-be corrective to Nishida's philosophy is itself highly questionable. How can we accept that history can be rendered rational in such a way? How could Tanabe, in his own historical circumstances, so idealize the state as a vehicle for realization of the absolute? We can also question his almost exclusive preoccupation with the *Japanese* state as the ideal mediator in the dialectical advance toward the most desirable "universal." Tanabe's argument here is reminiscent of the enterprise of Watsuji Tetsurō we earlier examined. Both manifest resistance to the West's subjection of all humans and their cultural activity to its own criteria of judgment. For Tanabe, humans are primarily conditioned not by the genus, but by the species to which they belong. Naturally, such an assertion invites the observation that Watsuji is closer to the mark: it is certainly culture, and not species (with its implication of race), that is the prime conditioner. However, we can at least understand Tanabe's choice of concept by recalling how racial belonging and cultural allegiance had, in a long period of national isolation, become associated in myth and fused in the State Shintō ideology. Even by the most eminent of thinkers, Japan's particularity continued to be seen as ethnically based, a matter of the blood.

Deteriorating personal relations between Nishida Kitarō and Tanabe Hajime prevented explicit dialogue between them on these issues, but we know that Nishida was very sensitive to the charge of being indifferent to history, a point on which he had been criticized also by Marxists such as Miki Kiyoshi and Tosaka Jun. Nishida's later works, such as *Tetsugaku no kompon mondai (The Fundamental Problems of Philosophy)*, unsurprisingly evidence a singleminded effort to re-present his philosophy from a historical standpoint, while remaining faithful to its main tenets.

> I . . . concretized the idea of place as a *dialectical universal* and gave that standpoint a direct expression in terms of *action-intuition*. That which I called in *[An Inquiry into the Good]* the world of direct or pure experience I have now come to think of as the world of historical reality. The world of action-intuition— the world of poiesis—is none other than the world of pure experience. (xxxii–xxxiii)

It is, of course, a unique view of history that Nishida is evolving and since it also lends itself to misrepresentation, we shall here set out his intentions as clearly as possible.

We have seen that for Nishida, as in Zen Buddhism, individual self-fulfillment is achieved by dissolving the duality of subject and object and thus achieving a state of awareness free from the ego's interference. Only thus can genuine self-realization be achieved, and only thus can the world's self-realization be accomplished through us. The place of absolute nothingness is the place where all human beings can come together in a common awareness and also a shared peace (for it is, Nishida believes, on the level of the conflicts of ego that wars occur). This leads to the notion of the "ethical state." On the collective level, the ethical state will be the state that facilitates the self-realization of the individual and of the world in these terms. Nishida's conception of such a state is evident in several late works: the 1938 lecture *Nihon bunka no mondai (Problems of Japanese Culture)*, the 1941 *Kokka riyū no mondai (The Problem of the Raison d'Etre of the State)*, the 1944 *Kokutai*, and the 1945 *Bashoteki ronri to shūkyōteki sekai kan (The Logic of Place and the Religious World View)*.

Just as Nishida tends to set up a schematic contrast between the dualistic outlook subtending Western philosophy and a holistic vision behind Eastern religio-philosophy, so he perceives (much as Okakura Tenshin had before him) corresponding contrasts in the nature of states, their rationales, and their policies. Pervaded by dualistic thinking, the Western

nations have operated primarily in the realm of ego; it was their subjectivist policies deriving from subjectivist nationalism that led to rifts
among peoples and imperialist squabbling. Likewise, it is within the subjective self that the West elaborated historicist ideologies that engendered
national delusions of grandeur. Against this erroneous thinking and its
catastrophic consequences, Nishida sees Japan as a nation with a unique
role. The collective renunciation of self he sees as corresponding to loyalty to the Imperial House, representative not of any relative ego-centered
power but instead of the eternal present.

On this point, Pierre Lavelle has written some excellent pages, and we
shall content ourselves with examining his demonstration, which is
amply supported by statements from Nishida himself, as when Nishida
says, "The culmination of the Japanese mind finds itself in actuality qua
absolute. The Imperial House is, for the Japanese people, an absolute reality" (*Kokutai*, in Lavelle, 147). Throughout Japanese history, the Imperial
House, Nishida tells us, "has been the being of nothingness: it has been a
contradictory self-identity" (*Nihon bunka no mondai*, in Lavelle, 147).

Lavelle notes the broad similarity of these ideas and the ideology
underpinning national policy, as expressed in the following excerpt from
a Ministry of Education text:

> That the Imperial Throne is coeval with Heaven and Earth
> means that the past and the future find their factual unity in the
> present. . . . Our history is the development of the eternal pre-
> sent that is always flowing through it. (*Kokutai no hongi*, in
> Lavelle, 147)

Here too *Kojiki* lore fuses with Buddhist nihility (Confucian loyalty to
be invoked to the amalgam). The Imperial House is the focal point of the
collective effort to realize a nation that is not subject but predicate. In religious terms and as a nation, Japan is thus qualitatively different from
other states. Nishida can thus write: "Our *kokutai* does not content itself
with giving impetus to religious forms, but necessarily transcends them"
(*Furoku ichi*, in Lavelle, 147). The emperor system corresponds to what, for
Nishida, is philosophically valid, and in his eyes it is therefore of universal value; "The Imperial Way must become universal" (*Gakumonteki hōhō
(The Academic Method)*, in Lavelle, 162). Loyalty to the Imperial House
thus becomes a moral imperative in the project of a transformation that
has implications beyond Japan's borders:

> Our activities can be based only on the idea expressed by "the
> entire nation at the service of the Imperial House". . . . This is
> why our nation's morality necessarily consists of the formation

of the historical world. To sacrifice one's self entirely, to conse-
crate one's activities to this construction, to become in all entirety the builder of a historical world going from that which is created to that which creates—such is no doubt the radiant
quintessence of our national morality. (*Nihon bunka no mondai*,
in Lavelle, 148)

Insofar as Japan has become a "creative force of eternal values, a subject of
the historical creation of the world," it can be regarded as a "real state."
The state has thereby become an "ethical substance" (*Kokka riyū no mondai*,
in Lavelle, 149). Not that this state itself is an absolute. It is rather a medium: the "real state" being grounded in religion, where adherence to state
morality represents profound religious action.

All the foregoing allows us to appreciate the perspective from which
Nishida supported, in his capacity as adviser to the Shōwa Research
Society, the "eight corners, one roof" policy of "reconstructing" East Asia
under Japanese leadership. It also explains his support for military
action, seen as a means of assisting other Asian nations (oppressed by
the West or hampered by their own errors, or both) to restore "Eastern"
culture—to realize themselves—under the tutelage of the nation in
which that Eastern culture had evolved to its finest form. War for
Nishida amounted to a moral and religious enterprise. Ultimately it
would be beneficial on a global scale: Nishida writes frequently of
Japan's role in installing a new world order. Where the secular Western
nations had long made war on the basis of petty national interest, devoid
of religious motive, Japan's war would, in a sense, be a war to end all
wars. Not an aggressive war, but a war designed to reveal the others to
themselves:

It is precisely this ability to empty oneself to embrace the other
that is the principle of our country's particular subjectivity. By
utilizing this ability, the radiant quintessence of the *kokutai* can
be illustrated in the world. (*Sekai shin-chitsujo no genri (The
Principle of the New World Order)*, in Lavelle, 159)

Whatever differences we may point to between the philosophies of
Nishida Kitarō and Tanabe Hajime, the *kokutai* became for both of them,
as also for Watsuji Tetsurō, a focal point. In the case of all three, despite
initial aims of demonstrating cultural particularity, the imperial loyalty
that emerged as integral in their thought implied an exclusivist position
that, on the surface at least, had all the colorings of ultranationalism.

Inevitably, this, together with less subtle Hegelian schemes of minor
figures such as Kōyama Iwao and Kōsaka Masaaki, provoked allegations

that the Kyōto school was characterized by "fascist" thinking and militarist collaboration. With regard to the two thinkers we are discussing, however, there is insufficient evidence to support such an appraisal, at least if we judge from stated intentions. Rather the contrary, as Nishida makes clear:

> We must most carefully guard against the subjectivization of Japan. It would serve only to transform the Imperial Way into a tyranny, into imperialism. (*Nihon bunka no mondai,* in Lavelle, 161)

At the center of Nishida's nationalism there is always the civilized ideal of the world-formative project, and even if this implies a military execution, Nishida stated his abhorrence of military activity that did not rise to this ideal and serve it. The brute military power that in his view subverted Japan's worthy ideals aroused Nishida's indignation and opposition (thus occasioning threats to him by extremists), and in March 1945 he expressed the country's coming downfall as "the natural consequences of the doings of those arrogant and reckless hicks who don't look at the world." It was a "fundamental mistake," he declares, "to have identified the national polity with military power" (letter to Nagayo Yoshirō, in Yusa, 208).

Tanabe Hajime too had little in common with the ultranationalists. James Heisig, in Tanabe's defense, cites his criticism of Heidegger for that thinker's Nazi sympathies, and his celebrated assistance to Jaspers when the latter was under Nazi threat. Certainly, at least in its initial expression, Tanabe's philosophy, too, implied not blind submission to the state as it is, but instead a carrying over of each individual's moral sense to the accomplishment of the state as he felt it ought to be. As Heisig notes, however, Tanabe himself went farther than to say he had been merely misconstrued.

> As the tensions of World War II grew ever more fierce and with it the regulation of thinking, weak-willed as I was, I found myself unable to resist and could not but yield to some degree to the prevalent mood, which is a shame deeper than I can bear. (in Heisig, 284)

For all our defense of the two dominant figures of the Kyōto school based on their actual intentions, two observations must be made: first, that their schemes were dangerous nonetheless insofar as they posited an ideal to be achieved, by force if necessary, beyond current reality, and perhaps despite reality itself. In this sense, did their systems not contain within themselves a seed of tyranny from the moment they set up an equation of ends and means? Second, it is difficult not to deplore, in such eminent and influential men, the naiveté that allowed them to believe, especially amid the telling realities of wartime Japan, that the mass of their fellow citizens could comprehend and would share in their idiosyncratic and abstruse projects. How can we explain such blindness? Thinker Umehara Takeshi has said:

> There are two types of philosophers. One type generates ideas within himself, like a silkworm spinning silk. The other type creates ideas through the sensation of touch, through contact with external objects. (Ōe and Umehara, 17)

If this is so, the Kyōto school thinkers appear to have belonged to the former type. Their refined moral sense and singleminded devotion to philosophy appears to have insulated them from worldly insights that too are necessary for a genuine wisdom.

A student of Nishida making his name outside the Kyōto school was Miki Kiyoshi (1897–1945). Yet another to make the long journey to Germany to study under the author of *Being and Time*, Miki was quick to apply Heideggerian perspectives himself in his 1926 *Pasukaru niokeru ningen no kenkyū (A Study of Man in Pascal)*, which predated Heidegger's masterwork by a year. With time, however, this influence was increasingly nuanced by reservations. In particular, Miki "criticized Dilthey's and Heidegger's views of man as emphasizing the subjective, affective aspect, and failing to grasp sufficiently the aspect of action that engages the world" (Yuasa, 164).

Thereafter, he embraced Marxism in his early thirties and became a prominent theorist writing in the journal *Shinkō kagaku no hata no moto ni (Under the Banner of the New Science)*, which sought "a new theoretical position that, rejecting the basis of modern science in a universal nature, would synthesize knowledge instead around the principle of nature as a societal category" (Doak, xxii). Progressively estranged from orthodox Marxists, Miki, in thus trying to restore humanistic values to the dialectic process, eventually arrived at his own distinctive logic, laid out in the 1939 *Kōsōryoku no ronri (The Logic of the Power of Imagination)*.

From the mid-1930s, in accordance with this logic, he expressed the view that a new Asian humanism could, under Japan's guidance, become the basis for a new cooperative East Asian ideology. This, he thought, would nullify capitalistic inequities by rejecting the individualism from which the class system had arisen. It was with this position that Miki joined the Prime Minister's think tank, the Shōwa Research Society, in

1936 as a cultural adviser. While supporting the Japanese invasion of China the following year as the first step toward his humanistic Asian community, Miki was soon forced to realize that the military were leading Asia, not toward any imaginatively liberating community, but to devastation and deeper division. His death in 1945 came after he had been imprisoned for sheltering a Communist sympathizer.

With Japan's defeat in the same year a sorry era in the country's intellectual history was brought to a close. In 1924, Sun Yat-sen had said that as Japan grew stronger through modernization, it would have to choose between becoming "the hawk of Western-style might or the tower of Eastern right" (Jansen, 72). In the end, it seems, the hawks found a convenient gathering place on the tower, nourishing themselves with the grandiose arguments laid out within, learning to masquerade even as doves.

> War . . . is not by any means intended for the destruction, over-powering, or subjugation of others; and it should be a thing for the bringing about of great harmony, that is, peace, doing the work of creation by following the Way. (*Kokutai no hongi*, in Tsunoda et al., vol. 2, 284)

William LaFleur has perhaps expressed it best. Referring to the liberal thinkers of the Taishō period, he writes: "Many . . . especially the philosophers, seem to have unintentionally become patsies and ideological front-men for others who were playing a harder, deadlier game" (234).

CHAPTER 5

BEYOND MODERNITY

The postwar years were a time of sober reflection on the role of philosophy, past and future.

> Deprived during the war of all freedom of thought, the Japanese seemed in the immediate postwar period to turn in great numbers towards philosophy. Those who studied it or were interested in it were so numerous, and so great was their hunger for reading, that when the editor Iwanami published Nishida Kitarō's *An Inquiry into the Good*, already before dawn a long queue had formed at the doors. (Nakamura Yūjirō, *Philosophie*, 80, our translation)

The public read Nishida and other Kyōto school philosophers anew, but for many, the school's most recent writings appeared all too close to the now discredited imperial supremacist orthodoxy. It was a general preoccupation. The inability of prewar thought to resist ultranationalism became the first concern of *sengo shisō* (literally "postwar thought," and used generally for the period from 1945 to the 1960s). In this climate, Marxism (returning in force after years of persecution) and democracy (installed with the American Occupation) became favored directions.

Along with other intellectuals who had become road companions of the military, some Kyōto school writers painfully reviewed themselves the implications of their political stance, and their expressions of regret and repentance led to what Maruyama Masao called the "community of contrition." The symbolic text par excellence of this last is Tanabe

Hajime's 1946 *Zangedō to shite no tetsugaku (Philosophy as Metanoetics)*. In this work of disillusion, the self is painfully aware that it is inescapably relative and so unable to achieve by itself a conversion to absolute nothingness. Elevating the nation as species to absolute status had been a grave mistake. No longer could historical praxis be regarded as decisive in the attainment of the desired conversion. Indeed, it appeared that conventional speculative philosophy as a whole offered no effective recourse: "[T]he rational philosophy from which I had always been able to extract an understanding of history . . . has left me" (26). Hence Tanabe's new metanoetic position: the only way the relative self might consummate the conversion it seeks is through a "philosophy that is not a philosophy." Metanoesis is "the ultimate conclusion to which the critique of reason drives us" (19–20). The self, he concluded, has no choice but to recognize its own impotence and surrender itself to *other-power*, where this latter is not the "other" of a self-other duality, but, in keeping with the outlook of Shinran (1173–1263), the founder of the Jōdo Shin Sect of Pure Land Buddhism and one of Tanabe's major influences, something sensed as an all-embracing grace.

Reactions to Tanabe Hajime's repentance and his new "non-philosophy" predictably ranged from sympathy to scorn. Most contemptuous of all were the Marxists, for whom Tanabe's new position, with its implication of a complete retreat from history, was merely a consummation of the Kyōto school's aberrant idealism. In reality, Tanabe was not utterly apolitical. He wrote a number of essays after the war in favor of social democracy, and in hindsight, we might rather commend him for renouncing so early the sort of historicist wishful thinking that the Marxists were to adhere to for a few more increasingly uncertain decades. But this was, after all, the period when Marxism remained for many, as for Jean-Paul Sartre as late as 1957, the "philosophy of our time . . . unsurpassable because the circumstances that engendered it have not yet evolved beyond it" ("Questions de méthode," 44, our translation). This affirmation belied a difficulty, of course, which was to draw a convincing *trait d'union* between existentialism and Marxism. In Japan too, the incongruence of existentialism and social engagement (characterized by Miki Kiyoshi's preoccupations with Heidegger and Marx) had never been satisfactorily resolved. Sartre's attempts to reconcile ontology and ethics (in *L'Existence est un humanisme* [Existentialism is a Humanism]) and his Marxist conversion were thus highly pertinent for many Japanese intellectuals. The postwar existential malaise and social confusion exacerbated the recurrent problems of assessing the role of the individual with regard to society, a matter highlighted in a long-running debate in 1947 and 1948 on *shutaisei* (subjectivity). Was the individual a creative maker of history (the view of Maruyama Masao) or simply an agent of dialectical historical change (the view of orthodox Marxists)? With this focus on the autonomy and collective responsibility of the individual, the issue of identity was once again highlighted with painful acuity.

Beneath the flurry of immediate controversy the question of identity was related to a more significant and long-standing issue: Japan's attitude to modernity. From Meiji days, the quandary of the intellectual had been to wander uneasily between imported theory on the one hand, and on the other, experience embedded in the indigenous culture. Turning West, he might make the futile attempt to assimilate the European systems, falsely interpreted as being reality itself, and suppress everything in his experience that such systems neglected or depreciated; turning toward home, he might regain a holistic concordance, but within an ambiguous shadow-world where the echoes of ancient voices, whispering still of a divine belonging, had increasingly been taken up by new voices in strident tones.

In his 1949 *Nihirizumu (The Self-Overcoming of Nihilism)*, Nishitani Keiji (1900–1991) wrote that Europeanization (and later, Americanization) had led to Japan's spiritual decay, and to an emptiness that was "the natural result of our having been cut off from our tradition" (175). To overcome this first alienation implied restoring the holistic culture that had been repudiated in the Meiji Restoration, and, as we have observed, such a reaction was already evident in the late nineteenth century. Ultimately, however, fidelity to holistic traditions became subsumed within ultranationalism. With Japan's defeat, condemnation of the ultranationalists' military adventure and the preoccupation with Marxism on the one hand and democracy on the other (the latter accompanied by its own infectious pop culture) accentuated the estrangement of Japan from its own intimate past.

Meanwhile, even as it was being imported in the Meiji era the would-be replacement European culture was itself being undermined by a nihilist crisis. For this reason, Nishitani pronounced European nihilism too a "pressing problem" for Japan, even if it might appear a distant issue, culturally as well as geographically. Japan's postwar crisis of identity and values may, for some, have assumed novel expression (in, for example, existentialist *angst*), but we recognize within it the familiar fundamental issue of Japanese values versus modernity, with both options appearing problematical. This is an issue that subsists even today (though, as we shall see, there are signs that it may soon become obsolescent). Let us review the two opposing positions, that is, of those who believe Japan should reject modernity and of those who feel the country should embrace it.

The "overcoming of modernity" was the subject of a series of debates held by the *Bungakkai* (Literary Society) in Kyōto in 1942 in which several members of the Kyōto school took part. Where, in the 1930s, the Japanese romantic movement had expressed its antimodern position primarily in terms of a longing for Japan's lost cultural integrity, most of the Kyōto intellectuals (Nishitani among them) saw the overcoming of modernity as a just cause of war. As they saw it, Japan's military had a double mission: to end the Western colonial incursion in Asia and to free Asia from the Western intellectual hegemony that had left the Japanese, among others, alienated from their own cultural past.

The antimodern project enunciated in these debates was swept up in Japanese military expansionism, but later the critic and sinologist Takeuchi Yoshimi (1910–1977) restated what he saw as its valid elements, distilling from the debate texts the central problem of Japan's relationship with modernity, and proposing a fresh solution. Identifying modernity with the "self" of Europe, Takeuchi called for Asia to shake off its alien modernist self-image and to see itself afresh in the context of its own culture. He felt moreover that "to realize superior Western cultural values, the West (had) to be entrapped once more by Asia" (in Najita and Harootunian, 771).

Meanwhile, modernist universalists, both in and outside Japan, have always taken the contrary line that Japan should be drawn "into the world." This was the position of Maruyama Masao (1914–1996), a prominent political scientist, noted for his *Chōkokka shugi no ronri to shinri (The Logic and Psychology behind Ultranationalism)* of 1946. Maruyama felt that Japan had "not yet succeeded in fully achieving (modern thought)" ("Modern Thought," 188–190) and, following Fukuzawa Yukichi, prescribed a movement from *wakudeki* (superstition, credulity) to *shutaisei* (flexible subjectivity). Noting all this, J. Victor Koschmann points out that for Maruyama, "modern subjectivity is not merely an epistemological mechanism, but also an anti-authoritarian strategy" (129–130).

For Westerners, accustomed from early education to the valuing of individualism and the development of personal autonomy, it is perhaps not easy to conceive of what Maruyama's concept of *shutaisei* meant for most Japanese. We should not forget that in Japan the identity of the individual had long been defined principally by social position and allegiance at various levels, and that moreover the supreme allegiance to the Imperial House had been strengthened progressively in the prewar period by the *kokutai* ideology. Thoughts and values had thus largely been formed by conventions imposed by the community and manipulated by the state according to perceived national interest. Recalling all this, we can better measure the difficulty of the transformation of mentality, and hence politics, that Maruyama strove to effect. Where before the war the Japanese had en masse absorbed the nationalistic ideology, postwar Japanese must develop a strong subject *(shutai)*, permitting both personal independence and the exercise of free participation in society as a whole. Only then would Japan have a chance of establishing genuine democracy. On the surface, it might appear that Maruyama failed. In 1950 he declared that "at present there is no democracy worth defending in Japan" (Maruyama, *Gendai*; in Kersten, 269), and as the Cold War progressed, he was branded a Leftist, despite being attacked in 1960 by the New Left in the person of Yoshimoto Takaaki. The latter observed in postwar Japan the relentless advance of free capitalistic enterprise rather than any liberation of the citizen, and felt Maruyama's analysis and aspirations were deluded. For all this, Maruyama's scholarship continues to be a touchstone for Japanese democrats, and, as we shall see, there are signs that in the very different social climate of the turn of the century, the value of *shutaisei* is becoming officially acknowledged. The game is not yet over.

We have been reviewing antimodern and pro-modern positions. In the immediate postwar period, these two options could not but be fiercely antagonistic. To be antimodern was to run the risk of being branded antidemocratic, nostalgic for the nationalistic values now indissociable from the military disaster. To be pro-modern was fine as a refusal of the immediate past, but was (as in the corresponding period of progress in the Meiji period) not consonant with deeply felt Japanese convictions. For all the allergy to imperial supremacism, the nation was not suddenly ripe for a thoroughgoing modernist/rationalist conversion.

In short, Japanese identity was caught in a Hobson's choice with high passion on both sides over what the country should stand for, and this explains something of the character of Japan even today: a nation taken in hand by "modern reformers" but where alien values have encountered a strong conservative element that has kept democratization superficial. Resentment on the part of the antimodern element occasionally surfaces in reactionary political comments that the public face *(tatemae)* of a would-be modern democracy is forced to condemn (but the condemnation itself is, significantly, usually tardy and minimal).

This reactionary underside has been more visible in extreme forms of the so-called *nihonjinron* discourse, a genre purporting to explain Japan and the Japanese. There is a longstanding tradition of *nihonjinron*, going back to such pioneering works as Basil Hall Chamberlain's 1890 *Things Japanese* and Miyake Setsurei's *Shinzenbi Nipponjin (The Japanese: Truth, Goodness and Beauty)* of the following year. However, as Japan's modernization intensified in the 1960s and '70s there was an unprecedented surge of *nihonjinron* output characterized by radical, sometimes absurdly crude, assertions of Japanese uniqueness. Focusing mainly on this, Peter Dale wrote that the *nihonjinron* exhibit three "major assumptions or analytical motivations":

[T]hey assume that the Japanese constitute a culturally and socially homogeneous racial entity; . . . they presuppose that the Japanese differ radically from all other known peoples; . . . they are consciously nationalistic, displaying a conceptual and procedural hostility to any mode of analysis which might be seen to derive from external, non-Japanese sources. (Introduction)

Certainly one can identify in Japanese scholarship a vast body of pseudo-knowledge that, while responding to the nostalgia for an established sense of Japanese identity, is packaged in the language and style of genuine research.

Such *nihonjinron* discourse has been seen by some purely as a retreat into a stubborn *sakoku* (closed country) attitude, in other words, as an attempt to "finish the incomplete wartime project of removing Japan from the alien matrix of 'modern' (read 'Western') historical discourse by trying to declare it once and for all ahistorical, eternal, and unchanging" (Pollack, 81). Reading this, we recall the similar criticism directed long before at Motoori Norinaga, who, in rebutting other scholars, reported that one of them objected that he wanted to "put our country outside the universe" (Tsunoda, et al., vol. 2, 22).

The consensus models of the *nihonjinron* of this type have been stoutly challenged both by "conflict theorists," who emphasize the dissension within Japanese society, as evidenced by demonstrations on social issues such as pollution, and "control theorists," who, inspired by Foucault and others, attribute Japan's alleged high degree of homogeneity not to innate characteristics but to power relations.

Such challenges have obliged *nihonjinron* writers with higher academic pretensions to seek new themes and strategies. Whether they can succeed in perpetuating or propagating consensus myths no doubt depends on how far these correspond to the fundamental needs and hopes of their readership and how far they offend critical awareness. That those in power, at least, can see such myths as strategically viable has been shown by Marilyn Ivy, in her essay "Consumption of Knowledge." Faced with "the ever-increasing speed of information" in the postmodern era, she writes, "[T]he state increasingly attempts to circumscribe the capitalization of knowledge and to appeal to meta-narratives of (discredited) legitimation" (25). One detects the implication that such a strategy may become the old guard's desperate last resort. For a highly informative discussion of the *nihonjinron* and related issues, the reader should consult her *Constructs for Understanding Japan.*

All this does not mean that we should dismiss *every* Japanese claim to distinctiveness, or uniqueness. The nationalist claims of Japanese racial uniqueness with their implication of biological superiority or existential privilege have made many observers, especially foreigners, allergic to *any* claim of widespread distinctiveness about Japanese people and their behavior (see, for example, Dale's *The Myth of Japanese Uniqueness*, a work with a highly justified demystifying purpose, but trawling with a very wide and fine net). Yet it is important to focus the critical attack, that is, not to shoot down any and all attempts to describe the distinctive dynamics of Japanese society in themselves, but rather to discredit the elusive ghost of the nationalistic mythology, voicing notions of genetic superiority, divine privilege, or radical racially conditioned uniqueness, that may lurk within. We need valid explanatory descriptions of Japanese social dynamics because these are, taken as a whole, unique, and are certainly fundamentally different from those in any Western country, a point we can acknowledge without yielding in the least to notions of racial supremacy. Even if the ghost of the nationalist mythology were hunted out of descriptions of Japanese social dynamics, we would still be left with realities such as "insider/outsider relations" and *amae* (the latter explored in Doi Takeo's 1971 *Amae no kōzō*, translated as *The Anatomy of Dependence*) that may well have preceded that ideology. These could, of course, still be criticized on some other basis (see for example the psychiatrist's critique of Japan's bureaucracy sketched by Miyamoto Masao in his *Straightjacket Society*).

In retrospect, we can see that in the face of increasing modernization in the 1960s and 70s, certain Japanese writers instinctively sought to present evidence to support their sense of having no deep connection with the modern and its values, including democracy. (Unlike Maruyama Masao, they saw democracy not as a universal value but as one more symptom of this invasive modernity.) The recourse nearest at hand (a self-evidence for those educated prewar) was in fact nothing but a set of received ideas (Japanese homogeneity; uniqueness of a vaguely superior kind) that had been molded by and had outlasted the *kokutai* ideology and its enterprise of forming a homogeneous Yamato state. The result was an exchange of exasperation, largely between Westerners who were demanding rational clarity and these Japanese evoking the past in the name of cultural independence. Amid all this, constant reference by nationalist proponents to the myths of uniqueness and homogeneity, along with unremitting reference to these same myths by critics of Japan's social dynamics led to a dialogue of the deaf, which lapsed only when it was overtaken by new realizations.

Whether clarifying or mystifying, the wellspring of the *nihonjinron* genre is clear: we see here an assertion of identity by a nation that has felt itself misunderstood, misinterpreted by a powerful outsider. Yoshino

Kōsaku attributes the preoccupation with Japanese uniqueness that has long characterized Japanese nationalism to a "series of historical events that have stimulated [Japanese thinkers] to define and redefine Japan's identity in relation to the more central civilization, first of China and then of the West" (199).

Insofar as Japan remained deferential to Western civilization regarded as "central," it would be on the defensive, its self-image framed in Western terms. We recall here the early Meiji situation in which, despite obscure convictions of spiritual superiority, Japan also felt uncomfortably backward with regard to the West, primarily on account of material progress. In an effort to overcome Chinese "superstitions" and emulate the West's scientific achievements, the nation rapidly embraced positivist thinking.

Yet this deference to the modern was never unanimous and it was not long before figures such as Nishida Kitarō were reasserting the worth of Japan's traditional culture by undercutting Western logic's pretensions to universality. Nishida can be seen in this sense as Japan's most prominent precursor to more recent demystifiers of modernist claims. When critic Miyoshi Masao writes in the 1980s that "the signifier 'modern' should be regarded as a regional term peculiar to the West" (in Pollack, 87), he is merely re-expressing what Nishida had intimated decades earlier.

Pointing up the particularist character of the West's universalist claims, Nishida pursued the ideal of a more truly universal archetype, consistent with the Japanese holistic outlook. In *Nihon bunka no mondai (Problems of Japanese Culture)*, he wrote, "We cannot take any one culture and call it *the* culture."

> Human culture . . . must have what is called an archetype, in relation to which different cultures are to be understood and compared. (860–861)

We now know that from the affirmation of an archetype of Oriental culture, the Kyōto school thinkers arrived at various historical schemes of dubious practical significance. But this in no way discredits the holistic vision common to their points of departure, and the notions of "pure experience" and "absolute nothingness" continue to inform the school's postwar writings. Thus, Nishitani Keiji, after hinting at the greater depth of Nāgārjuna's nothingness compared with Western nihilism in *Nihirizumu (The Self-Overcoming of Nihilism)*, asserts anew the "standpoint of *Śūnyatā* (nothingness)" in the mid-fifties essays that came to comprise *Shūkyō to wa nanika* (translated as *Religion and Nothingness*).

The consistent fidelity to Buddhist thought we observe here should at least lend a nuance to the accusation that Japan, facing modernity, has merely sought refuge in a premodern intellectual policy of *sakoku*. Does the withdrawal from the "modern matrix" derive from an immature refusal to "face the facts" or from an astute alternative perception of reality?

For the eminent poet and literary critic Yoshimoto Takaaki (1924–), also known as Yoshimoto Ryūmei, the very notion of a universal model is a fantasy. The defect of Japan's *sengo shisō* (postwar thought), in his view, was its studious application of foreign criteria to the country, followed by various perceptions that it somehow failed to "measure up." Marxist and democratic ideas he came to see as equally culpable in this sense, both offering a model to which reality would be forced to conform. Countering his own earlier ideological enthusiasms (as a supporter of the imperial doctrine and, from 1945, a Marxist sympathizer), Yoshimoto, in a new metamorphosis initiated by *Gisei no shūen (An End to Fictions)* in 1960, took the position that the intellectual's role in effecting social transformation should be not to indoctrinate the masses in revolutionary ideologies or indeed to inculcate "enlightened thinking," but rather to articulate the very concrete realities of the masses in their humble everyday life. In contrast to Maruyama Masao, he believes that only in this sphere can personal autonomy (*jiritsu*) be possible. Human behavior, Yoshimoto asserts, manifests three forms of fantasy: individual, dual and collective. Of these, he privileges the second, for there where individual fantasy (in narcissism) and collective fantasy (in conceptions of the state) lead to alienation, in the couple and in the family, the individual can find genuine fulfillment. This communalistic anthropology we can trace through the 1965 *Gengo ni totte bi to wa nanika (What is Beauty for Language?)*, the 1968 *Kyōdō gensōron (Collective Fantasies)* and the 1971 *Shinteki genshōron josetsu (Introduction to a Theory of Psychic Phenomena)*. Yoshimoto's consistent criticisms of both Marxism and democracy as a social philosophy made him a major influential figure for the 1960s New Left Movement, though he was later criticized for being fundamentally romantic, moved by a Nietzschean ressentiment. In the 1970s powerful new critical tools began to render such attitudes passé.

Here, of course, our plot takes an ironic turn. Japan's attempts to cope with the modern may whimsically be compared with the earthlings' encounter with the Martians in H. G. Wells's *The War of the Worlds*. The earthlings are invaded by a seemingly unstoppable foe, but in the end the Martians are stricken where they stand by a microbe within. Nowadays we might see European essentialist metaphysics presenting a similar spectacle, like a giant cadaver stretching, yet transfixed, across the history of Western thought, ever being eaten away within by the relentless microbes of deconstruction.

The ailment had been long threatening. In the eighteenth century, F. H. Jacobi coined the term *nihilism* after identifying the vulnerability of

Western metaphysics latent in Kant's *Critique of Pure Reason*. Two centuries later, Gilles Deleuze draws his own conclusions:

> When Kant puts rational theology into question, *in the same stroke* he introduces a kind of disequilibrium, a fissure or crack in the pure Self of the "I think," an alienation in principle, insurmountable in principle: the subject can henceforth represent its own spontaneity only as that of an Other, and in so doing invoke a mysterious coherence in the last instance which excludes its own—namely that of the world and God. A cogito for a dissolved Self: the Self of "I think" includes in its essence a receptivity of intuition in relation to which *I* is already an other. It matters little that synthetic identity—and, following that, the morality of practical reason—restore the integrity of the self, of the world and of God, thereby preparing the way for post-Kantian syntheses: for a brief moment we enter into that schizophrenia in principle which characterizes the highest power of thought, and opens Being directly on to difference, despite all the mediations, all the reconciliations, of the concept. (58)

On the same issue, Nishitani Keiji writes:

> Since [Kant's] time, the process of awakening to subjectivity has progressed rapidly, arriving at the notion of ecstatic existence within nihility, that is, at the notion of subjectivity in Existenz. The same subject now comes to exist within nihility "essentially," that is, in such a way as to disclose its very "existence" in nihility. (*Religion and Nothingness*, 111)

With the dissolving of the self, world views constructed with the aid of the concept of substance are rendered secondary, arbitrary, revealed in their very nature as constructions; ultimately, this development culminates in the "decentering" effected by structuralism and postmodernism. Would-be centers come to lose their cachet of justification. Their pretensions of a superior vantage point are exposed, their projects of expansion and subsumption discredited.

With the translation of writers such as Foucault, Lacan, and Lévi-Strauss in the 1970s, such ideas were actively explored and re-expressed by Japanese thinkers, and the result was a shift away from the "postwar thought" that had drawn its primary inspiration from people such as Marx, Sartre, and Merleau-Ponty. The new wave of French ideas yielded the critical foundation that Yoshimoto Takaaki, for all his originality, had lacked, and a major watershed was created. In considering Japanese intellectuals who were active in this development, we should give special attention to Karatani Kōjin (1941–) and Yamaguchi Masao (1931–).

Karatani Kōjin was swift to grasp the full implications of the latest French thought, and he was among those most instrumental in communicating it to the Japanese intelligentsia. In his first work, the 1969 "Ishiki to shizen" ("Will and Nature"), on writer Natsume Sōseki, he had already emphasized that the human will can be grasped rationally, but is itself neither rational nor completely analyzable. Five years later we find him writing a critique of Marx, the 1974 *Marukusu sono kanosei no chūshin (Marx: The Center of His Possibilities)*, in which the influence of poststructuralism (and supremely, beyond this, of Nietzsche) is clear: Marx's claim to have rendered clarity to human existence with the aid of economic analysis is affirmed to be of the same order as metaphysical systems developing from a weak will. For all Marx's declaration that it was necessary to change the world, he had done nothing but impose upon the world a new interpretation. That said, Karatani has since been careful to mark his divergence from those of his contemporaries in whom he feels postmodern inspiration has obscured political and social realities. At a time when Marxism has suffered a dramatic retreat within the Japanese intellectual milieu, he calls for a supple rereading of *Das Kapital*. Rejecting the "Hegelian Marx," Marxism as constitutive *Idee*, Karatani advocates a Kantian review of communism as regulative *Idee*. In this he shows the influence of his erstwhile teacher, and major Marxist theorist, Uno Kōzō (1897–1977). Such an approach appears to Karatani all the more urgent in that Japan in his eyes and according to his own definition remains to this day a "fascist" society.

Yamaguchi Masao, for his part, must be credited with having brought a poststructural thoughtscape to Japan's cultural anthropology. Societies and their vision, he showed, develop around a consensual center, with all "misfit" elements rejected to the margins (the relative nature of the center's judgment of the misfits being conveniently concealed within a would-be absolutely defining vocabulary). This representation of the process by which societies evolve their *Weltanschauung* indicates that there is no essential center, and thus no ultimately authoritative interpretation. The world views of particular societies are constructions, all too human in their biases. Here Nietzsche (of the *Genealogy of Morals*) and his European descendants (such as Georges Bataille) find in Yamaguchi a passionate Japanese successor, willing moreover to apply his findings in a fresh analysis of his own society. His 1975 landmark work *Bunka to ryōgisei (Culture and Double Meaning)* is more specifically indebted to Lévi-Strauss and, as the title suggests, the Ricoeur of *Le conflit des interprétations (The Conflict of Interpretations)*, but manifests a wide-ranging curiosity and original insight. Setting out his poststructuralist tenets with ample examples, Yamaguchi takes time out along the way to deliver a telling deconstructive blow to conventional Japanese anthropology (as represented by Yanagita Kunio), urging that the discipline be engaged within universal perspectives.

The intellectual watershed we are here concerned with is also quintessentially illustrated by a joust between Hasumi Shigehiko (1936–) and Yoshimoto Takaaki in the July 1980 number of the revue *Umi*. Referring to Yoshimoto's critical method in the latter's *Higeki no kaidoku (The Interpretation of Tragedy)*, Hasumi questioned the idea of literary "truth," and, following Nietzsche, ascribed this notion to merely aesthetic ideals. Literature, he declared, simply compensated for a lack, and Yoshimoto had only been romantically constructing his own shelter over nihility. Thus placing his stake in the ground, Hasumi laid his own claim to Japan's intellectual poststructuralist territory, within which he has since become a major literary and film critic. In fairness to Yoshimoto Takaaki, it must be added parenthetically that for all the criticisms he received from Hasumi, as also from Yamaguchi, for his "truth claims," he too continues to be a prolific intellectual force, and has himself taken up postmodern themes.

Finally, it is impossible to refer to the arrival of poststructuralism in Japan without mentioning *Kōzō to chikara: kigōron o koete (Structure and Power: Beyond Semantics)*, a 1983 work by Asada Akira which re-presented this new wave of critical theory in a manner accessible to a mass audience, and became a phenomenal bestseller.

The effect of the introduction by the above writers and others of structuralism and poststructuralism was that Japanese antimodern intellectuals found themselves furnished with a ready made-in-the-West new challenge to the Occidental tradition, a challenge enthusiastically joined. Nakamura Yūjirō (1925–), versed not only in French philosophy but also in "peripheral" cultures (notably that of Bali), was especially well placed to recognize the opportunities. In the pertinent article to which we have already referred, he credits Western structuralism with having opened the way for him to break through the "aporias" of Japanese philosophy. Structuralism, he says, "opens a way that, through language, illuminates the unconscious and allows us to grasp the stake and sense of figures of rhetoric hidden beneath logic" (*Philosophie*, 88). In radicalizing Heidegger's critique of metaphysics, and undermining the "logocentric tendency influential in Western metaphysics" on which Western ethnocentrism is based, structuralism has also, he adds, led to an intellectual acknowledgment of an "anti-philosophical mode of knowledge"; in so doing it has enabled the reevaluation not only of "unorthodox Western thought," but also, crucially for the Japanese philosopher, of non-Western thought.

> Oriental thought, whose irreducibility to Western knowledge was obvious and prolifically emphasized, has been able to be put in relationship with this Western knowledge and has been able to gain its legitimacy as philosophy. (*Philosophie*, 88–89)

It is important to emphasize that this irreducibility of Oriental thought to Western knowledge does not mean that Oriental thought is reduced to what we characterized in our first chapter as philosophy in the broad sense, as opposed to Western knowledge, which is characterized as philosophy in the narrow sense. Rather, it involves a reevaluation of Oriental philosophy in the narrow sense. Japanese philosophy—at its deepest level uncomfortable with Indo-European logocentricity—had nonetheless evaluated itself and been evaluated according to the criteria of a logocentric tradition that was for centuries privileged in Western thought (extending from Plato and Aristotle through Descartes, Kant, and Hegel to Husserl). Internalizing the judgment of this mainstream, lesser Japanese thinkers might yield to the implication that their philosophy should obey logocentric imperatives or else be in error, deficient, irrelevant, or in any case marginal.

Of course, the claims of reason had been challenged before within Western thought (by Pascal against Descartes, by post-Enlightenment romantics, by Kierkegaard against Hegel and Nietzsche against traditional metaphysics, by Bergson in his response to Kantian skepticism). But with the contemporary deepening self-critique of Western metaphysics, fundamental perspectives of philosophy in the narrow sense in the West have been significantly modified. The logocentrist tradition's domination has ended, while opposing currents, such as the "intuitive" thought of writers such as Kierkegaard and Nietzsche, have gained favor. As Deleuze says, "The task of modern philosophy has been defined: to overturn Platonism" (59). And again: "Kierkegaard and Nietzsche are among those who bring to philosophy new means of expression. In relation to them we speak readily of an overcoming of philosophy" (8). Of course, Kierkegaard and Nietzsche had long been acknowledged as philosophers of a kind, but in a canon where logocentrism was a referential touchstone, they had merely occupied the margins. On the contrary, structuralism, and to a greater degree postmodernism, has given such thinkers an indubitable place at the very heart of Western philosophy reconsidered. In *Marges de la philosophie (Margins—of Philosophy)*, Derrida cites Hegel's injunction that "the Eastern form must . . . be excluded from the History of Philosophy" (101). For Hegel, as Derrida makes clear, Oriental scripts are inferior in that they merely act as graphic representation, lacking the capacity of phonetic writing to transmit the authentic speech of "presence," the voice of the logos. With Western philosophy now itself more readily acknowledging the representational limits of reason, and shifting its emphasis toward the value of the intuitive, many Japanese philosophers, deeply akin to the move, have felt justified, included.

We have named Nishida Kitarō as a forerunner to recent demystifiers of modernity's universalist claims. With the West's own questioning of its modernist past now familiar to Japanese intellectuals, the value of Nishida's own antimodernist legacy has gained even wider recognition. His project of emancipation from the invasive framework of modernity is reaffirmed for current Japanese thinkers as an instructive precedent. Nakamura Yūjirō himself is a case in point. Declaring that he has "finally" recognized the importance of Nishida, he writes that the Kyōto school founder showed philosophy is possible outside the West and need not be based on the Greek model.

Given all the above, it is hardly surprising that since the 1970s the challenge to modernity has become a commonplace, putting into question the entire relevance of modernity to Japan and other cultures that suffered from the Western incursion. Naturally, this *mise en question* extends retrospectively to become a justification for entire "local" philosophies as independent traditions and a vindication of their stances of resistance to being defined within the Western cultural lexicon. Hence the recent redrawing of the terrain by Japanese intellectuals, as noted here by David Pollack:

> What [Asada Akira and Karatani Kōjin] have discovered of late is not so much that Japan has been catching up with the latest Western ideas as that the West has perhaps only belatedly begun to come around to a "postmodern" position that has existed in Japan ever since the seventeenth century, if not before. (76)

Miyoshi Masao will go as far as to say that "the term 'postmodern' seems to have been invented just to describe Japanese society" (146).

Postmodern implications concerning the role of language in cultural formation inspire the same author to observe:

> Particularities of the Japanese language no longer merely dictate the parameters of expression: language now shapes the very *logic* of representation.
>
> For example, the Japanese language, and so Japanese literature, rejects Western Aristotelian notions of sequence and temporality: paratactic rather than syntactic, arithmetic rather than algebraic, the *shōsetsu* is the expression not of order and suppression, as the novel is, but of space, decentralization, and dispersal. (153–154)

Pondering this, might we not nominate Samuel Beckett, that precursor of postmodern expression, as also the most accomplished Western practitioner of the *shōsetsu*? Similarities in style evidence a convergence of vision.

Needless to say, with the decline of Eurocentric modernity favoring a more holistic outlook, the way was open for a greater commonality of philosophical concerns between Japanese and Western thought. Such a resemblance is indeed evident in the perspectives of Western postmodern thinkers and those, similarly outlined in Western terms, of the Kyōto school. In both one finds an antipathy to logocentrism, and the "dethroning" of the rational subject with, in turn, recognition of the limits of the usefulness of reason in representation of reality, a distrust of what we might call congealed concepts. The final emphasis is on the *pre*conceptual, on becoming and univocity. Deleuze harks back to Duns Scotus, Nishitani to Nāgārjuna, and both accord an important place to Nietzsche and Heidegger.

In keeping with Deleuze's statement that philosophy is now dedicated to the overturning of Platonism, these common elements East and West imply a radical redefinition of philosophy and its role compared with those in the former mainstream of Western convention. For Nishida and his successors as for Deleuze, philosophy is no longer a statement corresponding to reality, a restating of reality in words (as it was for Leibniz, or for Hegel with his synthesis of concept and existence). It is instead a "way" where the thinker elaborates a landscape of rationality merely to situate and guide the reader on a path where intellectual argument will ultimately scatter into poetic reflection and the sighting of intuitive truths. Clearly, if this is the role of philosophy, again it renders pertinent as philosophy the entire Buddhist tradition. We too, the authors of this book, find here our own justification. Where Japan's traditional thought was oft deemed obscure, ambiguous, bereft of logocentrism's estimable clarity, we, disabused of the "long error," can affirm it resolutely as philosophy in that discipline's most esteemed sense.

What is more, the shift of Western philosophy toward areas explored by the Kyōto school suggests a future shift of focus *beyond* to the Kyōto school's antecedents. Foucault in 1970 imagined the opening of a Deleuzian era of philosophy. But might Western philosophy, weary from its long platonic detour and refreshed with Derridean insights, even find itself on a path toward Nāgārjuna? Certain scholars are alert to this possibility. A 1984 text by Robert Magliola, *Derrida on the Mend*, points the way, as we see in this remark by Steve Odin:

> Magliola argues that *différance* as the interplay of identity and difference or presence and absence is equivalent to Nāgārjuna's Buddhist notion of *Śūnyatā*, since it constitutes a Middle Way between the "it is" of eternalism and the "it is not" of nihilism. (in Fu and Heine, 5)

Alas, the West has never fully exploited the philosophical possibilities in that direction, despite Schelling, despite Schopenhauer, despite Nietzsche's own prophetic—if not always well-informed—interest in Buddhism. We say "never fully exploited," for the references to the Asian traditions on the part of Western thinkers do remain few. And yet these words occasion a digression, for there are those who would have it that considerable exploiting has occurred, but without due acknowledgment being given.

We return here to the case of Heidegger. The affinities of Heidegger's expression and concerns with those of Japanese intellectuals, we have already noted. Some diligent detective work, however, has suggested that we are here in the presence of more than mere affinity. A strong case has been made for Heidegger's having been, as it were, an East Asian in disguise. With rigorous scholarship, Reinhard May lays out compelling evidence that, in the words of Graham Parkes, "a major impetus for Heidegger's new beginning (as he himself calls it)—for the trajectory of a path of thinking that is to lead beyond (or around or beneath) Western metaphysics—came from non-Western sources about which he maintained an all but complete silence." (in May, x) May himself writes more pointedly of a "clandestine textual appropriation of non-Western spirituality," holding that Heidegger "appropriated wholesale and almost verbatim major ideas from the German translations of Daoist [Taoist] and Zen Buddhist classics" (xviii).

While Heidegger reportedly claimed he learned more from the Chinese than the Japanese, he had numerous opportunities to enquire about Japan, not least in his encounters with the likes of Kuki Shūzō, Tanabe Hajime, and Miki Kiyoshi, detailed by Parkes in his essay, "Rising Sun over Black Forest" (in May, 79–117). Yet, Parkes emphasizes, the only work in which Heidegger is known to have explicitly written about Japanese ideas is the text "Aus einem Gespräch von der Sprach—Zwischen einem Japaner und einem Fragenden" (rendered by Parkes as "From a Conversation on Language: Between a Japanese and an Inquirer"), which appeared in *On the Way to Language* as late as 1959, some three decades after Heidegger's fecund conversations with those figures who were, or were to become, major Japanese thinkers. Both May and Parkes tend to see this text as at least partly confessional.

If all the foregoing is true, then we are faced with an intriguing possibility—Japanese philosophy already residing within Western thought, yet without acknowledgment. In the absence of references to his hidden sources, the best Heidegger will have done for comparative studies of Western and East Asian philosophy is to emphasize the importance of the transcultural. As Heidegger writes in "Hölderlin's Erde und Himmel," from the 1958–1960 *Hölderlin-Jahrbuch* 11,

What is changing [in Europe] is able to do so only thanks to the preserved greatness of its beginning. Accordingly the present state of the world can receive an essential [*Wesenhaft*] transformation—or even just the preparation for it—only from its own beginning. . . . The present as something waiting over against us becomes the great beginning only in its coming towards the small [*zum Geringen*]. But nor can this small something remain any longer in its Western isolation. It is opening up to the few other great beginnings that belong with their Own to the Same of the beginning of the infinite relationship, within which the earth is held. (36, in May, 48)

Indeed, one cannot magically step from one subjectivity to another; there is no bridge of forgetting from one cultural tradition to another, only a path on which fresh reflection may supersede old ideas. In this light, Heidegger may have felt that any explicit focus on Tao, Zen, and their exponents would be counterproductive, distracting his readers with exotic names. Whatever the motives, his decision not to refer explicitly to Chinese and Japanese influences did little to bring about a Western recognition of the East Asian tradition as such, something Heidegger's own reference to Western isolation would seem to render regrettable. Had the author of *Being and Time* fully acknowledged his East Asian influences, the Western philosophical tradition as a whole would have been recontextualized and obliged to redefine itself with reference to that multiplicity of philosophical beginnings he refers to.

Such has not occurred, and the contrast between the West and Japan in terms of intercultural curiosity remains striking. A diligent concern with Western, and especially French thought will be evident in even a random survey of contemporary names in Japanese thought: we might cite the place of Freud in Kishida Shū, the debt to Derrida, Deleuze, Foucault, and Barthes in Hasumi Shigehiko, the decisive influence of Kristeva in Nakazawa Shinichi. Japanese bookstores abound in translations of and critical works about Western philosophy, with postmodern French thought remarkably dominant. Meanwhile, how few are the works by Western thinkers that take account of Japanese philosophy and its Asian antecedents! A notable exception, of course, is Roland Barthes's *L'Empire des signes (The Empire of Signs)* in which Japanese realities become in part pretext for and in part apt illustration of postmodern themes. Facing an image of a Chinese Buddhist monk, we find these words: "The sign is a fracture that only ever opens on to the face of another sign" (66, our translation). Thus is the wisdom of the monk expressed in the language of semiotics: there is no essence, only an essential emptiness. In chapter 2 we indicated how late Mahāyāna Buddhist schools appear to argue against one another, not for the sake of replacing one theory with another, but rather to prevent any theory from being taken too seriously, or rather to prevent practical advice on how to avoid theorizing being taken as yet another theory! Barthes also shows himself well aware of linguistic limitations on intellectual inquiry:

> It is derisory to want to contest our society without ever having thought through the limits themselves of the language by which . . . we claim to contest it: it amounts to wanting to destroy the wolf while settling back comfortably in its throat. (16–17, our translation)

This little work of Barthes, however, was a precious rarity, its author an adventurous dissenter amid what we might call the West's own intellectual *sakoku*. As far as we can see, Deleuze's *Différence et répétition (Difference and Repetition)*, for example, contains not a single reference to Asian thought, even though one can sense the Buddhist tradition standing just beyond this book, like a great irony. Since *L'Empire des signes*, Derrida's references to Japan in works such as *De la grammatologie (Of Grammatology)* have incited a review of Japanese thought, seen as developing independently of logocentrism, but the kind of intercultural focus envisaged by Magliola above will probably remain marginal until residual resistance to the postmodern erodes within the West itself. Habits at the discredited center are dying hard.

In the religious domain, more dialogue has occurred. One finds in the West increased interest and participation in holistic lifestyles that draw on similar or identical inspiration to that which moved the Kyōto thinkers. Zen Buddhism, partly through the efforts of D. T. Suzuki and more recently Abe Masao, has gained adherents around the world, albeit often in unconventional forms (the international repute of the highly original Zen thinker Hisamatsu Shinichi is worthy of mention in this regard). Figures in the Christian tradition who held a holistic, rather than dualistic, view of creation have been given new attention (a salient case is that of Meister Eckhart, much admired by Suzuki and Nishitani and nowadays much referred to in postmodern theology). All this suggests a convergence of preoccupations such as would logically, at some point, result in a burgeoning curiosity in the West with regard to the Kyōto school (and particularly Nishitani, relatively the most accessible for the Western reader). Should this occur, there may well be a flow-on into the philosophical domain from the theological side such that Nishida's philosophy would find a hospitable reception in postmodern philosophy. Yet, as we have shown, there are good reasons for postmodern philosophy itself to take the initiative.

We have been detailing the convergence we see in the representation of reality by prominent Western and Japanese thinkers. Let us now imagine this. We have climbed to a point high above Kyōto (it could be Athens, or Vancouver). We look up from our reading of *Hataraku mono kara miru mono e* (it could be *Différence et répétition*) and we meditate on the wisdom to which so many intellectual paths may lead. The concepts shaping our meditation become fluid, like eddies in a stream, soon to be dispelled. We listen to the water flow. We fall silent. And yet, far below, we hear too the hum of the city to which we must return. In our hearts we have learned the value of silence, and it is this silence we calmly resolve to carry back to the city. But, as we descend, the tumult of the city grows. We re-enter the daily network of human relations, expectations, and conflicts. As John Caputo would have it (in *Against Ethics*), we discover ourselves *within* obligation. As we descend, questions of choice arise that silence alone may not resolve.

Thinkers East and West have shown the way to what Nishitani would call a *real* depiction of the real, purged of representational fallacies. But morality and the law typically seek within representation their own unchallengeable justifications, objective grounds they can point to for their own undisputed authority. They call for a truth where description itself implies prescription. "Truth"—even "truth" *sous ratures* (truth "crossed out")—appears forever a touchstone in human quests for a commonality. It is the supporting evidence that can be referred to and deferred to. This basis of commonality has been envisaged in different ways. In Zen, the word is a betrayal. In the West, the Word, we were told, was "Truth." Now, we have seen, in the West excessive claims of language are in question. Deleuze again, echoing Heidegger: "The history of the long error is the history of representation, the history of the icons" (301). Moreover, the word has been unveiled as dogma of particular interests. These may be those of the individual philosopher ("la pensée de l'homme, c'est sa nostalgie," as Camus once wrote). Or they may be those of what Caputo terms the "hyperbolic Other." Henceforth, quests for ultimate touchstones and self-justifications in metaphysics will be ironically undermined. The "dissolving" of the notion of truth in the Nietzschean assertion that there are only interpretations leads to perspectivism, the idea of the word as private play. At the limit, the postmodernist sees a world where subjectivities are condemned to perpetual conflict. This has the consequence of lending credibility to the implication of Buddhism and the contention of the Kyōto school that the only human commonality lies in the "pre-self."

Yet, if this is so, what consequences follow for us who must descend to the city? If, after a long, tortuous, and verbose passage, the West is finding an affinity with Zen Buddhism, what, if anything, might the latter offer with regard to *moral* perspectives for those in the West in their post-modern disillusion? Clearly, the Buddhist-inspired historical projects of the prewar and war years have been discredited. Nishida, we now see, attempted, overreachingly, to end the "alienation" of selves and to realize the commonality of the "pre-self," the community of pure experience. In the postwar years, Nishitani's similar project offered little advance in concrete political terms. Certain commentators have moreover questioned Nishitani's postwar silence about his own wartime support for the "co-prosperity sphere." As for Watsuji Tetsurō, his *Rinrigaku* began promisingly enough by refuting the notion that the self is at its most authentic an atomistic individualism (of the sort that leads to perspectivism), and positing instead a relational commonality that is our ontological and ethical "foundation." Encouragingly too, this latter is in theory a degree less abstract than Nishida's "place of absolute nothingness." As Robert E. Carter puts it, when the term "absolute nothingness" is used by Watsuji, "his emphasis is on *nothingness* as immanent in society and in the individual, not as *absolute* in Nishida's sense of a transcendent *as well as an immanent* nothingness" (346). However, ultimately, this distinction made little difference in political terms. While asserting the transcultural "objectivity" of certain moral imperatives, Watsuji failed to show how his "socio-ethical unity" would not itself become acquiescence to totalitarianism; indeed, his own conduct underlined that very weakness. For all the considerable interest of Watsuji's ontology, the postmodernist, mindful of the excessive claims of totalitarian philosophies, must ultimately find his ethics disappointing.

But such projects aside, what is left? It is sometimes objected that Zen, whatever its aesthetic rewards, is morally an escapism, itself a form of nostalgia, one more position we may take in the quest for comfort within the often inhospitable milieu in which we must fashion our lives. According to this view, Zen may leave evident the futility of violence committed in the name of principles hatched by the rational self, thus engendering a passive peace, but it also offers little incentive to act with regard to the suffering of others.

It must not be forgotten, however, that already in the Buddhist doctrine of *er ti* (the doctrine of two truths) we find the idea that morality is culturally relative; in the absolute sense no things exist (*śūnyatā*) and morality is transcended, but in the relative and culturally contextualized sense the monk has a moral obligation to use the money he has been given to purchase cabbage in the market for the monastery and not on something for himself.

A similar reminder is to be found in Alan W. Watts's *The Way of Zen*. As Watts puts it, "Zen lies beyond the ethical statement, whose sanctions must be found, not in reality itself, but in the mutual agreement of human beings" (167). He adds:

> In the culture of the Far East the problems of human relations are the sphere of Confucianism rather than Zen, but since the Song dynasty (959–1278) Zen has consistently fostered Confucianism and was the main source of the introduction of its principles into Japan. It saw their importance for creating the type of cultural matrix in which Zen could flourish without coming into conflict with social order, because the Confucian ethic is admittedly human and relative, not divine and absolute. (167–168)

Indeed so. So what of the encounter between postmodernism and Confucianism? Is there *here* a "postmodern ethic" the perspectivist can embrace, genuinely founded on the "mutual agreement of human beings," immune to deconstruction? As we have noted, some would have it that Japan is already inherently postmodern, with the implication that there is no "construction." It is not for us to disprove this by, for example, attempting our own deconstruction of Confucianism. But we can at least hypothesize a moment. How, for example, might the postmodern feminist approach that aspect of the "five ethics" imported to Japan as part of neo-Confucianism that states that the husband, as superior, is (ought to be?) the guiding rope for the subordinate wife? There she might be, excavating the texts, scrutinizing the reminiscences of the disciples of Confucius, finally confronting the man himself, his personal dispositions, his misogyny.

Our suspicion that Confucianism *can* be deconstructed, along with the observation that Zen accommodated it quite comfortably, will lead us here to a useful distinction between Zen and postmodernism. Reviewing our musings on ethics to this point, one point is clear: philosophy East and West appears, as much as by the definitional love of wisdom, to be motivated by a common quest for authenticity. The Zen-inspired thinkers we have encountered could not conceive of authenticity without emptiness, nothingness. There may be no "truth," but we come closer to the point of *knowing* there is no truth by clearing away our illusions. Postmodern demystification proceeds in a similar manner. The move to insight is expressed negatively. We advance by unraveling the pretenses, by demystifying. In this, we observe that Japan's Zen and the West's postmodernism have in common the objective of undermining false representations of the real, based on what we earlier called "congealed concepts." They are both, in their way, "stripped down" positions.

Yet there is a difference. The practice of Zen has as its goal the individual's "pure experience." It is a training in view of arresting the habitual drift of the mind toward conceptualization. In its reluctant, succinct, didactic utterances, it is enough for it to cite single concepts for "deconstruction." This focus on single, unconnected concepts renders Zen fundamentally unconcerned with power relations in the society at large, even if an individual adept, outside Zen practice, may be socially "engaged." Given this, Zen is at risk of being an accomplice to tyranny in a way that postmodernism is not. We have already observed that this was precisely the case with certain thinkers of the Kyōto school. The Zen element in the Hegelian schemes of Kyōto school philosophers was impotent to undercut the pretensions of those systems. Unsurprisingly, then and since, thinkers primarily concerned with the nitty-gritty of sociopolitical doings have criticized such a position as being, wittingly or not, an abstention, an escape, a nostalgic retreat from messy complication to pure simplicity.

The deconstructive stance of postmodernism is, on the contrary, concerned primarily with complexes of concepts spuriously posited as justifications of power. Having emerged on a continent lately so ravaged by the excesses of reason, Western postmodernism has a highly developed sensitivity to such extravagance. It has been all the more eager to follow the lessons of Nietzsche and assume the role of parasite, always undermining reason's excessive claims, ever exposing disguised interests and motives.

Postmodernism has no magic recipe for a peaceful unity, but it does thwart division resulting from attempts to realize a commonality on particularist terms (which would unavoidably be hegemonic, and in most instances a case of hubris). If there is one feature of postmodernism that is outstanding, it is its overall humility (even if this is not a quality of all its proponents). It reminds us always that we are within something greater than ourselves. Here again, we are reminded of John Caputo's views on obligation: "Obligation transcends me; it is not one of my transcendental projects. If an obligation is 'mine' it is not because it belongs to me but because I belong to it" (8).

There is wisdom here akin to Buddhism and to Nishida Kitarō's affirmation that experience precedes the individual. Postmodernism sees philosophy shunning private "descriptions" of reality laden with hidden agendas, and paradoxically coming closer and closer to actual description of what occurs, recognizing that *all* descriptions entail interpretation and may be subtended by prescription, and acknowledging that it can never succeed in any ultimate or permanent deconstruction—nor yet in any reconstruction.

Although Zen, too, ironically undercuts the move to conceptualization, and thus to the pretensions this can engender, after making its point it is content to lapse back into silence. As we have shown, it does not regard as its business any analysis of fallacious constructions. Such analysis, being also reliant on a lexicon of concepts, would be for Zen a self-betrayal. In this sense, for all the assertions that Japan has long been postmodern, it has not yet fully exercised the kind of ironic analysis that comes with Western postmodernism, even if deconstruction is nowadays a ubiquitous theme in Japanese academia. We noted earlier that the question has even been raised whether European-style deconstruction is possible in Japan. Both in a celebrated exchange of views with Derrida and in his 1981 *Inyu to shite no kenchiku* (*Architecture as Metaphor*), Karatani Kōjin has stated that deconstruction is inapplicable in Japan because "in Japan, the will to architecture does not exist—a circumstance that allowed postmodernism to blossom in its own way. Unlike in the West deconstructive forces are constantly at work in Japan" (xlv). The debate on this continues, but if European-style deconstruction does have a role even in Japan, might we not find that instead of Zen providing the decisive moral directions for the West that some hope for, it will be the effect of the West's postmodernism on Japan that will be the more profound? Certainly, Nakamura Yūjirō, for one, sees here a real opportunity. The Japanese, he insists, should avoid seeing postmodernism as just another intellectual trend and instead apply it in social analysis.

> The question is how to grasp the substrata of the modern. The most appropriate course would be to take up the emperor system as a problem of Japanese culture, but nobody's willing to do it even though it's vital for the Japanese to question their own culture. If people simply become captive to the word *post*, then all sorts of moral phenomena will be as one. In Japan especially, the proliferation of moral phenomena is rapid. (Japanese Thought, our translation)

Of course, it must be acknowledged that the moral consequences *anywhere* of postmodern philosophy are still a matter of fierce debate. Optimistically, John Caputo believes that the justice of postmodernism will make itself felt in between the "cracks" of the law. Respect for difference will make for greater case-by-case empathy, and hence greater justice. Encouraging as such a reading is, we might still ask whether postmodernism can combat injustices other than metanarratival hubris or the ideological oppression of minorities or the law's too highhanded approach to the individual case. In addition, it would no doubt be important to determine how much of the sense of obligation we "receive" is itself a cultural relic, floating chunks of metanarrative, echoes of religio-moral imperatives that are imperceptibly fading, for if the convictions that led to the laws being framed and respected should decay, then might the postmodern in a later stage merely be winking

ironically, thus comparable to the Zen practitioner closing his meditative eyes to the world?

Whatever one's outlook on this, it is hard not to agree with Nakamura
Yūjirō that postmodernism's deconstructing role is as relevant and valuable to Japan as to the West. Japan too has its ideologies to demystify, its
mythologies to expose, its justifications of power to unravel. How could
we not recall here the precursory texts of Andō Shōeki, who declared
moreover that he was writing not for his own generation but for those
who would come two hundred years hence?!

Japan may, as has been asserted, have been "postmodern" before its
time (Western time, of course) in its notion of the real representation of the
real and its questioning of Eurocentrism, but centers of power within the
country remain largely intact. As evidence of this, we may cite not only
the mystique surrounding the imperial family, but also the preponderance
of bureaucratic power rather than democratic initiative, and the enduring
marginalization of some residents of Japan on account of race (Koreans,
Ainu) or class background *(burakumin)*. These issues are not being entirely neglected by Japanese intellectuals: one can cite, for example, the
impressive 1998 *"Nihonjin" no kyōkai (The Boundaries of the "Japanese")* by
Oguma Eiji, which explores the implications the notion "the Japanese"
has had for Ainu, Okinawans, and others on Japan's cultural periphery.
On the whole, however, Japan appears to be behind the West (if the word
behind is allowed to have any meaning), not in the sense that it evidences
worse injustices, but in the sense that the critique of those injustices is less
developed. Whatever the difference between organization of Western
society and Japanese society, certain similarities appear to hold in terms of
problems of controls and freedoms. The recognition of this confirms the
demystifying task for postmodernism in Japan too. We might even surmise that accomplishment of this task would lead to a breakdown in the
frequent caricatural division between East and West. In the modern era
we saw mutual intolerance, European colonialism encountering a hostile
and ultimately rigid Japanese response. However, the West is now different. The way is open to tolerance of "world philosophies" and the dispos-
al of old stereotypes.

Most of all, in the postmodern era the Japanese may at last be able to
affirm their difference, dare we say it, their uniqueness, in a way that will
be sympathetically received. Japan is stubbornly and reclusively premodern, say some, in that it is reluctant to accept that its local interpretation of
reality can be subsumed within more general accounts. But it should be
clear by now that we must not assume that all cultures can or should be
judged in terms of a would-be universal model. It thus makes no sense to
describe Japan as "premodern." At the same time, we assert that there is a

trend toward greater cultural commonality of which each particular culture is henceforth obliged to take account. The coming into contact and interaction of contrasting worlds is irreversible (and the fact that the West's modernist exploration and development impelled this is secondary). These particular worlds have diverse cultures and as a result the mythologies of each have been relativized. Indeed the West's own would-be universalism has also been revealed as a particularism, forcing the West to revise its own interpretation of itself.

But when we say "relativized," what do we mean? Relativized as what? As unrelatable absolutes? Is not this relativization an absolution? Not being subject to any universalist judgments, can we conclude that anything goes, that any particularism, any exceptionalism, is beyond challenge? We can still see such a response by some in Japan, and usually by those who, anachronistically, are still carrying on the antimodern struggle. This response can be seen in the rewriting of history, whether in school textbooks or in the spate of 1995 movies in which Japan was shown as having won the war fifty years earlier. But postmodernism has shown us that all would-be absolute myths are man-made, human, all too human in origin. And they are elaborated largely according to a similar recipe. In Japan, such myths have led to an exclusiveness in the Japanese consciousness that has much hampered the awareness of and the naming of that country's philosophy as one amid a multiplicity that have emerged from human nature in general.

Postmodern demystification allows, on the contrary, the prospect of the Japanese (and not just philosophers) stating clearly: "We do not identify fundamentally with the modern, but at the same time we are finally breaking free from the ultranationalist abuse of our ancient myths." When more Japanese writers are engaged in deconstructive projects that complement those of foreign critics such as Herbert Ooms and Carol Gluck, we envisage an ongoing archaeology of ideas meticulously laying bare each step in the contrivance of the State Shintō ideology, exposing its motives and deceits, defanging it, so that the Shintō deities might finally be released back into their former habitat of innocuous legend. The notion of Japanese selfhood will similarly profit, the self being seen as partaking of human nature in general, rather than as being the unit of a mythified ethnic collectivity taken as an absolute. For if postmodernism vindicates Japan in its particularity, it vindicates Japanese individuals all the more in *their* particularity with regard to society, and in kinship with individuals of other races and nations.

Here too, there is a convergence with the West. Millennial schemes inspired by Spenglerian romanticism or Hegelian logic having traumatized the twentieth century, we find at last a newfound preference for the pragmatic and provisional use of reason. In postmodernism, the dissension of an astute minority, expressed early by writers such as George Orwell in *Nineteen Eighty-four*, Camus in *L'Homme révolté (The Rebel)*, and Raymond Aron in *L'Opium des intellectuels (Opium of the Intellectuals)*, has developed into a systematic mainstream critique. This critique similarly indicts Japan's historicist philosophies, where, for all the talk of banishing rationalist excess and creating a unity based on pathos, one senses the ghost of Hegel creeping in at the back door. Caputo says it well when he writes that he will content himself with a "minimalist metaphysics" that "limits itself to the 'es gibt' " (224). If Japan fully assimilates the postmodern movement, can coming Japanese philosophers do anything other than follow such a lead?

Of course, it remains a moot point how long it might take before Japanese intellectuals fully apply deconstructive perspectives. The atmosphere of academic conservatism in which most young Japanese philosophers are trained encourages acquisition of specialized knowledge rather than interdisciplinary free-thinking, and so deconstruction has simply furnished another chamber in the ivory tower, rather than being applied as an effective means of investigation. A second point is that in Japan, as elsewhere, postmodernism's own excesses have caused it to lose much appeal and credibility. It is in the very nature of postmodernism to be iconoclastic, but the most revolutionary (some would say the most simplistic) of its proponents take anticonceptuality to the point where we are left with nothing but a shallow subjectivism, leading to an unprincipled pragmatism. This position evinces the familiar retreat from grave disillusion to extreme skepticism (although postmodernism would not take as its own the latter term). There is no truth; therefore there are only interpretations. There is no transcendent morality, and not even a universally common ground for morality; thus, consensus views prevail, unchallenged by any rational critique. In this guise, postmodernism hardly seems fit to make meaningful ethical statements. Indeed, it comes to seem just one more symptom of the confusion, implying (contrary to its initial motivations) that mystification of one kind or another may even be necessary for moral order.

Of course, as we have noted, the function of postmodernism is never in any case to promote a comprehensive moral program of its own. Characteristically aloof, it will, even at the best of times, hold little appeal for those who seek directives. Yet Japan is a country where at the turn of the century there is, precisely, a prevailing sense of a lack of direction. In the immediate postwar period, the nation's pride was largely invested in economic reconstruction, culminating in bullet train lines, the 1964 Tokyo Olympics, and the 1970 Osaka Expo. The pride in such achievements, however, came to be accompanied by an undertow of shame when Japan was perceived abroad as a mere "economic animal." The self-contempt this engendered at home led to a greater concern for cultural and spiritual values, and among many there was a knee-jerk reaction away from the modernity seen as subtending material development and back to primitive *nihonjinron*. As we have seen, in the 1970s poststructuralism brought the possibility of a fundamental emancipation vis-à-vis both the matrix of beliefs concentrated in State Shintō ideology and the West's logocentric modernism, but this opportunity has yet to be fully exploited. Thereafter, in the late 1980s the "bubble economy" briefly generated a sense of economic invincibility accompanied by nouveau riche arrogance, but the major slump that followed sapped the country's confidence, and a series of spectacular crimes, most notoriously the sarin gas attacks in 1995 engineered by the religio-terrorist cult Aum Shinrikyō, brought citizens and intellectuals alike to talk of a moral crisis, or a moral void. The era of economics, it was said, was over; the next age would be that of philosophy. Of course, whether it would ever be agreed which philosophy is another issue.

On July 31, 1999, Japan's largest-selling newspaper, the *Yomiuri Shimbun*, published excerpts of conversations among four intellectuals it had invited to informally sum up Japanese thought in the twentieth century. Although two of the participants (Nakamura Yūjirō and Umehara Takeshi) one can term without demur "philosophers," the newspaper paradoxically presented their informal discussions under the title *Tetsugakusha wa fuzai shiseikan yuragu gendai* (in an age of uncertainty, facing life and death without philosophers). It is a title that curiously echoes Nakae Chōmin's declaration of a century earlier that impoverished thinking deriving from a paucity of philosophy was the source of the country's social woes. The content of these excerpts, however, suggests not a lack of philosophy so much as the lack of any one philosophy sufficiently dominant to command authority. While we cannot take the discussions of these four thinkers as being exhaustive, they are worth a moment's attention insofar as they underline the durability of major contradictions we have referred or alluded to throughout our treatment of Japan's post-*sakoku* philosophy.

A familiar argument we can distill first from these talks is that holism and communalism are to be favored against the dislocations resultant from "modernist" dualism and individualism. In the major Okakura-Nishida-Watsuji line of thinking we saw the development of an effort to expose and cast off the error of logocentrism, and to privilege "emptiness" in elaborate schemes where Japan took its place as an exemplary nation of the here-and-now. Yet it is important to note that the sense of loss and urge to regain that motivated such projects is a much broader phenomenon in Japanese society. Umehara Takeshi (1925–), one of the foremost students of Japan's cultural history, has repeatedly returned to this theme of holism. Contemporary Japanese, he laments, have become alienated, whereas in the country's ancient culture they were (and in the Ainu culture still are) creatures among other creatures, an integral part of nature. Chatting to his fellow guests for the *Yomiuri* article, Umehara notes that when the Darwinian theory of evolution arrived in Japan, the Japanese were not surprised in the least. That humans had evolved from (and belonged to the same family as) apes they took as a matter of course. In numerous newspaper articles, treatises, plays, and stories, Umehara continues to communicate to today's Japanese in a very direct way what he sees as the wisdom of the past. Similar concern to preserve holistic modes of representing reality can be seen in a wide range of other intellectuals, including psychiatrist Kimura Bin (1931–) body-mind theorist Yuasa Yasuo (1925–), and the Catholic philosopher Sakabe Megumi (1936–).

A second argument in the *Yomiuri* articles, running counter to the first, is that a "strong subject" must be developed to prevent the submerging of the individual in the group. This is a long-standing view, expressed by Fukuzawa Yukichi and the novelist Natsume Sōseki, and reprised in the writings of Maruyama Masao, but it has recently been given topical relevance by the social disruptions caused by the Aum Shinrikyō. While responding to holistic needs within a society characterized by fragmentation and alienation, Aum developed its own (im)morality, mostly according to the dictates of the guru, and without independent points of reference. Spectacular though Aum's emergence was, we should not regard it as merely an aberration. Rather, it can be viewed as an extreme but logical outcome of Japan's holistic beliefs and group dynamics. The Buddhist "emptying" of the self already implies a "giving over" of the individual to nothingness. If the individual does not "kill the Buddha," in the person of the guru, this giving over to nothingness can easily coalesce with a giving over of the disciple to the guru and to the cult, with the loss of moral independence this implies. This feature of the Aum sect parallels a similar deficiency in the Buddhist-based ethics proposed by Nishida Kitarō. The designation of the Imperial House (focal point of the state) as the place of absolute nothingness means the move to selflessness is, at the same time, a giving over to the collectivity. The will of the individual is in effect nullified in selfless obedience to the Imperial House. We can hold great respect for Nishida as a "cultural liberal" (Tosaka Jun's words), that is to say, a thinker who aspired to emancipate Japan culturally by way of a re-expression of its most intimate, holistic values. Yet the schemes he and others under his influence elaborated to this end manifest a disturbing moral and political passivity.

In fact, of course, Nishida here was reflecting the ambient ideology of his time, where already the very identity of the individual had progressively been absorbed in the concept of the *kokutai*. When Maruyama Masao sought to elucidate the problem of Japan's war responsibility, he unsurprisingly focused on this point. As Rikki Kersten writes,

> Maruyama claimed that the dominant characteristic of prewar and wartime society was a lack of perceived distinction between the individual and the state. The state maintained this by employing the *kokutai* ideology as a psycho-cultural tool which defined morality in terms of power. Rather than a preserve of the individual, morality was defined by the state, and all values were national values: "the real locus of Japanese morality was not in the conscience of the individual but in the affairs of the nation." (31)

Furthermore, says Kersten, referring to wartime atrocities,

> As the Emperor was the ultimate value, acts committed in his name acquired the aura of sanctity. The greater the proximity to the ultimate value, the more the act was morally justified. (31)

Hence Maruyama's conclusion that the triumph of totalitarianism and the behavior it engendered can be ascribed to an inadequacy of personal and social autonomy. The problem was one of "weak subjectivity." Interestingly, and no doubt partly in response to the Aum affair, the Japanese Ministry of Education moved in the late 90s to encourage critical thinking among school children.

We notice again how closely all the above parallels current controversies in Western philosophy, despite differences in the specifics. The holism advocates' rejection of the modern, its dualism, its hubris, parallels the West's postmodern *mise en question* of logocentricity, and the metanarratives this has spawned. Yet at the same time, there is a recognition that an excessive diminution of the subject can lead to the point where there is no longer any place for reasoned critique. A consensus view of truth then prevails, implying an acquiescence to the existing power structure. We can well imagine the dismay with which Maruyama might have read Lyotard's discrediting of narratives of emancipation in *La condition postmoderne (The Postmodern Condition)*. Where Maruyama advocated an enlightened subjectivity over superstition, Lyotard's analysis effectively reversed the very progress from superstition to rationality that became a prime belief of modernity.

It follows that for both Japanese philosophy and postmodernism (and not only for ethics, though that is our focus here), the central issue becomes that of the subject, and in particular, what place, if any, can be accorded to reason.

If we are to see in Japan a creative ethics of self and community, rooted in the "strong subject," as Maruyama ceaselessly urged, then precisely what form is that subject to take? How is the relationship between the personal subject and the collective subject to be understood? Also, how are we to take account of this subject in ontological terms? If the Buddhist teachings instruct us that the true way is that of "emptying" the self, then what validity can we accord the self as subject? In Heidegger's terms, what is the origin of reason? What can the place of rationality be after all concepts have been put under suspicion? Caught amid Buddhist selflessness, Confucian loyalty reviewed by the samurai and enshrined in the national consciousness, and frequent misinterpretations in Japan of the postmodern subject as a mere "anti-subject," the Japanese subject's self-definition is difficult indeed. The continuing significance in Japan of the problematic of the subject *(shutai)* is illustrated by the fact that more than two hundred pages of the October 1998 issue of the prestigious philosophical journal *Gendai Shisō* were given over to the theme *Shutai to wa nanika (What is the Subject?)*.

As we have seen, the West faces similar questions. While postmodernism has done much to undermine and forestall conceptual excesses, the so-called metanarratives, the historicisms, the grand schemes of Absolute Reason, it has also raised the specter of nihilistic irrationality. Against postmodernism's most iconoclastic proponents, we observe diligent efforts of others to save the values of enlightened critique (Habermas, Adorno). In *Beyond Interpretation*, Gianni Vattimo evinces alarm at the trivialization perspectivism has led to in hermeneutics and poses the question, "How does hermeneutic ontology speak about truth?" before proceeding to consider the "reconstruction of rationality." The large questions of the origin and the limits of reason have been posed anew (by Derrida, notably) and however theoretical these questions may be, the answers we give will affect our lives in concrete ways. What of the *provisional* concepts we use in our everyday morality, in the law? To what degree can these concepts be readmitted as trustworthy in our personal judgments and our social intercourse? In postmodernism's postrevolutionary era, the discussion is likely to be concentrated on this difficult middle ground, and it is a discussion to which Japanese philosophy (by reason of its long and distinctive—some have said inherently "postmodern"—experience) has much to add.

CHAPTER 6

CONCLUSION

We must return now to the key question that we asked in our opening chapter: Why, in the face of foreign intellectual and cultural challenge, has there been no acknowledgment *en bloc* of that body of work we have been examining as Japanese philosophy?

That there is such a thing as Japanese philosophy, in the narrow sense of the term as we defined it in chapter 1, we have made abundant demonstration. At their most original, Japanese Buddhism, Japanese Confucianism, Japanese philosophy of Western expression all exhibit common traits, predilections, exigencies that set them apart from their alien inspiration. Tracing these recurrent features through centuries of reflection, we have shown that for all the frequent critical emphasis on the aspect of importation, it is rather the ever-consistent *modification* of the received ideas that merits our attention. Seen in retrospect, this consistency of modification provides the shape and identity of a very distinctive body of thought.

Yet, as we saw in chapter 1, there is a marked disinclination, not least in Japan itself, to recognize Japanese philosophy as a genuinely independent tradition. The prevalent tendency remains instead to disclaim, to deny. In exploring the reasons for this, one may do well first to revisit the most influential of the disclaimers. Nakae Chōmin's famous remark on the supposed lack of Japanese philosophy up to his own day has for a century been quoted repeatedly and taken as deciding the issue. Yet if we recall the circumstances in which that statement was made and the personality of its author, we find ample grounds to reject such uncritical acquiescence. First and foremost, the translator of the *Social Contract* was a fervent idealist preoccupied throughout his literary and political careers by the defense and promotion of popular rights. His ideal of philosophy, in consequence, was a discipline that through careful reflection would lay down principles of social justice. Now, it may be true that no Japanese has produced an elaborate, liberal personal philosophy in the manner of Rousseau. Yet, clearly this is hardly an exhaustive definition of philosophy! In the assertion that there had never been any philosophy in Japan, Nakae Chōmin's specific ideal of philosophy leads him to an assertion that, taken as a general statement, is false.

When Nakae Chōmin says that the National Learning scholars had done nothing but study ancient texts and imperial mausoleums, he fails to do justice to the philosophical content of the writings of Motoori Norinaga, whose revaluing of ancient texts was accompanied by a rigorous critique of the speculative constructions of human reason. For all his devotion to the *Kojiki*, Motoori uses philosophy to challenge philosophy, and in a way that has postmodern resonances. When Nakae Chōmin says that the Confucianists had merely advanced new interpretations of the sages, he vastly undervalues the significance of those interpretations. The Japanese, after all, did nothing less than reject the founding notion of Zhu Xi that the ultimate reality of the world is the abstract, unchanging *li*, a position that would have seemed an enormity to most Chinese scholars. Even the speculation of the Koreans, remember, had occurred within the fundamental *qi/li* dualism of Zhu Xi. How too, one might ask, could Nakae Chōmin dismiss in a phrase the subtle and complex arguments Ogyū Sorai employs in his radical criticism of neo-Confucianism (for example, in his reevaluation of Xunzi against Mengzi)? Is there not here real originality? An originality that is, moreover, philosophical in our technical sense? As for the Buddhists, when Nakae Chōmin concedes that some had shown originality but only within the limits of their own religion, we cannot but again see a depreciation of real philosophical achievement: it was, to take one example, no mean feat for Kūkai to synthesize the major schools of Buddhism into a single schema. And, as we saw, Dōgen's "dropping off mind and body" offered an important new interpretation of Zen Buddhism.

The essence of Nakae Chōmin's position is that Japanese had for the most part rehashed old, and mostly imported, ideas. Yet, and we do not wish to labor the point, if Buddhism and Confucianism arrived all at once as ready-made thought systems, a factor that contributed to the perception of them as foreign, Japanese Buddhism and Japanese Confucianism differed from their antecedents on account of the initial selection of what to assimilate, specific local interpretations of what was imported, and all the subsequent refashioning of these philosophies within Japan itself. It would, we consider, be a similarly ludicrous caricature to see early modern scientific empiricism (Hobbes, Galileo) as simply re-editing ancient Greek and Roman atomic theory. Such a view, moreover, is refuted by the very foreignness that Chinese or Korean scholars point to in *their* readings of representative Japanese Confucian and Buddhist texts.

All these considerations lead us to smile at the oft-repeated affirmation that in Japan's philosophy, "everything is importation, imitation." Had Nakae Chōmin known continental Buddhism and Confucianism in detail, would he have been so vehement in his declaration? Can we really imagine concepts, in their passage from one culture to another, maintaining their pristine original identity in the new environment? Are we to deny any cultural and individual distinctiveness at all and reduce the receiving "thinker" to a mere robotic role in the transmission of the identical? Clearly we cannot. We said in our opening chapter, and illustrated it in the course of our text: importation and imitation across cultural boundaries always engenders something different. There may be a passivity in the fresh creation, as when the untraveled, the monocultural, in assimilating a foreign idea, unconsciously and spontaneously refashion it according to their own mindscape. Yet this very re-acclimatizing of philosophies in a different cultural environment is already a process in which originality *necessarily* arises—even before that foreign idea is taken up by a genius such as Dōgen or Ogyū Sorai or Nishida Kitarō. No, we repeat. In the pre-Meiji thought to which Nakae Chōmin primarily refers, as in the most original thought that was to appear after his death, we note again and again a compelling consistency of modification, and it is in this consistency that we discern the Japaneseness of this tradition.

Of course, the circumstances in which foreign thought was apprehended by Japanese altered significantly in the years after the arrival of Perry's "black ships" in 1853. As we have shown, at the arrival of Buddhism and Confucianism, a deliberate modification, with attendant changes of emphasis, occurred at the very moment of selection. The Japanese took only what they felt they needed and were comfortable with. Japanese Buddhism fully accommodated Shintō, and Japanese Confucianism complemented them both in a harmonious whole. In contrast, we observe that the importation of Western thought occurring after Japan reluctantly opened up to the outside world introduced a deep cultural dissonance. The rationalism seen as underpinning scientific progress ran directly counter to enduring Japanese sensibilities. However, such progress was perceived by many as being a paramount necessity if Japan was to be able to build a nation capable of defending itself against the European colonial powers. Hence, in the first decade or so of the Meiji era, much of the importation of Western civilization was (in a manner

reminiscent of the cases of Confucianism/Buddhism) government-direct-
ed, under the slogan *bummei kaika* (civilization and enlightenment). Then,
through the individual initiatives of the likes of Fukuzawa Yukichi,
"Westernization," "modernization," "liberalization" took on a life of their
own. Unsurprisingly, this development appeared and felt quite un-
Japanese to the traditional-minded, and a reaction soon set in. Amid the
flood of Western thought entering the country at this time, we see, to
some extent, a bipolar process of selection, with egalitarians such as
Fukuzawa and Nakae Chōmin himself championing European liberal
thought, and conservatives making their own choice from the Western
libraries as well as reverting to Confucian values, and ultimately allying
these latter to Shintō. As we saw in chapter 4 and chapter 5, the polariza-
tion between "modernizers" and defenders of traditional Japanese values
was to be the single most enduring feature of the Japanese intellectual
milieu. Also, as we saw in referring to Okakura Tenshin, the paradigm of
"overcoming modernity" emerged very early, even if the elaboration of
philosophy to this end took somewhat longer.

What, then, can we say of all this Japanese philosophical activity that
owed its development to the arrival of Western civilization? To be sure,
there have been countless "isms" of European provenance: positivism,
neo-Kantianism, neo-Hegelianism, Marxism, existentialism, structuralism, and more. From its emergence in the Meiji era, Japan's Western-
style philosophy has often seemed to serve simply as a "relay station"
for these incoming waves of Western isms, successive trends in
European thought. Here again, the Japanese have often "slanted" the
foreign philosophies in a distinctively Japanese way, and were not
always aware of their own biased reading (just as Westerners are not
always aware of their biased readings of non-Western philosophies).
However, for as long as the imported ideologies and theories merely
became the career pickings of scholars (and we can nod in agreement
when Nakae Chōmin, Nishida Kitarō, Ōe Kenzaburō and Nakamura
Yūjirō lament this tendency), little original philosophic production was
likely.

Where those aspiring to social reform—people such as Fukuzawa
Yukichi or Nakae Chōmin himself in the Meiji period or Marxists such as
Uno Kōzō or postwar democrats such as Maruyama Masao—re-edited
Western concepts or ideologies for the Japanese context, in order to "bring
Japan to modernity" or express Japan in modernist terms, we can point to
a greater degree of intellectual input. And yet, here too, because the core
ideas being expressed were of Western coinage and pointed to Western,
would-be universal models, however much applied to the Japanese case,
this philosophy was not fundamentally Japanese.

Clearly, the greatest innovation was always going to come from those who experienced most acutely the cultural contradictions arising in the Meiji era: if Japan's age-old culture and authentic identity (as they saw it) were to survive, then the nation's beliefs and values would need to be re-expressed, against the West, and against Western representations perceived as fallacious, yet in Western terms. Clearly here, originality was a condition sine qua non. Those seeking to reassert Japanese values against the Western incursion, those who sought to "overcome modernity," had perforce to engage Western thought in a fresh manner.

From the final brooding pages of Okakura Tenshin's *The Awakening of Japan* to the postwar declarations of Nishitani Keiji and beyond, we have seen how this last, and most distinctive, current of Japanese thought is characterized by a sense of dislocation and loss, accompanied by the longing to regain, to reassert. What is lamented most of all is the loss of on the one hand that sense of oneness with nature that characterized both the Shintō and Buddhist world views, and on the other the tight sense of community that prevailed before the coming of Western individualism. Hence, just as important as the project to "overcome modernity" is the aspiration to "restore the holistic." This mainstream movement of Japanese thought has by itself been decisive in fashioning the overall reception (in weighting the canon, if you will) of Western thought in Japan. Hegelianism not only arrives as a prestigious Western current of thought, but finds its own rapport with Buddhism and provides a communitarian corrective for those who are uncomfortable with Western individualism. The thinkers of "pure experience" (William James, Mach, etc.) are sufficiently close to Zen to be accorded a role in the arguments of Nishida's *Zen no kenkyū (An Inquiry into the Good)*, that antimodernist text par excellence. And in Heidegger, the Japanese all but discover themselves. The author of *Being and Time* instantly garners enormous respect. And yet, as we have observed, the very criticisms made of Heidegger go even farther to reflect the same profound convictions and exigencies to which we are referring. In more recent times, French structuralism and poststructuralism, as we have seen, were embraced as a form of vindication. On the other hand Anglo-American "analytic" philosophy of the 1950s and '60s scarcely made a dent in Japanese consciousness.

Japan, with an intellectual tradition thousands of years old, had striven to transform itself in less than five decades from a semifeudal state to a modern nation. In retrospect, if we may be permitted the metaphor, we see these would-be restorers of holism instinctively drawn to Hegel, Heidegger et al. as allies in the effort to find a way out of the Western cultural labyrinth—in which they so suddenly found themselves estranged—and thus back to their instinctive cultural "home." In remapping the labyrinth in his own manner, Nishida Kitarō becomes the supreme indigenous guide, and with his direction Miki Kiyoshi, Nishitani Keiji, and others trace their own paths towards emancipation.

We repeat: according to this conception, the double-goal of this particular (and major) current of Japanese thought has long been clear—the overcoming of modernity and the restoring of holism. Such thought has been characterized by the belief that since modernity was essentially foreign, the language of modernity, all the thought produced wrestling with the problems that arrived with modernity, were similarly foreign.

We have said that it is *this* philosophy, engendered by the imperative to overcome modernity, that diverges most from Western "originals" and therefore emerges as the most "originally" Japanese. Let us not for all that slide into the inviting stereotype. In this perspective, we may easily be led to an image of the Japanese philosopher, having vanquished the logos and all the modernist complications it has brought, sitting meditatively at the end of his interminable effort, bowl of green tea before him, calligraphy brush at his side. It is an image occurring readily to those who associate Japanese philosophy uniquely with Zen Buddhism.

However, we have seen that this "philosophy of overcoming modernity" does not hold the entire field. Those who question it ask, Was modernity a wholly Western phenomenon? If it was, is modernity still Western? If modernity arrived all at once from abroad, did it not become one more phenomenon of Japan, *Japan's* modernity? A Japanese modernity that is, moreover, precisely because of the attitudes it engendered, a modernity in its details uniquely Japanese. Thus, a Japanese problem that Japanese thinkers have had to approach in philosophy that is, necessarily, Japanese. The concept of *shutaisei* (subjectivity) and its relation to Western notions of enlightenment illustrates this specificity. Japanese postmodernism would similarly cut out its own different career, be charged with different tasks, and this within universal perspectives. Thus, a Japanese philosophy that is engaging modernity. This too is Japanese philosophy. For philosophers of such persuasion, whose principle exigency is social action, thinkers of Zen inspiration may be considered with impatience, denounced for their *inactivity*, their *retreat from social issues*, their *nostalgic escapism*, their *resort to mystification*.

Such a dichotomy is an ancient one, of course. Problems of society did not begin with modernity. Thinkers who are engrossed in problems of society and concerned with ethics rather than ontology have manifested such impatience through the ages, from Socrates to Confucius.

In any case, the point is made: whether trying to "overcome modernity" or "engage modernity," Japanese thinkers have been active in a uniquely Japanese sphere where original philosophy has resulted.

So why, again, in a world where we have seen the emergence of "Arabic philosophy," "African philosophy," "Korean philosophy," among many others, has there been no Japanese acknowledgment of this body of work we identify and denote as "Japanese philosophy"?

In answering this, we can say first that Japan's "modernist" philosophies, to the very degree that they derive from Western models, have diminished specificity as being Japanese. They can only assert a specific Japaneseness in the details. Such imported thought, however internally modified, cannot touch the essential (or should we say ironically, the nonessential) of the issue. If we seek what is inherently distinctive in Japan's philosophy, it is rather in that other tradition, the lineage of Dōgen and Nishida, that we find it. And we affirm this without in the least yielding to Orientalist stereotypes.

In chapter 1 we put forward a series of preliminary theories and hypotheses, but from the ensuing account, one point has become especially clear: faced with incursive modernity, Japan responded not so much with philosophy in the sense of abstract statements about being, but rather myth and a nonrational, aesthetic, preferably taciturnly expressed vision, where philosophy as reasoned argument was only the way to the Way, a detour through borrowed expression. As Abe Masao has written:

> To generate a creative synthesis of Eastern and Western philosophy, one must include but go beyond the demonstrative thinking that is characteristic of the West and both arrive at unobjectifiable ultimate reality and give it a logical articulation by conceptually expressing the inexpressible. (in Abe's Introduction to Nishida's *Zen no kenkyū [An Inquiry into the Good]*, x)

This at least (the philosophy of Nishida and his ilk) was philosophy that touched the essential. Before Nishida, Japanese Western-style philosophy barely qualifies as "Japanese philosophy," not because it is not "philosophy" but because it is only marginally "Japanese," and, as we remarked above, the same is true of later philosophy that draws primarily on Western models. With Nishida and his successors, Japanese philosophy becomes more centrally "Japanese," but perhaps less clearly "philosophy." Indeed, some question whether existentialism, especially that of Kierkegaard and Nietzsche, should count as "philosophy." And the same question could be raised of a great deal of "postmodern thought": is it philosophy? If we think of mainstream, traditional philosophy as being predominantly rational, analytic, and systematic, then existentialism, postmodernism, and the Kyōto school all seem antiphilosophical. But this is an internal debate within philosophy itself. One of the central questions philosophers perennially ask themselves is, "What is philosophy?"

"Philosophy" is itself an essentially contested concept. Is the critique of rationalism an oxymoronic argument against argument, or is it a harbinger of a new philosophy to come? Is it the death of philosophy or the beginning of a new style of philosophy? In the midst of that intense and ongoing debate, the outcome is simply "too close to call."

For ourselves, we assert that in its language, its style, and even its conclusions, the philosophy that arose in Japan from this synthesis of Eastern and Western thought can be termed Japanese philosophy but only with qualifications. It is philosophy, and by Japanese, but the Japanese element of it entails a discreet nullification of the project itself. The language and style were borrowed from a Western tradition whose conventional purpose was to (fallaciously) make statements about Being founded on concepts of substance. The objective of Japanese philosophy texts' discursive journey through Western culture was above all to expose such Western error. This philosophy would ideally never embark on a conceptual line of its own. Requiring no voice, it would be present only as contestation, ultimately intent on nullification.

Japanese "thought" displays here its fidelity to a centuries-old objective, what the West would conventionally have called a nonphilosophic goal. It is problematic to speak here of assertion, assertion itself involving a coloration that the self is not supposed to have. We find ourselves here at the core of the long philosophical tradition we have surveyed. A profound aspiration within Japanese culture is, after all, to be selfless. And in such a case, self-defense can only be self-betrayal (unless, perhaps, it is accompanied by self-sacrifice). Takeuchi Yoshimi has written in similar terms:

> There is no *resistance*, that is, there is no wish to maintain the self (the self itself does not exist). The absence of resistance means that Japan is not Oriental. But at the same time, the absence of the self-maintenance wish (no self) means that Japan is not European. This is to say, Japan is nothing. (130)

Japan is not Oriental, in that it has taken on appearances, procedures, customs proper to Western modernity, and beneath this there is in any case no Oriental *essence*. Nor yet is Japan European; it has not assimilated the "self-maintenance wish" that modernity presupposes as normal.

In keeping with this, we affirm that quintessentially Japanese philosophy too is nothing, wherever it goes. The commitment to the unconceptualized, to "pure experience," requires philosophy only as a means to counter ways of thinking that erroneously posit a coherence in the realm of the concept, in the logos. This recalls the Buddhist use of philosophy that we encountered in chapter 2. As soon as one begins to say anything, even to say that all things are empty (*śūnyatā*), or to say that reality transcends all conceptual categories, philosophical issues appear to arise that can only be answered by more philosophy! The goal of all this is to transcend philosophy, to achieve silence. But as Samuel Beckett also discovered, given who we are, we can only *talk* ourselves into silence. In its critique of Western concept-based schemas of Being, the Japanese thought we are here concerned with follows just such a course. Such philosophy typically has as its task negation, deconstruction. And this being so, in the very moment of its expression, it cannot but imply its own superfluity. In the final analysis, all conceptual demonstration is self-defeating, *de trop.* Hence the most refined expressions of Japanese philosophy, such as Zen's *kōan* or the Sekitei garden at Kyōto's Ryōanji, in which several rocks amid raked sand bring home to us the suchness of things and, if we meditate a little, cease even to speak of suchness.

At this point, Japanese philosophy lapses into the silence where it finds its maximal authenticity. The philosophy within the philosophy is itself *de trop.* In this sense, the Sekitei is close to the desirable "degree zero of philosophy." Insofar as such philosophy tends toward this degree zero as an ideal, were we wrong earlier to affirm it as philosophy? Of course not, for like all ideals, this one exists only because of preponderant contrary realities. Even the Sekitei garden has its didactic function. Philosophy has been used as a means to achieve this goal of nullification, and even philosophy as nullification is also philosophy and valuable as such. It is valuable as deconstruction, whether for the individual alone or the individual in his or her social function. Recall our discussion in chapter 2 of the difference between the Zen monk's final realization of the truth of Zen and his initial starting point thirty years earlier; though both are expressed in the very same words, "seeing mountains as mountains and waters as waters," there is a world of difference between them and a difference that is philosophical. However, unless by allusiveness and discreet irony, to assert this tradition of philosophy vis-à-vis the modernist incursion would be, we repeat, to contradict, to betray, the most deeply felt intimations of Japanese identity.

To be sure, Taishō period philosophers and ideologues of various persuasions gave an apparent "form" to this inherently formless Japanese identity, with the imperial family at the focus of national loyalty, but the imperial family was, precisely, envisaged as symbolic of the eternal present (read the nothingness beyond the concept), and as suggested above, the nation's self-assertion had overtones of self-sacrifice. To use an expression common in Nishida's later writings, there is here a "contradictory self-identity." The notion of "self" itself is a contradiction.

We said that quintessentially Japanese philosophy is nothing, wherever it goes. So far the very nonassertive manner of such thought has limited its reception abroad. Meanwhile, the development of postmodern philosophy in the West has carried further the Nietzschean and Heideggerian review of the notion of Being, and in keeping with this has scrutinized anew the meaning of nihility. At the same time, redefinition of the subject has become once more a central concern for Western thinkers, paralleling the ongoing preoccupation in Japan with the *shutai* (subject). In these ways, the concerns of Japanese philosophy, on the one hand, and Western philosophy, on the other, are closer than ever before. Given this, does not the love of wisdom require that in the West, as in Japan, thinkers, notions, quests from both traditions be fully recognized in a broadened and shared field of inquiry?

It is our hope that the present work will contribute not only to the familiarization of Western readers with the philosophy of Japan, but also to the global career of the term *Japanese philosophy*, as designating a distinctive local body of thought offering pertinent perspectives on issues of universal interest.

REFERENCES

Abe, Masao. 1988. Nishida's Philosophy of 'Place,' *International Philosophical Quarterly* 28.

Arima, Tetsuo. 1969. *The Failure of Freedom: A Portrait of Modern Japanese Intellectuals.* Cambridge: Harvard University Press.

Aron, Raymond. 1955. *L'Opium des intellectuels.* Paris: Calmann-Lévy.

Asada, Akira. 1983. *Kōzō to chikara: kigōron o koete (Structure and Power: Beyond Semantics).* Tokyo: Kōsō Shobō.

Asada, Akira, Jacques Derrida, and Karatani Kōjin. 1984. Discussion: The Ultra-consumer Society and the Role of the Intellectual (Chōshōhi shakai to chishik-ijin no yakuwari), *Asahi jaanaru (Asahi Journal)* (25 May).

Barshay, Andrew E. 1988. *State and Intellectual in Imperial Japan: The Public Man in Crisis.* Berkeley: University of California Press.

Barthes, Roland. 1970. *L'Empire des signes (The Empire of Signs).* Geneva: Albert Skira.

Beasley, W. G. 1963. *The Modern History of Japan.* New York: Prager.

Berque, Augustin. 1976. *Le Japon: Gestion de l'espace et changement social.* Paris: Flammarion.

———. 1986. *Le Sauvage et l'artifice: les Japonais devant la nature.* Paris: Gallimard.

Brown, Delmer M. 1955. *Nationalism in Japan.* Berkeley: University of California Press.

Camus, Albert. 1965. *L'Homme révolté (The Rebel, 1951).* Paris: Éditions Gallimard et Calmann-Lévy.

Caputo, John. 1993. *Against Ethics.* Bloomington: Indiana University Press.

Carter, Robert E. 1996. Interpretative Essay: Strands of Influence. In Watsuji Tetsurō, *Rinrigaku,* Trans. Yamamoto Seisaku and Robert E. Carter. Albany: State University of New York Press.

Chang, Chunmai (Carson Chang). 1925. *Science and the Philosophy of Life.*

Chapman, William. 1991. *Inventing Japan: The Making of a Postwar Civilization.* New York: Prentice Hall.

Collinson, Diane, and Robert Wilkinson. 1994. *Thirty-five Oriental Philosophers.* London: Routledge.

Dale, Peter. 1986. *The Myth of Japanese Uniqueness.* New York: St. Martin's Press.

Deleuze, Gilles. 1994. *Difference and Repetition.* Trans. Paul Patton. London: The Athlone Press.

Derrida, Jacques. 1982. *Margins—of Philosophy.* Trans. Alan Bass. Chicago: Chicago University Press.

———. 1974. *On Grammatology.* Trans. G. C. Spivak. Baltimore: Johns Hopkins University Press.

Doak, Kevin Michael. 1994. *Dreams of Difference: The Japan Romantic School and the Crisis of Modernity.* Berkeley: University of California Press.

Dōgen. 1958. Body and Mind *(Shōbō genzō zuimonki).* In *Sources of Japanese Tradition,* ed. Tsunoda, de Bary, and Keene, vol. 1. New York: Columbia University Press.

———. 1958. Contempt for Scriptures *(Eto).* In ibid., vol. 1.

———. 1985. *Moon in a Dewdrop: Writings of Zen Master Dōgen.* Ed. Tanahashi Kazuaki. San Francisco: North Point Press.

———. 1958. Realizing the Solution *(Genjō kōan).* In *Sources,* op. cit., vol. 1.

Doi, Takeo. 1973. *The Anatomy of Dependence (Amae no kōzō).* Trans. John Bester. Tokyo: Kodansha.

Dumoulin, Heinrich. 1988–1989. *Zen Buddhism: A History.* Trans. James Heisig and Paul Knitter, 2 vol. New York: Macmillan.

Franck, Frederick, ed. 1982. *The Buddha Eye: An Anthology of the Kyōto School.* New York: Crossroad.

Fu, Charles Wei-Hsun, and Steven Heine, eds. 1995. *Japan in Traditional and Postmodern Perspectives.* Albany: State University of New York Press.

Fujiwara, Seika. 1958. Zhu Xi Studies *(Shushi gakuha).* In *Sources of Japanese Tradition,* ed. Tsunoda, de Bary, and Keene vol. 1 New York: Columbia University Press.

Fukuzawa, Yukichi. 1973. *An Outline of a Theory of Civilization.* Trans. Dilworth and Hurst. Tokyo: Sophia University Press.

Fung, YuLan. 1952–1953. *A History of Chinese Philosophy.* Trans. Derk Bodde, 2 vol. Princeton: Princeton University Press.

"Gendai Nihon no shisō" ("Contemporary Japanese Thought"). *Gendai Shisō (Revue de la pensée d'aujourd'hui),* vol. 8, no. 15, December 1980.

Gluck, Carol. 1985. *Japan's Modern Myths.* Princeton: Princeton University Press.

Green, Thomas Hill. 1890. *Prolegomena to Ethics.* London: Clarendon Press.

Hardacre, Helen. 1986. Creating State Shintō: The Great Promulgation Campaign and the New Religions, *The Journal of Japanese Studies* 12.

Harootunian, H. D. 1989. Visible Discourses/Invisible Ideologies. In *Postmodernism and Japan,* ed. Miyoshi Masao and H.D. Harootunian. Durham: Duke University Press.

Hasumi, Shigehiko, and Yoshimoto Takaaki. 1980. Hihyō ni totte sakuhin to wa nanika (What is a Literary Work for the Critic?), *Umi* (July): 236–266.

Hayashi, Razan. 1958. The Confucian Way. In *Sources of Japanese Tradition,* ed. Tsunoda, de Bary, and Keene, vol. 1. New York: Columbia University Press.

———. 1958. Conversations with Three Korean Envoys. In *Sources,* ibid., vol. 1.

Heisig, James W. 1990. The Self That is Not a Self. In *The Religious Philosophy of Tanabe Hajime,* ed. Taitetsu Unno and James W. Heisig. Berkeley: Asian Humanities Press.

Hirata, Atsutane. 1958. The Land of the Gods, from *Summary of the Ancient Way (Kōdō taii).* In Sources of Japanese Tradition, ed. Tsunoda, de Bary, and Keene, vol. 1. New York: Columbia University Press., vol. 2.

Huish, David. 1977. Aims and Achievements of the Meirokusha: Fact and Fiction, *Monumenta Nipponica* 32.

Irokawa, Daikichi. 1985. *The Culture of the Meiji Period.* Princeton: Princeton University Press.

Itō, Jinsai. 1958. The Life Force as the Ultimate Reality, from *Boys' Questions (Dōri-mon).* In *Sources of Japanese Tradition,* ed. Tsunoda, de Bary, and Keene, vol. 1. New York: Columbia University Press.

———. 1958. Love as Supreme Virtue, from *Boys' Questions (Dōri-mon).* In *Sources,* ibid., vol. 1.

———. 1958. "The Primacy of Confucius and the Analects," from *The Meaning of Terms in the Analects and Mencius (Gomō-jigi).* In *Sources,* ibid., vol. 1.

Itō, Tōgai. 1958. "The Devolution of Confucianism," from *Changes in Confucian Teaching, Past and Present (Kokon gakuhen).* In Sources of Japanese Tradition, ed. Tsunoda, de Bary, and Keene, vol. 1, New York: Columbia University Press.

———. 1958. "The Neo-confucianist's Erroneous View of Human Nature," from *Critique of the Doctrine of Returning to One's Original Nature (Fukusen-ben).* In ibid., vol. 1.

Ivy, Marilyn. 1989. "Consumption of Knowledge." In *Postmodernism and Japan,* ed. Miyoshi and Harootunian. Durham: Duke University Press.

Japan: An Illustrated Encyclopedia. 1993. Tokyo: Kodansha.

Jansen, Marius B. 1954. *The Japanese and Sun Yat-sen.* Cambridge: Harvard University Press.

Karatani, Kōjin. 1995. *Architecture as Metaphor (Inyu to shite no kenchiku, 1981).* Trans. Sabu Kōso. Cambridge: Massachusetts Institute of Technology Press.

———. 1978. *Marukusu sono kanosei no chūshin (Marx: The Center of his Possibilities).* Tokyo: Kodansha.

———. 1969. Ishiki to shizen: Sōseki shiron, *Gunzou* 24, no. 6.

———. 1993. *Origins of Modern Japanese Literature (Nihon kindai bungaku no kigen).* Trans. Brett de Bary. Durham: Duke University Press.

Kashiwahara, Yūsen, and Sonoda Kōyū , eds. 1994. *Shapers of Japanese Buddhism.* Trans. Gaynor Sekimori. Tokyo: Kosei.

Keene, Donald. 1969. *The Japanese Discovery of Europe, 1720–1830.* Stanford: Stanford University Press.

Kersten, Rikki. 1996. *Democracy in Postwar Japan: Maruyama Masao and the Search for Autonomy.* London: Routledge.

Koschmann, J. Victor. 1989. Maruyama Masao and the Incomplete Project of Modernity. In ed. Masao and Harootunian. *Postmodernism and Japan.* Durham: Duke University Press.

Kūkai. 1958. The Difference between Exoteric and Esoteric Buddhism *(Ben Kemmitsu Nikyō-ron).* In *Sources of Japanese Tradition,* ed. Tsunoda, de Bary, and Keene, vol. 1. New York: Columbia University Press.

———. 1958. Memorial on the Presentation of the List of Newly Imported Sūtras. In ibid., vol. 1.

———. 1958. Recapitulation of the Ten Stages of Religious Consciousness. In ibid., vol. 1.

———. 1958. Testament. In ibid., vol. 1.

———. 1958. The Transmission of the Law. In ibid., vol. 1.

Kumazawa, Banzan. 1958. The Development and Distribution of Wealth, from *Daigaku Wakumon.* In *Sources of Japanese Tradition,* ed. Tsunoda, de Bary, and Keene, vol. 1. New York: Columbia University Press.

Lafleur, William R. 1990. A Turning in Taishō: Asia and Europe in the Early Writings of Watsuji Tetsurō. In *Culture and Identity: Japanese Intellectuals during the Interwar Years,* ed. J. Thomas Rimer. Princeton: Princeton University Press.

Lavelle, Pierre. 1994. The Political Thought of Nishida Kitarō, *Monumenta Nipponica* 49.

Liang, Shuming. 1922. *The Civilizations of Orient and Occident and Their Philosophies.*

Light, Stephen. 1987. *Shūzō Kuki and Jean-Paul Sartre: Influence and Counterinfluence in the Early History of Existential Phenomenology.* Carbondale and Edwardsville, IL: Southern Illinois University Press.

Lyotard, Jean-François. 1979. *La condition post-moderne.* Paris: Minuit.

Magliola, Robert. 1984. *Derrida on the Mend.* West Lafayette, IN: Purdue University Press.

Maruyama, Masao. 1964. *Gendai seiji no shisō to kōdō.* Tokyo: Miraisha.

———. 1974. *Studies in the Intellectual History of Tokugawa Japan.* Trans. Mikiso Hane. Tokyo: University of Tokyo Press.

———. 1976. Modern Thought (Kindaiteki shii). In *Senchū to sengo no aida, 1936–57.* Tokyo.: Misuzu Shobō.

Matsunaga, Alicia, and Daigan Matsunaga. 1976. *Foundation of Japanese Buddhism,* 2 vol. Los Angeles and Tokyo: Buddhist Books International.

May, Reinhard. 1996. *Heidegger's Hidden Sources*. Trans. Graham Parkes. London and New York: Routledge.

Miura, Baien. 1958. The Disinterested Study of Nature, from a letter to Asada Gōryū. In *Sources of Japanese Tradition*, ed. Tsunoda, de Bary, and Keene, vol. 1. New York: Columbia University Press.

Miyamoto, Masao. 1994. *Straightjacket Society (Oyakusho no okite)*. Tokyo: Kodansha.

Miyoshi, Masao, and H. D. Harootunian, eds. 1989. *Postmodernism and Japan*. Durham: Duke University Press.

Miyoshi, Masao. 1989. Against the Native Grain: The Japanese Novel and the "Postmodern" West. In ed., Miyoshi and Harootunian. *Postmodernism and Japan, ibid*. Durham: Duke University Press.

Morris, Ivan. 1975. *The Nobility of Failure*. New York: Holt, Rinehart and Winston.

Motoori, Norinaga. 1958. The Error of Rationalism, from *Arrowroot (Kuzubana)*. In *Sources of Japanese Tradition*, ed., Tsunoda, de Bary, and Keene vol. 2. New York: Columbia University Press.

———. 1958. The Fact of Evil, from *Precious Comb-box (Tama kushige)*. In ibid.

———. 1958. Love and Poetry, from *Observations from Long Years of Apprenticeship to Poetry (Sekijō shishuku-gen)*. In ibid.

———. 1958. The True Tradition of the Sun Goddess, from *Precious Comb-box (Tama kushige)*. In ibid.

———. 1958. Wonder, from *Arrowroot (Kuzubana)*. In ibid.

Nagao, Gadjin. 1989. *The Foundational Standpoint of Mādhyamika Philosophy*. Trans. John Keenan. Albany: State University of New York Press.

Najita, Tetsuo, and H. D. Harootunian. 1976. Japanese Revolt Against the West: Political and Cultural Criticism in the Twentieth Century. In *The Cambridge History of Japan*, vol. 6. Cambridge: Cambridge University Press.

Nakae, Chōmin. 1961. Ichinen yūhan, *Nakae Chōmin, Ōsugi Sakae, Kawakami Hajime Shū; Gendai Nihon bungaku zenshū 3*. Tokyo: Chikuma Shobō.

Nakai, Tōju. 1958. The Divine Light in the Mind *(Yōmei gakuha)*. In *Sources of Japanese Tradition*, ed. Tsunoda, de Bary, and Keene, vol. 1. New York: Columbia University Press.

Nakamura, Hajime. 1964. *Ways of Thinking of Eastern Peoples*. Ed. Philip Wiener. Honolulu: University Press of Hawaii.

Nakamura, Yūjirō. 1999. *Shisō: Kyōto zadankai* (Japanese Thought: An Informal Discussion in Kyōto), *Yomiuri Shimbun*, July 31.

———. 1983. *Nishida Kitarō*. Tokyo: Iwanami shoten.

———. 1995. Une Philosophie japonaise est-elle possible? *Ebisu*, no. 8 and *Hermes, Tokyo*, no. 48.

Nishida, Kitarō. *An Inquiry into the Good (Zen no kenkyū)*. Trans. Abe Masao and Christopher Ives. New Haven: Yale University Press.

———. 1958. The Problem of Japanese Culture (*Nihon Bunka no mondai*). In *Sources of Japanese Tradition*, ed. Tsunoda, de Bary, and Keene, vol. 2. New York: Columbia University Press.

———. 1958. The Problem of Japanese Culture *(Nihon bunka no mondai)*. In ibid.

———. 1970. *Fundamental Problems of Philosophy*. Trans. David Dilworth. Tokyo.

———. 1973. *Art and Morality*. Trans. David Dilworth and Valdo Viglielmo. Honolulu: University Press of Hawaii.

———. 1973. *Intelligibility and the Philosophy of Nothingness*. Trans. Robert Schinzinger, 1958. Westport, CT: Greenwood Press.

———. 1973. *Nothingness and the Religious World View*. Trans. David Dilworth. Honolulu: University Press of Hawaii.

———. 1987. *Intuition and Reflection in Self-Consciousness*. Trans. Valdo Viglielmo et al. Albany: State University of New York Press.

Nishitani, Keiji. 1985–1986. The Days of My Youth: An Autobiographical Sketch, *FAS Society Journal*.

———. 1982. *Religion and Nothingness (Shūkyō to wa nanika)*. Trans. Jan Van Bragt. Berkeley: University of California Press.

———. 1986. The Starting Point of My Philosophy, *FAS Society Journal*.

———. 1990. *The Self-Overcoming of Nihilism (Nihirizumu)*. Trans. G. Parkes and S. Aihara. Albany: State University of New York Press.

———. 1991. *Nishida Kitarō*. Trans. Yamamoto Seisaku and James W. Heisig. Berkeley: University of California Press.

Nolte, Sharon H. 1987. *Liberalism in Modern Japan*. Berkeley: University of California Press.

Norman, E. Herbert. 1949. *Andō Shōeki and the Anatomy of Japanese Feudalism*. Tokyo: Asiatic Society of Japan.

Nosco, Peter, ed. 1984. *Confucianism and Tokugawa Culture*. Princeton: Princeton University Press.

Odin, Steve. 1995. Derrida and the Decentered Universe of Ch'an/Zen Buddhism. In *Japan in Traditional and Postmodern Perspectives*, ed., Charles Wei-Hsun Fu and Steven Heine. Albany: State University of New York Press.

Ōe, Kenzaburō. 1989. Japan's Dual Identity. In *Postmodernism and Japan*, ed. Miyoshi and Harootunian. Durham: Duke University Press.

Ōe, Kenzaburō, and Takeshi Umehara. 1973. [in conversation] in *Japanese Literature Today* 20.

Oguchi, Eiichi, et al., eds. 1973. *Shūkyōgaku jiten*. Tokyo: Tokyo Daigaku Shuppankai.

Oguma, Eiji. 1998. *"Nihonjin" no Kyōkai (The Boundaries of the "Japanese")*. Tokyo: Shinyōsha.

Ogyū, Sorai. 1958. Distortion of the Way through Ignorance of the Past, from *Distinguishing the Way (Bendō)*. In *Sources of Japanese Tradition*, ed. Tsunoda, de Bary, and Keene, vol. 1. New York: Columbia University Press.

Okakura Tenshin (Kakuzō). 1984. The Awakening of the East. In *Collected English Writings*, 3 vol. Tokyo: Heibonsha.

———. The Awakening of Japan, in *Collected English Writings, ibid.*

———. 1984. The Ideals of the East. In ibid.

Ooms, Herbert. 1985. *Tokugawa Ideology: Early Constructs, 1570–1680*. Princeton: Princeton University Press.

Orwell, George. 1949. *Nineteen Eighty-four.* London: Secker and Warburg.

Ōtsuki, Gentaku. 1969. *Rangaku kaitei* (Dutch Studies). In Donald Keene, *The Japanese Discovery of Europe, 1720–1830*. Stanford: Stanford University Press.

Parkes, Graham, ed. 1987. *Heidegger and Asian Thought.* Honolulu: University of Hawaii Press.

Piovesana, Gino K. 1981. Contemporary Japanese Philosophy. In *Asian Philosophy Today*, ed. Dale Riepe. New York: Gordon and Breach.

———. 1968. *Recent Japanese Philosophical Thought 1862–1962: A Survey.* Tokyo: Enderle Bookstore.

Pollack, David. 1986. *The Fracture of Meaning.* Princeton: Princeton University Press.

Radhakrishnan, Sarvepalli. 1931. *Indian Philosophy*, vol. 2. London: George Allen and Unwin.

Reischauer, Edwin O., and Albert M. Craig. 1973. *Japan: Tradition and Transformation.* New York: Houghton Mifflin Co.

Rimer, J. Thomas, ed. 1990. *Culture and Identity.* Princeton: Princeton University Press.

Sakai, Naoki. Return to the West/Return to the East: Watsuji Tetsurō's Anthropology and Discussion of Authenticity, *Boundary 2* 18.

Sakamoto, Hyakudai. 1993. *The Japan Foundation Newsletter* 21.

Sakuma, Shōzan. 1958. Reflections on My Errors *(Seiken-roku).* In *Sources of Japanese Tradition*, ed. Tsunoda, de Bary, and Keene, vol. 2. New York: Columbia University Press.

Sansom, George. 1958. *A History of Japan,* 3 vol. Stanford: Stanford University Press.

Sartre, Jean-Paul. 1946. *L'Existentialisme est un humanisme.* Paris: Éditions Nagel.

———. 1957. Questions de méthode, *Les Temps Modernes* 139.

Shutai to wa nanika (What is the Subject?), *Gendai shisō (Revue de la pensée d'aujourd'hui)* 26, no. 12 (October).

Sugimoto, Yoshio, and Ross E. Mouer, eds. 1989. *Constructs for Understanding Japan.* London: Kegan Paul.

Sugita, Gempaku. 1969. Rangaku kotohajime. In Donald Keene, *The Japanese Discovery of Europe, 1720–1830.* Stanford: Stanford University Press.

Suzuki, Daisetz T. 1959. *Zen and Japanese Culture.* Rutland, VT, and Tokyo: Tuttle.

Swanson, Paul. 1989. *Foundations of T'ien-T'ai Philosophy: The Flowering of the Two Truths Theory in Chinese Buddhism.* Berkeley: Asian Humanities Press.

Takeuchi, Yoshimi. 1980. Kindai to wa nanika. (What is Modernity?) In *Takeuchi Yoshimi zenshū, (Complete Works of Takeuchi Yoshimi), vol. 4*. Tokyo: Chikuma Shobō.

Tanabe, Hajime. 1986. *Philosophy as Metanoetics (Zangedō to shite no tetsugaku)*. Trans. Takeuchi Yoshinori et al. Berkeley: University of California Press.

Tsunoda, Ryūsaku, Wm. Theodore de Bary, and Donald Keene, eds. 1958. *Sources of Japanese Tradition*, 2 vol. New York: Columbia University Press.

Umehara, Takeshi. 1996. *The Concept of Hell*. Trans. Robert Wargo. Tokyo: Shūeisha.

Unno, Taitetsu, ed. 1990. *The Religious Philosophy of Nishitani Keiji: Encounter with Emptiness*. Berkeley: Asian Humanities Press.

Vattimo, Gianni. 1997. *Beyond Interpretation*. Trans. David Webb. Stanford: Stanford University Press.

Watsuji, Tetsurō. 1935. *Climate and Culture: A Philosophical Study (Fūdo)*. Trans. Geoffrey Bownas. Westport, CT: Greenwood Press, 1988.

———. 1948. *Koeber Sensei*. Tokyo: Kōbundo.

———. 1996. *Rinrigaku*. Trans. Yamamoto Seisaku and Robert E. Carter. Albany: State University of New York Press.

Watts, Alan W. 1962. *The Way of Zen*. Harmondsworth, Middlesex: Penguin Books.

Yamaga, Sokō. 1958. An Autobiography in Exile *(Haisho zampitsu)*. In *Sources of Japanese Tradition*, ed. Tsunoda, de Bary, and Keene, vol. 1. New York: Columbia University Press.

———. 1958. Essence of Confucianism, from *The Essential Teachings of the Sages (Seikyō yōroku)*, In ibid.

———. 1958. The Sage as a Moral Man *(Takkyo dōmon)*. In ibid.

Yamaguchi, Masao. 1975. *Bunka to ryōgisei (Culture and Double Meaning)*. Tokyo: Iwanami Shoten.

Yamazaki, Ansai. 1958. Collected Commentaries of Zhu Xi 's Regulations for the School of the White Deer Cave. In Sources of Japanese Tradition, ed., Tsunoda, de Bary, and Keene, vol. 1. New York: Columbia University Press.

———. 1958. Devotion and Righteousness. In ibid.

Yoshimoto, Takaaki. 1974 and 1978 *Yoshimoto Takaaki zenchosakusha (Collected Works of Yoshimoto Takaaki)*. Tokyo: Keisō Shobō.

Yoshimoto, Takaaki, Takeshi Umehara, and Shinichi Nakazawa. 1995. *Nihonjin wa shisō shita ka*. Tokyo: Shinchōsha.

Yoshino, Kōsaku. 1992. *Cultural Nationalism in Contemporary Japan: A Sociological Enquiry*. London: Routledge.

Yuasa Yasuo. 1987. Modern Japanese Philosophy and Heidegger. In ed. Parkes, *Heidegger and Asian Thought*. Honolulu: University of Hawaii Press.

Yusa, Michiko. 1991. Nishida and the Question of Nationalism, *Monumenta Nipponica* 46.

Printed in Japan
落丁、乱丁本のお問い合わせは
Amazon.co.jp カスタマーサービスへ

11421223R00126